THE GREATEST BATMAN STORIES EVER TOLD

VOLUME 2

BATMAN CREATED BY BOB KANE

DC Comics Inc., 1325 Avenue of the Americas,
New York, NY 10019
A Warner Bros. Inc. Company
Printed in Canada. First Printing.

Cover painting by Norm Breyfogle
Publication design by Dale Crain

This volume is dedicated to the spirit of the Golden Age of comics, which enabled a Bat-Man to protect the city from grotesque villains such as The Penguin or deadly antagonists as The Cat.

TABLE OF CONTENTS

OF FOWLS AND FELINES: FIFTY YEARS OF FELONY

By Martin Pasko

Not too long ago, a Warner Bros. executive addressing a large gathering spoke of how certain media had proclaimed 1990 The Year of the Bat, and he assured those media that 1992 would be an even bigger year for the Dark Knight. He then lovingly recalled, to hearty laughter from the crowd, the syndicated gag-cartoon panel about a TV news crew gathering on the front lawn of the only man in America who didn't own a Batman T-shirt.

So it would come as no surprise to me if by now you're so accustomed to seeing the Batman all over the place—on screens large and small, on billboards and in shop windows everywhere—that it's easy to forget: the Batman is not just *in* the comics, he is *of* the comics. Always has been, and probably always will be—a fair statement, I think, considering he's been published in that form continuously for almost 53 years.

As I listened to the gentleman from Warners speak, I couldn't help but feel a distinct jolt of *déjà vu*. Because we've been through all this before, ladies and gentlemen—though the first time it was on a somewhat smaller, and certainly sillier, scale.

In any event, we are living during the third period in the history of popular culture when the world has been seized by a paroxysm of Bat-mania. Which is why I don't need to acquaint you with th character.

I don't need to tell you that th hero created in 1939 by artist Bo Kane, with an assist from writer B Finger, is, unlike the many supe powered colleagues who followe him onto brightly colored comi book pages, a mortal crimefight who struggles and triumphs in th dark places. Not just the shadow alleys and back streets of a spraw ing city at night, but the Stygia corners of his own tortured soul.

I don't have to explain that h has conditioned himself to th peak of physical perfection and arguably the world's greatest dete tive, as well as a brilliant scienti and inventor and a master of th martial arts. I needn't remind yo that he has dedicated himself developing those skills and abi ties with but one purpose—to fu fill a vow made at the graves of h parents—and in so doing, cleanse his city of its rot of crin and corruption.

BRIAN STELFREEZE

Nor must I tell you that his vow was to avenge his parents, whose murder by a gunman's bullets in an alley when he was but eight years old changed the course of his life irrevocably. I don't need to say that in the crucible of that alley was forged an ineluctable avenging force. A masked and cloaked vigilante. "A creature of the night," as the world first learned in the pages of DETECTIVE COMICS #33, "black and terrible," that would strike terror into the hearts of the "superstitious and cowardly lot" of criminals he would face in the five decades to come.

The first time the awareness of these same facts was shared by most of the population of the planet was a little more than twenty-five years ago. And it is to memories of this time that I return each time I hear that term "Bat-mania." I can't describe the feeling as nostalgia; that word is reserved for memories bathed in a glow of contentment. But I, like many other preteens who were deeply into comic books at the time, quickly learned to loathe a mass-medium incarnation of one of our favorite comics characters—one that, as *Batman* editor Denny O'Neil has so rightly put it, "turned the character into a comedian."

Still, we remember the winter of 1966 as if it were yesterday, precisely because it was the year our worlds were suddenly rendered in the bold primary colors and spare, emphatic lines of the comic art form. For, on television, Batman stormed the beachheads of the pop-cultural landscape with an overnight smash-hit series. The show transposed intact the formal elements and conventions of the *Batman* comics to the film medium, where their ludicrous, jarring inappropriateness elicited laughter and gave the culture a definition of the neologism "camp" that was far more cogent than any Susan Sontag could provide.

It would be quite some time before anyone would again see the grim, mysterious hard-boiled detective-by-night that had been created by Kane in 1939 and, forty-six years later, would be re-invented by Frank Miller as The Dark Knight.

The TV series would, however, introduce an entire generation to an element of the mythology that had never been seen in any previous mass-medium version of the character. There had been no budget for it when the Batman was the star of two howlingly low-budget Columbia serials, in 1943 and 1949 respectively. Nor was there time, in 15-minute adventures, to explore this aspect of the character when he was heard on radio in the mid-1940's, as a guest star on *The Adventures of Superman* (in the person of Gary Merrill, later more famous as Bette Davis's husband and co-star in *All About Eve*). And it was a dimension of the Batman that had been largely missing from the comics, due primarily to shifts in popular taste, for roughly fifteen years.

I am of course referring to the inimitable "Rogues Gallery" of costumed villains.

Thanks to the television series, those colorful characters are as inextricably linked in the public imagination to the Batman character as Robin the erstwhile Boy Wonder or Alfred the butler. So it seemed only natural, after Jack Nicholson's fascinatingly perverse interpretation of The Joker in the first *Batman* theatrical feature, that director Tim Burton and his producers would choose to similarly revitalize the next two heavy hitters in this pantheon of villainy, The Penguin and The Catwoman—in the persons of Danny DeVito and Michelle Pfeiffer—in *Batman Returns*. Which in turn makes it only natural that DC's editorial board would choose to make the felonious fowl and feline the focus of this, the second collection of the greatest Batman stories ever told.

For me, the stories in this volume are old friends, to whom I'd recently been reintroduced in the course of doing research for Warner Bros. Animation's forthcoming *Batman—The Animated Series*, on which I'm delighted to be working as a writer/story editor. For obvious reasons, The Penguin and The Catwoman will appear in many of the half-hour adventures that begin airing weekdays in September of 1992 on the Fox network, beautifully rendered by some of the best animators in the field and delightfully voiced by Paul Williams and Adrienne Barbeau.

And so, during a recent visit to New York to search the vast DC archives for stories that might inspire our writers, I was approached by editor Mike Gold to provide this introduction. I found it not only informative, but even more fun than I remembered, to be able to track the development of these characters from their inception as I reread the stories contained herein.

While the various chronicles of the history of comic books are filled with fascinating firsthand accounts of how several of the *Batman* Rogues Gallery were created, there doesn't seem to be a consensus on where The Catwoman came from. That's probably because, unlike such villains as The Joker, The Scarecrow, or Two-Face, who over the years remained largely unchanged from their first, full-blown appearances, The Catwoman slowly *evolved*. And, as such inventive writers as Frank Miller, Mindy Newell, and Alan Grant, and such dazzlingly talented illustrators as David Mazzucchelli, J. J. Birch, Michael Bair, and Norm Breyfogle have demonstrated most recently, The Catwoman remains one of the most frequently redesigned and reinterpreted characters in the Batman mythology.

In her earliest appearances, she looked as she does in the first story in this volume, reprinted from BATMAN #1: an exotically beautiful, dark-haired young woman in a vaguely Oriental-looking dress. As you will see, in her debut she is quite specifically a jewel thief—a "cat burglar." There is no indication that her creators had even an inkling of the cat-o'-nine-tails, claw-like weapons, cat-shaped equipment, or feline-themed crimes that would later become her trademarks.

Even her name kept changing. She isn't even The Catwoman in her first appearance—merely "The Cat." Perhaps sensing that there was further work to be done, Kane and company returned to the drawing board immediately, and the character reappeared in the

JIM APARO

DAVE STEVENS

next two issues of BATMAN, referred to variously as the Cat Woman and the Cat-Woman. It wasn't until the mid-1940's that everyone seems to have settled on the simpler "Catwoman."

There was no such ambiguity, nor any similar mutability, about the rogue who took his first bow in the story beginning on page 28. Within a year of creating their slinky jewel thief, Kane, Finger, and Kane's assistant, illustrator Jerry Robinson—by now joined by inker George Roussos—would come up with a third distinctive adversary for their bat-cloaked hero. And the new villain would temporarily eclipse The Cat-Woman in popularity, if number of encores is any indication.

The pudgy, waddling, criminal connoisseur of the finer things in life, whose given name of Oswald Cobblepot would not be invented for at least another thirty years, returned in some thirty-three *Batman* adventures over the next quarter-century (thirty-*four* if you count a 1946 Sunday continuity for the *Batman* syndicated newspaper strip, reprinted in the first volume in this series). All this before 1966, when he began to enjoy an even greater notoriety thanks to the TV series.

The creation of this character, who in the 1940's became, after The Joker, the second most-frequently-appearing Batman villain, is just about the only positive thing I can think of ever having come from cigarette smoking. Just as Robinson has told of having found the inspiration for The Joker in a deck of playing cards, writer Bill Finger has shared with comics historians his recollection of how he created the character that came to be known, in the days when the floridly-phrased caption was in vogue, as the Bold Bird of Banditry, the Buccaneer of Birds, or The Man of A Thousand Umbrellas.

As one might suspect from Bob Kane's many, often wildly disparate accounts of how the Batman himself was invented (For, what storyteller can resist a good yarn? And when they ask you where you get your ideas, you have to tell them *some*thing), Finger's account might well be apocryphal. But, as he told it, in 1940 he was smoking a certain brand of Menthol cigarette whose trademark was a little cartoon penguin. One day while casting about for a story premise, he happened to glance down at the pack and found there the genesis of the second story reprinted in this collection, "One of the Most Perfect Frame-Ups."

Unlike The Catwoman, who made half a dozen appearances before hitting on the purple peek-a-boo-skirted costume and "purr-fidious" M.O. that ultimately defined the character, most of the familiar Penguin trademarks are in evidence in this story from DETECTIVE #58: the beak-like nose, swallowtail coat, monocle, top hat, cigarette-holder, and umbrella—they're all there.

As are the love of fine art, the taste for Shakespeare, and even a hint of the pompous, overblown manner of speech that would, in The Penguin's next appearance, take on a more indentifiably British flavor. Even the concept of his vast array of trick-umbrella weapons premiered at the same time he did, as you'll notice by the bullets, gas, and acid that his parasol dispenses in the first story alone.

Yet the conception of the character is just as clearly embryonic. Not yet in evidence, for example, is the Penguin's predilection for crimes using birds as weapons or planned around avian themes. This gimmick would not come into play until DETECTIVE #62 (Sept. 1942), in the story called "Crime's Early Bird." And in his first few appearances, The Penguin is quite clearly a cold-blooded murderer, rather than the comparatively benign bandit he later became. By the time he first met The Joker in the mid-40's ("Knights of Knavery," reprinted in the first volume), he seemed content to concentrate on theft, and by "The Riddle of the Seven Birds" in BATMAN #56 (Dec. 1949-Jan. 1950), he is described as a felon who has "never killed anybody."

By the early 1950's, when the Penguin was settling for terrorizing Gotham with mechanical mythical beasts (our fourth golden oldie, "The Penguin's Fabulous Fowls"), The Catwoman had finally become the character she is today—more or less. After four appearances wearing a costume topped by a grotesque cat's-head mask, and assuming a variety of aliases such as Marguerite Tone and Elva Barr, The Catwoman finally emerged in 1946 (in "Nine Live Has the Catwoman, " in BATMAN #35) in the cat-eared cowl that would remain her definitive appearance well into the next decade. But she hadn't stopped changing her hair color; she is blonde in the 1946 tale, after having appeared both as a sultry brunette and a raven-haired temptress.

In "The Secret Life of the Catwoman" (reprinted here), we first learned that her real name was Selina Kyle, and that she was the daughter of a pet shop owner when she lost her memory due to an injury sustained in a plane crash. When a blow to the head cured her amnesia, she renounced her criminal past and settled down to a quiet life as Selina Kyle, proprietor of (what else?) a pet shop...*and* of a still-unrequited love for the cowled crusader. It is from this retirement that she is goaded into emerging by the city's scorn in the 1954 story, "The Crimes of the Catwoman" replete with cat-signal, refitted kitty-car, and catboat.

The late 50's and early 60's are unrepresented in this volume, having spawned a *Batman* that was, in its way, even more surreal than the TV show to come. Those were the days of the impossibly square-jawed Batman and fey, spit-curled Robin, who were always shown in these arms-akimbo poses that made them less resemble human beings than bendable "action figures." These are the Batman and Robin who were always meeting pointy-eared "aliens from outer space," whose heads seemed to be drawn by tracing bowling balls and who came in almost as many colors as a Princess telephone.

During this period, Catwoman disappeared altogether—replaced for a time by an orange-and-yellow humanoid tabby imaginatively dubbed Cat-Man—and The Penguin made but two appearances, one in 1956 and another in 1963.

Already The Penguin's decline in stature, to that of a character you could never quite take seriously, had begun—a situation not helped by the scenery-chewing of Burgess Meredith in the TV series. As a kind of cultural artifact, we've included two Penguin tales from that period, during which editor Julius Schwartz, veteran writers like John Broome, Gardner Fox, and Ed Herron, and gifted artists like Sheldon Moldoff, Joe Giella, and (usually on covers) Carmine Infantino labored heroically to bring some of the old dignity back to this by-now rather silly buffoon.

In the mid-70's, Denny O'Neil, Irv Novick and Dick Giordano succeeded admirably as well, in "Hail Emperor Penguin," setting the stage for the brilliant writer-artist team of Steve Englehart and Marshall Rogers to recast the character as a formidable adversary in their memorable "Malay Penguin." Their lead was followed in the subsequent writing of Doug Moench, Joey Cavalieri, and Max Allan Collins, and the dynamic graphics of talents like Gene Colan, Klaus Janson, and the aforementioned Mr. Breyfogle, whose efforts from the 1980s under editors Len Wein and Denny O'Neil round out our collection. The tradition reestablished in that work continues today.

The Catwoman, too, was ill-served by television, beginning with a costume redesign—replicated in "Catwoman Sets Her Claws for Batman"—featuring something that looked like a cross between an overgrown domino mask and harlequin glasses, which had the unfortunate effect of making Julie Newmar's head look like the back of a '61 Biscayne. Numerous redesigns and reinterpretations of the character followed; one by Frank Robbins can be seen herein, in the featurette from 1974. But in the early 80's under editor Wein, The Catwoman returned briefly to her old, classic self, until the Miller-Mazzucchelli incarnation that debuted in the BATMAN: YEAR ONE series could set the standard of excellence that ushered the character into the 90's.

What lasting impact on the *Batman* mythology will be made by the big-screen versions of these characters served up by *Batman Returns* remains to be seen. But as you savor this second helping of the Greatest Batman Stories Ever Told, bear in mind that there are many more yet to be created. And you will probably someday be able to read them, in future editions of this series—because in this, the third Year of The Bat in as many decades, one thing is certain: whether you know him as the Caped Crusader, Masked Manhunter, Darknight Detective or simply The Dark Knight, the Batman's power to excite seems greater than ever. Indeed, it seems eternal.

THE DEADLIEST DUO

Foreword by Mike Gold

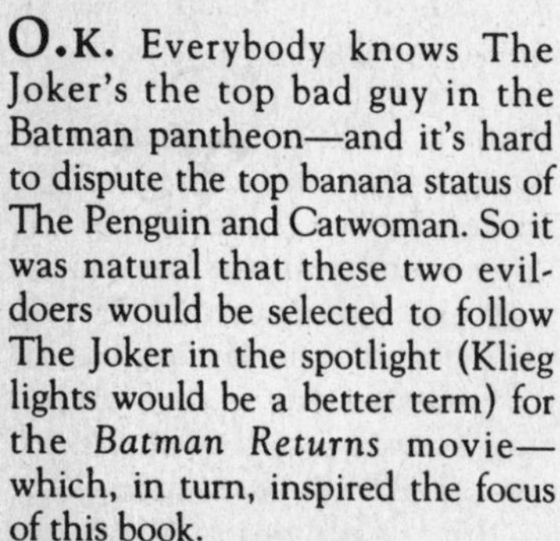

O.K. Everybody knows The Joker's the top bad guy in the Batman pantheon—and it's hard to dispute the top banana status of The Penguin and Catwoman. So it was natural that these two evildoers would be selected to follow The Joker in the spotlight (Klieg lights would be a better term) for the *Batman Returns* movie—which, in turn, inspired the focus of this book.

All of which is just fine by me, as The Penguin and Catwoman are my favorite blackguards, and they always were. But, for the life of me, I don't quite understand how they were able to achieve such a reaction. I figure I must have been born knowing about these scoundrels.

In doing the research needed to select these stories, Editors Bob Greenberger and Paul Kupperberg happened across an interesting revelation: there were hardly any Penguin or Catwoman stories published in the late 1950s and early 1960s. Actually, this was true of all of the big-name Batman villains: As I noted in the introduction to THE GREATEST JOKER STORIES EVER TOLD, when the Comics Code went into effect in the mid-1950s, DC decided to move away from the "traditional" villains into the realm of science-fiction inspired storylines. This also was in keeping with the motion picture trends of the time, where cheapo alien invasion stories brought them into the popcorn palaces in droves.

But I started reading Batman around 1957, and I was aware of The Penguin and Catwoman long before their stories were reprinted in those phenomenal BATMAN ANNUALs of the early 1960s. So where did this knowledge come from?

I can only guess that I was inspired by tales of legend expressed by my older sister, herself a comic book reader, or perhaps by an older cousin who had been a Batman reader since the early 1940s. Clearly, The Penguin and Catwoman were extremely memorable characters, and I suspect their sagas were "handed down" to me the way stories had been handed down for centuries before Gutenberg.

All I know is, I became their fan long before I became their reader. Somebody successfully communicated the wonderment that creates these legends.

When Editor Julius Schwartz reintroduced The Batman in 1964, he started to bring back all of the classic villains, establishing a rogues gallery that rivaled the one he and his creative crew had established in THE FLASH. All of a sudden the Joker, the Penguin, Catwoman, Two-Face, the Mad Hatter, and Scarecrow were back on the scene.

This wasn't a stab in the dark—Julie's instincts, as usual, were right on the money. When the folks at 20th Century-Fox started up their now-classic Batman television series less than two years later, they had a wealth of fantastic characters to exploit. Indeed, they led with The Riddler, a villain who had made but two appearances, both seventeen years prior to the launch of the television series. Although Frank Gorshin's entertaining and energetic performance in no way reminded older readers of Fred Astaire, the original inspiration for The Riddler's visual appearance, it was more than sufficient to burn the character into the viewers' minds and to establish the tone for the upcoming series.

It is no coincidence that the Penguin and Catwoman were among the most memorable television villains—not simply because the concept and the imagery of these characters was so significant, but because the actors who portrayed these villains were the cream of the crop. Burgess Meredith, one of America's most gifted and versatile performers, donned tuxedo, umbrella and body padding to transcend the limitations of the campy television series with his broad yet truly memorable creation. While the comic book Penguin was a formidable character, the post-television incarnation became a truly deadly adversary. Clearly the makeover was motivated, in part, by a desire to distance the Batman myth from the humorous atmosphere of the television series—yet the demand for the Penguin created by the show remained high for these ensuing two dozen years.

A penguin is a rather enigmatic animal: it is a bird, yet it does not fly; it swims, but is not a fish. Our Penguin is an extremely enigmatic villain: he dresses up in a tuxedo with tails, but he is no gentleman attending a dinner party. He is no gentleman at all.

Now, people dressed in tuxes often are referred to as wearing penguin suits, and as those of us who have seen *The Blues Brothers* know, it is not uncommon to refer to nuns as penguins as well. I am relieved to report that we have yet to come across an example of our Penguin being influenced by the latter reference.

He has been preoccupied with bird-themed crimes (and it's amazing that this narrow fixation did not impose undue limitations on his career), but his most enigmatic personality quirk is his fixation with umbrellas, a device not commonly associated with either fish or fowl. Of course, The Penguin's umbrellas tend to be cleverly-rigged instruments of death—or, in the case of the movie *Batman Returns*, a mode of transportation that compensates for this bird's inability to fly.

In other words, The Penguin is a pretty wacky guy—impressive because of his affectations more than his deeds, although in recent years his actions have grown much darker, consistent with the evolved mood of the contemporary Batman comics.

It has taken no less than three talented actors to create the part of Catwoman—Julie Newmar, the first to play the part on television, Lee Ann Meriwether, who played it solely in the 1966 theatrical motion picture, and Eartha Kitt, who imparted a strong, salacious quality to the character during the final season.

It was Kitt's downright sexiness that was most true to the evolution of Catwoman. In the aggregate, Catwoman has followed a rather twisted career path: a cat burglar who was The Batman's sworn enemy, it wasn't too long before she developed a romantic attraction to the Darknight Detective.

Such a desire certainly has its precedents in heroic fiction—the concept of the moody male hero sexually felling his female adversary is by no means unique. In the case of Catwoman, however, her attentions seemed to go beyond the cliché—and even beyond the typical identification-with-the-aggressor syndrome similarly typical of popular fiction. Her love was genuine; there was something pure about her emotions towards The Batman.

The sexually aloof Batman always has remained rather beyond such base desires—generally speaking. But most remarkably, The Batman often has found himself succumbing (in one form or another) to Catwoman's charms. Quite frankly, he seemed to find Catwoman more...appealing...than alter ego Bruce Wayne ever found his "legitimate" girlfriends, Julie Madison and Vicki Vale. It was this dichotomy that makes the Batman/Catwoman relationship fascinating.

Her feelings towards The Batman had a ping-pong effect on her résumé. Starting out as a villain, she took on the heroic role in an effort to prove her worthiness to the object of her desire. When things didn't work out, Catwoman found herself drifting back to a life of crime—and flowing back to the other side of the stream as a reflection of her moral ambiguity.

In the process, Catwoman's travails clearly illustrates the schizophrenic role of the so-called superhero: as vigilantes, costumed heroes blatantly ignore the very legal structure they purport to hold dear. Even those heroes who have been "duly deputized by the police" are a civil libertarian's worst nightmare, as they are in constant violation of the fourth, fifth, sixth, seventh, and eighth amendments to the United States Constitution. Viewing it from this perspective, The Batman is a hypocrite, whereas Catwoman merely possesses a confused soul.

You may notice that, unlike the previous books in our GREATEST STORIES series, this volume largely concentrates on stories from the past three decades. As noted, there weren't very many Penguin or Catwoman stories in the years that preceded Editor Schwartz's takeover and, quite frankly, the quality of many of those few stories was rather... varied. Additionally, we already reprinted a number of the better early Penguin and Catwoman stories in our earlier GREATEST

STORIES books. (Oddly, THE GREATEST BATMAN STORIES EVER TOLD, VOLUME 2 is actually the third BATMAN volume, the aforementioned GREATEST JOKER STORIES book being the *real* volume two. If the time comes when the decision is made to do a sequel to the Joker book, perhaps we should move to lettering this series: THE GREATEST BATMAN STORIES VOLUME D, or somesuch.)

I should further point out that the early Penguin and Catwoman stories are being systematically reprinted in order as part of the complete reprinting of the DETECTIVE COMICS and BATMAN series, in our ongoing ARCHIVE EDITIONS. In the interest of historical perspective, however, we did not let the availability of these ARCHIVES books stop us from reprinting (*re-reprinting?*) the very first Penguin and Catwoman stories in this book.

Fans of our little menagerie of evildoers can find a nearly endless supply of books reprinting other classic sagas, in addition to the other books in our GREATEST STORIES and ARCHIVE EDITIONS series. Recently, Kitchen Sink and DC Comics teamed up to produce BATMAN: THE SUNDAY CLASSICS, reprinting several Penguin and Catwoman newspaper strip stories (in color, no less) from the mid-1940s. In the mid-1960s, Signet books issued a number of paperbacks reprinting classic stories, in black and white (with panels rearranged to fit the 4" by 6 3/4" format). One of these volumes was dedicated to Penguin stories, and this paperback series was re-reprinted in 1989 by Titan Books of England with the addition of a Catwoman collection.

Two of the most significant Catwoman sagas of the modern period remain in print in trade paperback form: the Frank Miller/David Mazzucchelli/Richmond Lewis BATMAN: YEAR ONE, and the Mindy Newell/J.J. Birch/Michael Bair/Adrienne Roy CATWOMAN: HER SISTER'S KEEPER. Both stories feature an updated—some might feel controversial—view of the classic villain.

Furthermore, Batman initiator Bob Kane's autobiography, *Batman & Me* (Eclipse Books, 1989) contains his views and recollections as to the creation of these and other pillars of the Batman community.

These days, there is no shortage of Penguin and Catwoman stories from all five decades of Batman history. Young readers need not rely on television reruns or genetic imprinting to experience firsthand the sense of wonder generated by the classic super-hero/super-villain confrontations.

To those of you who are looking at the following stories as revisiting old friends, welcome back. To those of you who are coming across these mini-epics for the first time, I envy you.

Here's where the fun *really* starts.

BRENT ANDERSON

(DC Comics' Group Editor/Director of Development Mike Gold is the editor of the other volumes in THE GREATEST STORIES EVER TOLD series, including the forthcoming multi-volume GREATEST 1960s STORIES EVER TOLD set, and is the former Consulting Editor of the ARCHIVE EDITIONS series.)

Written by Bill Finger/Art by Bob Kane & Jerry Robinson/Lettering by Jerry Robinson

READING ABOUT THE TRAVERS YACHT PARTY, EH? IT SURE IS GETTING A LOT OF PUBLICITY! EVERYONE KNOWS ABOUT IT!
THAT'S THE TROUBLE EVERY CROOK IN TOWN WILL BE THINKING ABOUT STEALING THAT NECKLACE IF HE CAN!

DO YOU THINK THERE MIGHT BE TROUBLE? THAT SOMETHING MIGHT HAPPEN?
CALL IT A HUNCH! I'D LIKE TO BE ON THAT YACHT TOMORROW NIGHT, BUT I'VE ANOTHER JOB TO DO FIRST! I WONDER HMMM....

DICK, HOW WOULD YOU LIKE TO TAKE CHARGE OF THIS CASE UNTIL I GET THERE IN TIME TO HELP YOU? THINK YOU CAN DO IT ALONE?
ME? ALONE? AND HOW! LEAD ME TO IT!
BUT HOW WOULD I GET ON THE YACHT WITHOUT BEING SUSPECTED?
I KNOW A LOT OF PEOPLE. I'LL GET YOU A JOB AS A STEWARD THERE. FROM THEN ON YOU'RE ON YOUR OWN! NOW LISTEN CAREFULLY...

AND SO IT IS THAT YOUNG DICK GRAYSON IS ABOARD THE DOLPHIN...
BETTER KEEP MY EYES AND EARS OPEN. SAY, THERE'S MRS. TRAVERS... THINK I'LL EAVESDROP...

AH, DENNY. MY FAVORITE NEPHEW! WHERE HAVE YOU BEEN?
HELLO, AUNT MARTHA. I WANT YOU TO MEET MISS PEGGS. SHE IS A GUEST OF MINE! I HOPE YOU DON'T MIND MY BRINGING HER ABOARD?
2.

NONSENSE! GLAD TO HAVE MISS PEGGS!
THANK YOU! EVER SINCE I SPRAINED MY ANKLE DENNY HAS BEEN ESCORTING ME ABOUT! A FINE BOY, YOUR NEPHEW. A FINE BOY!

DICK "PUMPS" ONE OF THE REGULAR STEWARDS!
MUST BE A NICE FELLOW, HER NEPHEW, TO ESCORT AN OLD WOMAN AROUND LIKE THAT!
HUH, HIM? HE'S A RAT... PROBABLY HANGING AROUND TO GET SOME MONEY OUT OF HER! HE'S ALWAYS BORROWING DOUGH FROM HIS AUNT MRS TRAVERS!

THEY ALL TRY TO GET DOUGH OUT OF HER! SEE THAT GUY WHO JUST WALKED OVER? THAT'S HER DOCTOR... WALLACE. GAMBLES ALL HIS DOUGH AWAY... AND THEN HE BORROWS MONEY FROM MRS. TRAVERS! I BET HE OWES HER PLENTY!... PLENTY!

SOMETIME LATER AS DICK PASSES A CABIN...
VOICES! SOUNDS LIKE A QUARREL!
NO! I WON'T LEND YOU A CENT, ROGER AND THAT'S FINAL!
BUT I NEED IT TO COVER MY STOCK LOSSES! PLEASE!

JUST BECAUSE YOU'RE MY BROTHER, DOESN'T MEAN I MUST FINANCE ALL YOUR STUPID PLUNGES IN THE STOCK MARKET!
I'LL BE RUINED! AND YOU'LL BE THE CAUSE OF IT ALL! I'LL GET THAT MONEY SOMEHOW SOMEWAY!
WHEW! LOOKS LIKE THIS YACHT ISN'T THE SAFEST PLACE IN THE WORLD FOR A NECKLACE WORTH A HALF A MILLION DOLLARS!

AS HE TURNS A CORNER HE SEES DENNY FURTIVELY THROW A PAPER OVER THE RAIL!
IF EVER A GUY LOOKED GUILTY ABOUT SOMETHING, HE DOES! WONDER WHAT'S IN THAT PAPER?
3

BY A QUEER QUIRK OF FATE, THE WIND SEIZES THE PAPER AND TOSSES IT BACK ON DECK...
WHAT A BREAK! NOW TO READ IT!

THE LETTER!
Keep your aunt away from room! Will try then!
—The Cat

THE CAT!·· MRS TRAVERS IS KEEPING HER NECKLACE IN HER ROOM TILL THE BIG PARTY LATER!·· I'D BETTER GET TO THE ROOM RIGHT AWAY!

SUDDENLY A SCREAM SPLITS THE NIGHT AIR!
I'VE BEEN ROBBED! MY NECKLACE HAS BEEN STOLEN! HELP QUICK···
TOO LATE· THE CAT'S GOT HERE FIRST!

I HAD THIS PRIVATE DETECTIVE GUARDING MY SAFE·· AND WHEN I CAME HERE I FOUND HIM LIKE THIS! OH! MY NECKLACE GONE! OH DENNY, WHAT WILL I DO?
NECKLACE·· GONE??
DON'T WORRY, MARTHA·· WE'LL FIND IT FOR YOU!

HELLOOOO THERE! STAND BY!
AT THAT MOMENT A BOAT APPROACHES... CLEAVING THE MURKY WATERS!

SWIFTLY IT DRAWS ALONG SIDE THE YACHT·· ITS FORM INDISTINCT BECAUSE OF THE DENSE FOG!
WHAT DO YOU WANT? WHO ARE YOU?
COAST GUARD! WE'RE COMING ABOARD!

I'LL FETCH THEM HERE AT ONCE!
COAST GUARD!·· POLICE!·· THEY'LL FIND MY NECKLACE!
OF COURSE THEY WILL!
4

BUT INSTEAD OF THE COAST GUARD..QUITE THE REVERSE!
WH..WHY, YOU'RE NOT THE COAST GUARD!
YOU'RE A BRIGHT BOY! YOU MUSTA GOT HIGH MARKS IN SCHOOL!
RAISE YOUR HANDS HIGH, ALL OF YA!

GET THIS, CAPTAIN. IF ANY OF YOUR MEN JUST SO MUCH AS MOVES A FINGER I'LL SPRAY THESE PEOPLE WITH LEAD! WE'RE TAKIN' OVER THE BOAT!
CAPTAIN, TELL THE SAILORS TO LAY DOWN THEIR ARMS! WE DON'T WANT ANYONE HURT!
YES M'AM!

IN A FEW MOMENTS ALL THE CREW IS LOCKED BELOW AND THE GUESTS LINED UP ON DECK...
NOW MRS. TRAVERS... YOU CAN HAND OVER THAT NECKLACE OF YOURS OR... SAY, SHE GONE NUTS? WHAT'S SHE LAUGHING ABOUT?
YOU'RE TOO LATE! HA-HA-HA-IT'S ALREADY STOLEN!

WHAT'S THIS?.. HAND OVER THE NECKLACE!
IT'S TRUE. IT WAS JUST TAKEN WHEN YOU CAME! WE THOUGHT YOU WERE THE COAST GUARD AND MIGHT HOLD AN INVESTIGATION, BUT NOW...

CAN YOU IMAGINE THAT! SOMEONE STOLE IT BEFORE WE DID! WHATTA CROOK! YA CAN'T TRUST ANYBODY THESE DAYS!
AND WHILE WE'RE AT IT, WE MIGHT AS WELL TAKE WHATEVER ELSE IS AROUND...
COAST GUARD OR NOT, WE'RE STILL GONNA HOLD AN INVESTIGATION.. RIGHT NOW! C'MON BOYS.. FRISK EM!

AS ONE OF THEM APPROACHES A WOMAN...
A FRESH GUY, HUH? I'LL TAKE THAT OUTA YA!
OKAY, BABY, LET'S HAVE THAT BRACELET. C'MON, GIVE IT TO ME!
TAKE YOUR HANDS OFF HER, YOU DIRTY THIEF!

BUT HURTLING THROUGH THE AIR-DICK GRAYSON!
MUSTN'T PLAY WITH GUNS.. MIGHT HURT SOMEBODY!
5

I DON'T LIKE YOUR FACE. I'LL THINK I'LL CHANGE ITS APPEARANCE!
GET THAT KID!

YOU'VE GOT TO GET ME FIRST!

HEADLONG DIVE..
NOTHING LIKE A COLD PLUNGE!

RAIN OF DEATH FOLLOWS THE PLUMMETING FIGURE!

THE BOY'S FIGURE HITS THE WATER TO REMAIN BELOW!
DID YA GET HIM?
HE AIN'T COME UP YET!
SURE, BOSS, WE GOT HIM! WE DON'T MISS!
6

BUT THE GUNMAN IS WRONG-THERE ARE TIMES THEY DO MISS AND THIS WAS ONE OF THEM!
THINK I'D BETTER GET OUT OF THESE CLOTHES AND INTO CHARACTER!

UPON THE DECK OF THE "DOLPHIN", THE GUNMEN QUICKLY GATHER THEIR LOOT!
SORRY, BOSS, NOT ONE OF THIS BUNCH HAS THE NECKLACE ON 'EM!
WELL, WE CAN'T KICK, WE GOT MORE THAN THE NECKLACE IS WORTH IN DOUGH AND JEWELS IN THE BAG! WE OUGHTA SCRAM!
LET'S GO!.. THE COAST GUARD MAY BE HERE ANY MINUTE. C'MON!

A MOMENT LATER THE BOAT ROARS AWAY FROM THE WAKE OF THE YACHT!

WELL, WE CERTAINLY GOT AWAY WITH A NICE HAUL EVEN THOUGH.. ..SAY.. BOSS.. LOOK.. A BOAT AFTER US!
IT'S A FAST ONE. SHE'LL BE ON US IN A MINUTE.. GIVE 'EM A TASTE OF LEAD!

A HAIL OF LEAD GREETS THE BOAT.. BUT ON SHE COMES LIKE A HUGE JUGGERNAUT!
GIVE IT TO 'EM!
HE AIN'T STOPPIN' ..KEEPS RIGHT ON COMING!

AS THE PURSUING BOAT DRAWS NEAR, A FAMILIAR FIGURE LAUNCHES OFF.. BATMAN!

ABRUPTLY A HISSING SOUND AND..
WHAT TH'... A ROPE!!

FROM ATOP THE CABIN-ROOF.. ROBIN THE WONDER BOY!
SORRY YOU CAN'T TALK TO THESE MEN NOW.. THEY'RE A LITTLE TIED UP!
ROBIN!

THE GUNMEN ARE DISARMED!
HOW DID YOU GET HERE?
THE TRAIL GOT COLD ON MY OTHER CASE, SO I DROVE TO THE YACHT! WHEN I SAW THIS LAUNCH SPEEDING AWAY, I FIGURED SOMETHING WAS UP. SO HERE I AM!

ROBIN, I'VE ALWAYS WONDERED JUST HOW BRAVE A CROOK IS WITHOUT HIS GUN! I'D LIKE TO TRY A LITTLE EXPERIMENT AND YOU'RE GOING TO PROVE IT!
HOW?

I'M GOING TO SHOW THE KIDS OF AMERICA HOW YELLOW YOU RATS ARE WITHOUT YOUR GUNS! I'M GOING TO LET ROBIN HERE TAKE FOUR OF YOU ON. ALL AT THE SAME TIME!
THE GUY'S NUTS!

FOUR OF US AGAINST THAT KID! HA-HA-HA!
THAT'S MY PROPOSITION. TAKE IT?
AND HOW! JUST LET ME GET MY HANDS ON HIM!

A MOMENT LATER.. A STARTLING SCENE TAKES PLACE.. FOUR GROWN MEN PIT THEIR STRENGTH AGAINST THAT OF A LONE BOY!!
WE'LL KNOOK THE KID SILLY!
I'M AFRAID YOU'RE THE ONES WHO ARE GOING TO FEEL SILLY!

ROBIN ACTS WITH THE SPEED OF THOUGHT!
FANCY BUMPING INTO YOU BOYS.. WAY OUT HERE!
8

THEN A FIST THAT SHOOTS OUT WITH THE FORCE OF A PISTON-ROD!
COME, COME, BOYS, HOW ABOUT A LITTLE COMPETITION!

WHAT HAPPENED.. DID WE HIT A REEF?
COME ON, BOYS, GET UP.. JUST ONCE MORE..
TSK! TSK!

ONCE MORE A LAUNCHING ATTACK..BUT ROBIN IS READY..AND QUITE ABLE!
I'LL... PHHHFT!
I DIDN'T QUITE GET WHAT YOU SAID!

ANOTHER THUNDER-BOLT BLOW...THEN
HO HUM!

THE FRIGHTENED MEN SHOW THEIR TRUE COLOR!
HEY.. WHERE ARE YOU BOYS GOING?... LET'S PLAY SOME MORE!
N..NO! DON'T HIT ME AGAIN! I QUIT...YOU WIN!
T..TAKE IT EASY, KID!

HOW ABOUT THESE BOYS, BATMAN!
NOT A BAD IDEA!...WOULD YOU FELLOWS LIKE TO TRY A JOUST WITH THE KID!
N..NOT ME!
NO-NO-GET THAT KID AWAY FROM ME!
IF I ONLY HAD MY GUN...
9

WELL, KIDS, THERE'S YOUR PROOF! CROOKS ARE YELLOW WITHOUT THEIR GUNS!..DON'T GO AROUND ADMIRING THEM.. RATHER DO YOUR BEST IN FIGHTING THEM AND ALL THEIR KIND!

A MOMENT LATER WITH THE JEWELS IN THEIR POSSESSION AND THE MEN TRUSSED UP, BATMAN AND ROBIN SPEED AWAY....

AND THEN I PICKED UP THIS PAPER WITH THE MESSAGE FROM THE **CAT**!

LOOKS LIKE DENNY, MRS. TRAVERS' NEPHEW IS IN WITH THE **CAT**! TELL ME ABOUT THE PASSENGERS YOU SUSPECT MIGHT BE THE **CAT**!

...SO IT'S EITHER HER GAMBLING DOCTOR WALLACE OR HER STOCK-PLAYING BROTHER ROGER!

LOOKS THAT WAY, DOESN'T IT.. BUT YOU NEVER CAN TELL! NOW LISTEN..

ABOARD THE YACHT THE GUESTS ARE TRYING TO FORGET THEIR LOSSES BY HOLDING A MASQUERADE PARTY...

...AND NOW I WILL AWARD THIS CUP TO THE PERSON WHO HAS THE MOST ORIGINAL COSTUME..

WHY AREN'T YOU IN COSTUME, MISS PEGGS?

I'M TOO OLD FOR THAT SORT OF THING. BESIDES, MY ANKLE--IT BOTHERS ME TOO MUCH! THANK YOU FOR HELPING ME UP THE STEPS!

AT THAT MOMENT A FIGURE STEPS DOWN FROM THE STAIRWAY ONTO THE DAIS DRESSED IN A WEIRD COSTUME

...LOOK.. WHAT A STRANGE COSTUME!

HE OUGHT TO GET THE PRIZE!

HE'S DRESSED AS THE **BATMAN**. WHAT A CLEVER IDEA!

AN IRONICAL JOKE TAKES PLACE!!

IT HAS BEEN DECIDED THAT YOUR COSTUME OF THE **BATMAN** IS THE MOST ORIGINAL HERE TONIGHT.. THE CUP IS YOURS!!

THANK YOU. I ACCEPT THE CUP. AND NOW, IF I MAY, I WOULD LIKE TO FILL IT WITH...

...WITH DRINK, SIR?

...NO, DEAR LADY. WITH YOUR STOLEN PROPERTY! I HAVE RECOVERED IT. YOU SEE.. I REALLY AM.. THE **BATMAN**!

THE **BATMAN**.. HE R-REALLY IS... !!!

OUR MONEY AND JEWELS!

BATMAN.. IN PERSON. HOW THRILLING!!!

AT THAT MOMENT THE LOUD CLANGING OF A BELL IS HEARD --THE FIRE ALARM!

FIRE ALARM - THE SHIP IS ON **FIRE** - GET TO THE LIFE BOATS.

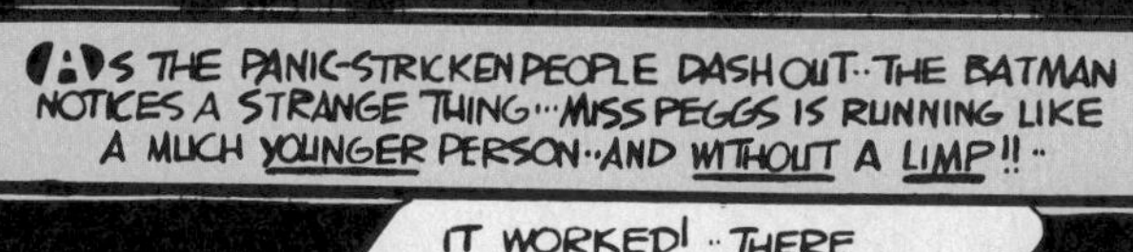
AS THE PANIC-STRICKEN PEOPLE DASH OUT··THE BATMAN NOTICES A STRANGE THING···MISS PEGGS IS RUNNING LIKE A MUCH YOUNGER PERSON··AND WITHOUT A LIMP!!··

IT WORKED! ·· THERE GOES MISS PEGGS··NICE LEGS FOR AN OLD WOMAN!

THE CAPTAIN APPEARS AND SHOUTS OUT WORDS THAT ALMOST HYPNOTIZE THE PEOPLE TO ORDER···
STOP!··THERE'S NO FIRE!·· IT'S A FALSE ALARM! SOME CRAZY FOOL MUST HAVE SET THE ALARM OFF AS A JOKE!!!

A FALSE ALARM··· I WONDER···THE BATMAN···HE'S AFTER ME!!··IT'S A TRAP!

BUT EVEN AS SHE DESCENDS THE STAIRS·· A FIGURE HURTLES AFTER HER!

ROBIN··THE BOY WONDER·· COMES THROUGH AGAIN!!··
MY MOTHER TOLD ME NEVER TO FIGHT WITH A LADY··BUT THIS TIME I'M MAKING AN EXCEPTION!!

THE BATMAN TAKES CHARGE!
···NOW I'M GOING TO SHOW YOU WHAT THE REAL CAT LOOKS LIKE!·· I'VE HEARD TALES ABOUT THE CAT BEFORE IN THE' UNDERWORLD!
I CAN HARDLY WAIT!

BLACK HAIR IS REVEALED UNDER THE GREY WIG!
FIRST··OFF WITH THE WIG!
YOU··· YOU···!!

THE MAKEUP WAX IS QUICKLY RUBBED OFF...
LET GO OF ME!
QUIET OR PAPA SPANK!
SWIFTLY THE SWADDLING FROCK IS REMOVED.. AND THERE IN THE PLACE OF OLD "MISS PEGGS".. A BEAUTIFUL YOUNG WOMAN
WELL, WHAT'S THE MATTER?.. HAVEN'T YOU EVE SEEN A PRETTY GIRL BEFORE?

WELL CAT, IT SEEMS WE'VE GOT YOU AT LAST!.. NOW LET'S TAKE A LOOK AT THAT BANDAGE!
WHAT'S THE USE.. I KNOW WHEN I'M LICKED!.. GO AHEAD!

THERE UNDER THE BANDAGE.. THE MISSING TRAVERS NECKLACE!!
WHEEW!... NO WONDER YOU WANTED TO STEAL THEM!.. THEY'RE PERFECT!.. A HALF A MILLION DOLLARS!

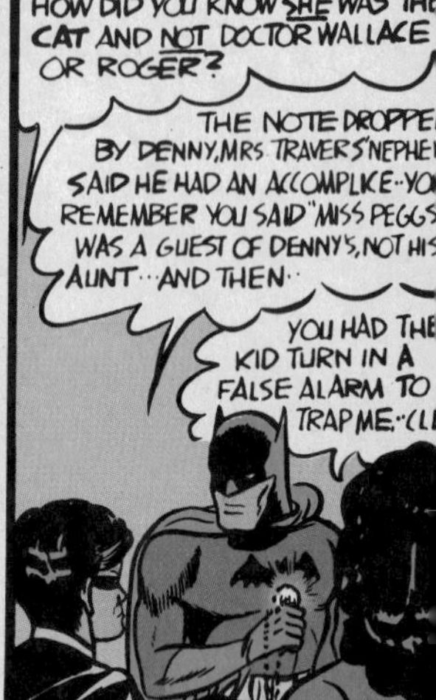
HOW DID YOU KNOW SHE WAS THE CAT AND NOT DOCTOR WALLACE OR ROGER?
THE NOTE DROPPE BY DENNY, MRS TRAVERS' NEPHE SAID HE HAD AN ACCOMPLICE.. YO REMEMBER YOU SAID "MISS PEGGS" WAS A GUEST OF DENNY'S, NOT HIS AUNT... AND THEN..
YOU HAD THE KID TURN IN A FALSE ALARM TO TRAP ME.

ABRUPTLY...
DENNY!
I'LL TAKE THAT, BATMAN!
12
..AS LONG AS YOU WANT IT... HERE!

BOY, HE'S OUT COLDER THAN A DEAD MACKEREL!
BATMAN ··· I WAS SUPPOSED TO GIVE DENNY HALF OF THE JEWELS ·· WHY DON'T YOU COME IN AS A PARTNER WITH ME! YOU AND I TOGETHER!

YOU AND I ·· KING AND QUEEN OF CRIME! ··· WE'D MAKE A GREAT TEAM! WITH YOU AS MY PARTNER WE ···
SORRY, YOUR PROPOSITION TEMPTS ME BUT WE WORK ON DIFFERENT SIDES OF THE LAW! LET'S GO!

WITH THE JEWELS GIVEN TO MRS. TRAVERS ·· AND HER NEPHEW LOCKED IN HIS CABIN ·· THE BATMAN AND ROBIN ARE HOME-WARD BOUND ··· WITH THE CAT!
WELL, WE'RE HOME. THERE'S THE WHARF NOW!
WHY DIDN'T YOU LEAVE ME BEHIND ON THE YACHT INSTEAD OF TAKING ME TO THE POLICE YOURSELF?
I'VE GOT MY REASONS!

SUDDENLY THE CAT LEAPS TO HER FEET AND ··
WATCH HER ·· SHE'S JUMPED OVERBOARD!
FANCY THAT!

AS ROBIN MAKES READY TO JUMP AFTER THE CAT ·· THE BATMAN CLUMSILY 'BUMPS' INTO HIM! ···
HEY!
OOPS ·· SORRY, ROBIN!

BY THE TIME THEY RECOVER, THE CAT HAS MADE GOOD HER ESCAPE!
TOO LATE ·· SHE'S GONE! ·· AND ··· SAY ·· I'LL BET YOU BUMPED INTO ME ON PURPOSE! ·· THAT'S WHY YOU TOOK HER ALONG WITH US ·· SO SHE MIGHT TRY A BREAK!
WHY, ROBIN, MY BOY, WHAT EVER GAVE YOU SUCH AN IDEA! ··· HMM ·· NICE NIGHT, ISN'T IT?

·· LOVELY GIRL! ·· WHAT EYES! · SAY ·· MUSTN'T FORGET I'VE GOT A GIRL NAMED JULIE! ·· OH WELL ·· SHE STILL HAD LOVELY EYES! ·· MAYBE I'LL BUMP INTO HER AGAIN SOMETIME ··
HMMM ..
BOB KANE

SO MANY OF OUR READERS HAVE WRITTEN US SUCH NICE LETTERS THAT WE HAVE DECIDED TO SHOW OUR APPRECIATION ···· THEREFORE ON THE BACK COVER OF THIS MAGAZINE YOU WILL FIND A FULL-PAGE AUTOGRAPHED PICTURE, SUITABLE FOR FRAMING, OF BOTH BATMAN AND ROBIN ·· THE BOY WONDER ····
THIS IS OUR WAY OF SAYING THANKS ····
Bob Kane

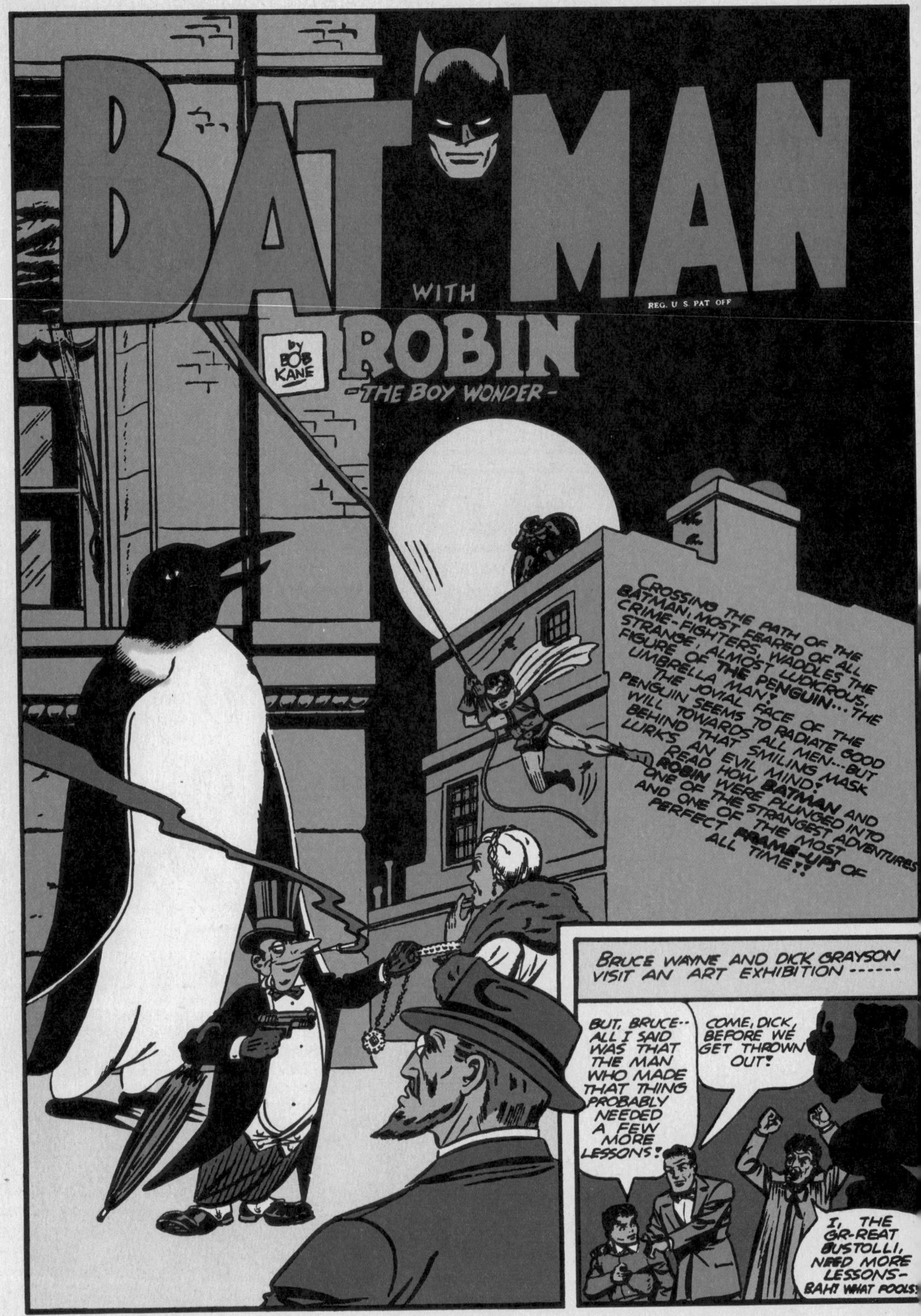
BATMAN
WITH
REG. U. S. PAT OFF
by BOB KANE
ROBIN
-THE BOY WONDER-
CROSSING THE PATH OF THE BATMAN, MOST FEARED OF ALL CRIME-FIGHTERS, WADDLES THE STRANGE, ALMOST LUDICROUS, FIGURE OF THE PENGUIN... THE UMBRELLA MAN! THE JOVIAL FACE OF THE PENGUIN SEEMS TO RADIATE GOOD WILL TOWARDS ALL MEN... BUT BEHIND THAT SMILING MASK LURKS AN EVIL MIND! READ HOW BATMAN AND ROBIN WERE PLUNGED INTO ONE OF THE STRANGEST ADVENTURES AND ONE OF THE MOST PERFECT FRAME-UPS OF ALL TIME!!
BRUCE WAYNE AND DICK GRAYSON VISIT AN ART EXHIBITION ------
BUT, BRUCE-- ALL I SAID WAS THAT THE MAN WHO MADE THAT THING PROBABLY NEEDED A FEW MORE LESSONS!
COME, DICK, BEFORE WE GET THROWN OUT!
I, THE GR-REAT BUSTOLLI, NEED MORE LESSONS- BAH! WHAT FOOLS!

DICK LEARNS THAT ART CAN BE EXPENSIVE.
YES, DICK, THESE TWO SMALL WATTEAUS ARE WORTH ROUGHLY A HALF MILLION DOLLARS BETWEEN THEM!
WHEW! MAYBE I OUGHT TO TAKE UP PAINTING!

BEAUTIFUL--MARVELOUS--GORGEOUS--
LET'S GO BACK. YOU REALLY MUST LEARN NOT TO LAUGH AT PEOPLE OR THINGS, BECAUSE THEY MAY BE----ER-ODD LOOKING!
PENGUIN

BUT, BRUCE, LOOK FOR YOURSELF!
HA! HA! HE DOES LOOK LIKE A PENGUIN AT THAT!

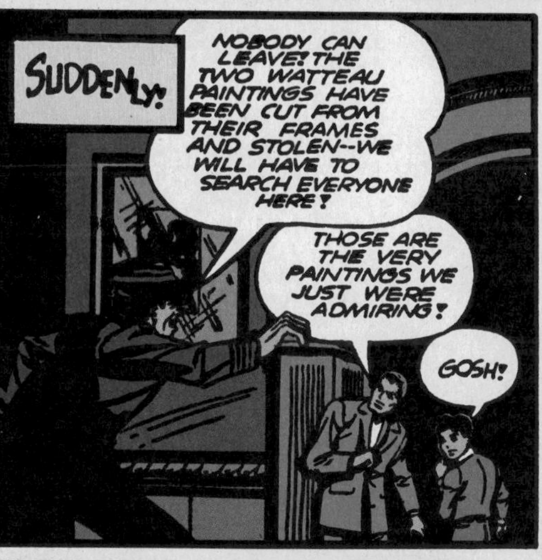
SUDDENLY!
NOBODY CAN LEAVE! THE TWO WATTEAU PAINTINGS HAVE BEEN CUT FROM THEIR FRAMES AND STOLEN--WE WILL HAVE TO SEARCH EVERYONE HERE!
THOSE ARE THE VERY PAINTINGS WE JUST WERE ADMIRING!
GOSH!

RICH MAN--POOR MAN--BEGGARMAN--AND THIEF--ALL MUST SUBMIT TO THE SEARCH!
I'M AFRAID THIS IS GOING TO BE--ER--EMBARRASSING!
I DON'T MIND A-BEIN' SEARCH! I ONLY HOPE -A DEY CATCH DA THIEF!
IT'S OUTRAGEOUS! IMAGINE SEARCHING ME!

CURSES! THERE GOES A MILLION DOLLARS!
COUNT PEREL! WHY, YOU'RE NOTHING BUT A PHONEY! GOODBYE!
LOOKS LIKE FINE FEATHERS DON'T ALWAYS MAKE FINE BIRDS!

BRUCE AND DICK SUBMIT UNCOMPLAININGLY TO BEING SEARCHED!
SORRY, MR. WAYNE, BUT WE GOTTA CHECK EVERYBODY!
PERFECTLY ALL RIGHT, JONES!
I'D TAKE OFF MY SHOES, BUT I'VE GOT A HOLE IN MY STOCKING.

THE GUARDS ARE BAFFLED AS THEIR SEARCH ENDS FRUITLESSLY!
SORRY TO DISAPPOINT YOU-HEE-HEE---DON'T YOU KNOW IT'S BAD LUCK TO OPEN AN UMBRELLA INDOORS?
HE AIN'T GOT THEM EITHER. THEY WOULDN'T HAVE FLOWN AWAY!

THAT NIGHT, IN A HOTEL OF THE BIGGEST RACKETEERS IN TOWN-- KNOWN SIMPLY AS THE BOSS-- A FAT FIGURE WADDLES IN!
PARDON ME-- BUT AREN'T YOU THE GENTLEMAN WHO CONTROLS ALL THE RACKETEERING IN THIS TOWN?
SAY-- YOU'VE GOT THE NERVE!
WHAT DO YOU WANT?

DID YOU HEAR OF THE HALF MILLION DOLLARS' WORTH OF PAINTINGS THAT WERE---ER--- STOLEN FROM THE ART EXHIBITION?
SHALL I DRILL HIM, BOSS?
WAIT A MINUTE-- LET'S HEAR HIS SPIEL!

HOLY SMOKE! BROTHER, YOU'RE IN--SAY, WHAT'S YOUR HANDLE?
OH--AH--I HAVE SO MANY! WHY NOT CALL ME THE PENGUIN? IT DOES FIT--- HEE-- HEE!

BEFORE LONG, THE PENGUIN DIRECTS THE ACTIVITIES OF THE BOSS' MOB!
THE WAY WE'LL PULL OUR JOB IS BY GOING THROUGH THIS ABANDONED GAS PIPE--AND COMING UP UNDER THE BANK HERE!
YOU TELL 'EM, PENGUIN!

NEWSPAPER HEADLINES CALL FOR ACTION AS A CRIME-WAVE THREATENS TO ENGULF THE CITY!
ORGANIZED CRIME THREATENS THE CITY
SUN
HAND OF CRIM MASTER SEEN BA OF SERIES OF ROBBERIES

NEXT DAY---AT THE STAHL AUCTIONEERING HOUSE---
IF I'M NOT MISTAKEN, THAT'S THE FATTY DICK AND I SAW AT THE EXHIBITION. THAT UMBRELLA-- MUST BE ATTACHED TO HIM!
EXCUSE ME--
THIS COLUMBIA DIAMOND IS THE FINEST WHITE STONE IN THE WORLD--

SUDDENLY--THE ROOM PLUNGES INTO DARKNESS--
SOCK!
BAM!

WHEN THE LIGHTS ARE TURNED ON!
THE DIAMOND--- THE GREAT COLUMBIA DIAMOND--- IT'S GONE!

FRENZIED VOICES FILL THE AIR AND PEOPLE MILL ABOUT EXCITEDLY--
SORRY-- I WAS SO EXCITED WHEN THE LIGHTS WENT OUT--I DIDN'T KNOW WHAT I WAS DOING!
WHAT'S THE IDEA-- TRIPPING ME?

SO SORRY YOU WERE INCONVENIENCED!
QUITE ALL RIGHT! ER--- NO HARM DONE!
I'VE GOT A HUNCH THAT KEEPS GROWING. EACH TIME I BUMP IN THAT LITTLE GUY, SOMETHING HAPPENS-- I THINK I'LL GO SLUMMING TONIGHT.

LATER--AT THE BOSS' HEADQUARTERS--
I INSIST ON MY USUAL SHARE OF MONEY FOR ROBBERIES I'VE PLANNED!
YOU'RE GETTIN' TOO BIG FOR YOUR SHOES-- I'VE GOTTA TEACH YA A LESSON SO'S YOU WON'T STEP INTO MINE!

AAAAGH!
THIS WAS BOUND TO OCCUR SOONER OR LATER--- MIGHT AS WELL GET IT OVER WITH NOW!
BANG

IF NONE OF YOU LADS OBJECTS--I'M YOUR NEW BOSS!
SURE-- IT'S OKAY WITH ME, MR. PENGUIN!
SURE!

THAT NIGHT, THE PENGUIN'S HENCHMEN DISCUSS PLANS IN A WATERFRONT DIVE!
DAT JOB DE PENGUIN PLANNED FER TONIGHT WILL BE A CINCH-- ALL WE GOTTA DO IS HEIST A LITTLE JADE IDOL FROM DE VAULT OF DAT STAHL AUCTIONEERIN' HOUSE!
PIPE DOWN, YA DOPE! SOMEBODY MIGHT BE LISTENING!

REMOVAL OF PUTTY AND A WIG REVEAL THE CLEAN CUT FEATURES OF BRUCE WAYNE--
HOW'D YOU MAKE OUT?
I FOUND OUT PLENTY-- AND YOU CAN'T GO WITH ME--YOU'VE GOT HOMEWORK TO DO!

THAT NIGHT--- THE BATMAN CLIMBS TO THE ROOF OF THE STAHL AUCTIONEERING HOUSE---

INSIDE THE TOP-FLOOR OFFICE OF THE STAHL AUCTIONEERS-- A SEARING FLAME PLAYS UPON THE METAL OF A GREAT, OLD-FASHIONED VAULT!

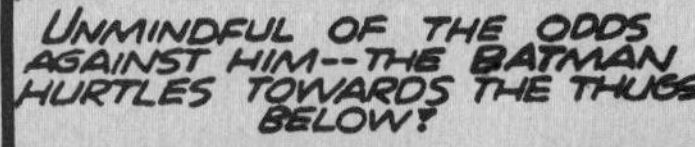
UNMINDFUL OF THE ODDS AGAINST HIM--THE BATMAN HURTLES TOWARDS THE THUGS BELOW!

IT'S THE BATMAN!

OOF!
THANKS FOR WAVING AT ME, BOYS! IT'S A BIT HOT IN HERE!
UGH!

BATMAN BENDS LOW AS THE DEADLY FLAME FROM THE ACETYLENE TORCH SHOOTS OVER HIS HEAD!
A WARM RECEPTION BATMAN! HAW!
AND YOU'RE NOT FOOLING, CHUM!

SNATCHING THE OIL PAINTING FROM THE WALL, THE BATMAN WHIPS ABOUT--
EVER GO IN FOR ART? YOU MAY FIND THIS A STRIKING EXAMPLE!

HA--HA-- A PICTURE NO ARTIST COULD DO JUSTICE TO. WELL, I COULD STAND AND ADMIRE YOU FOREVER, BUT---
5

--BUSINESS BEFORE PLEASURE!
OW!
UGH!

TSK! TSK! LOOK WHAT YOU'VE DONE TO MY POOR MEN! AH, WELL, I KNEW THAT WED HAVE TO MEET SOME DAY!
SO IT'S YOU?
BETTER SAY YOUR PRAYERS NOW, FUNNYFACE--
TOO BAD! A MARVELOUS PHYSIQUE COUPLED WITH A KEEN BRAIN--WE COULD GO FAR TOGETHER!

A SPRAY OF STRANGLING GAS SPURTS FROM THE PENGUIN'S DEADLY UMBRELLA!
BUT, ALAS, I'M AFRAID YOU'D NEVER APPRECIATE THE BEAUTY OF A SUCCESSFUL ROBBERY!

LUCKY FOR YOU LADS, I DECIDED TO DROP IN--NOW, PERHAPS YOU WILL COMPLETE YOUR ASSIGNMENT SO THAT I MAY GO HOME AND BROWSE THROUGH SHAKESPEARE!

THE INTERRUPTED ROBBERY NOW COMES TO A SUCCESSFUL ENDING..
HERE'S THE IDOL, MISTER PENGUIN!
AS THE IMMORTAL KEATS SAID-"A THING OF BEAUTY IS A JOY FOREVER!"

PENGUIN AND COMPANY LEAVE BY WAY OF THE SKYLIGHT---
THE POLICE WILL COME HERE AND FIND BATMAN. DOUBTLESS, THEY WILL DEAL WITH HIM STERNLY--IN THE INTERESTS OF JUSTICE! HEE! HEE!

IN ANSWER TO THE WAILING BURGLAR ALARM, THE POLICE SPEED TO THE SCENE-
THE JADE IDOL--IT'S GONE!
LOOK! THE BATMAN! MAYBE HE CAN EXPLAIN WHAT HAPPENED!
WE HAD BETTER TAKE HIM ALONG!

STILL DAZED, THE BATMAN IS TAKEN TO A LUXURIOUS MANSION-
WHERE AM I?-- WHY DID YOU BRING ME HERE?
JUST FORMALITY, BATMAN! WE WANT YOU TO TELL MR. BONIFACE WHAT HAPPENED TO HIS IDOL--

A PUDGY FIGURE TODDLES IN-- THE PENGUIN!
THAT'S HIM! I'D RECOGNIZE THAT MASK AND CLOAK OF HIS ANYWHERE--
AM I GOING CRAZY? HE'S--

BUT, MR. BONIFACE, YOU MUST BE WRONG! THIS IS THE BATMAN!
I DON'T CARE! HE'S BEEN THREATENIN ME FOR WEEKS! HE SAID I'D HAVE TO PAY HIM FO PROTECTION-- AND THAT HE STOO IN SO WELL WITH THE POLICE, THAT NOBOD WOULD BELIEVE M IF I COMPLAINED! I WANT HIM LOCKED UP!

DON'T WORRY, SIR--WE'LL TAKE CARE OF HIM!
THANK YOU-- I WAS SURE YOU'D SEE YOUR DUTY!
THAT GAS-- I CAN'T THINK--

AS THE POLICE VAN---CONTAINING THE BATMAN--GOES DOWN THE STREET, A SLEEK, BLACK CAR MOVES FROM IT'S POSITION ON THE CORNER!
NOW WE FINISH THE REST OF THE PENGUIN'S PLANS!

SUDDENLY-- THE BLACK CAR DELIBERATELY SIDESWIPES THE POLICE VAN--
CRASH!
7

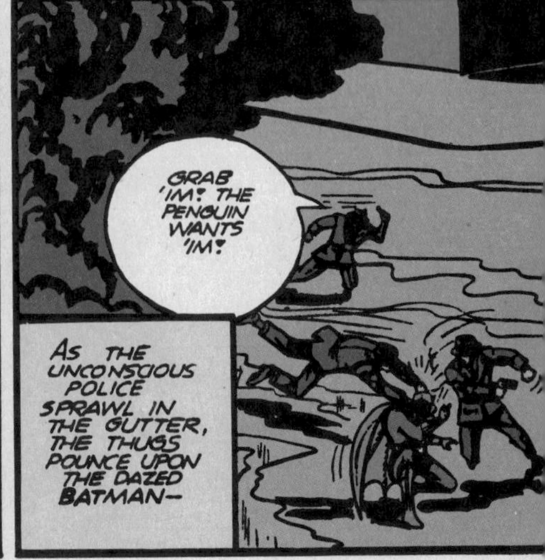
GRAB 'IM! THE PENGUIN WANTS 'IM!
AS THE UNCONSCIOUS POLICE SPRAWL IN THE GUTTER, THE THUGS POUNCE UPON THE DAZED BATMAN--

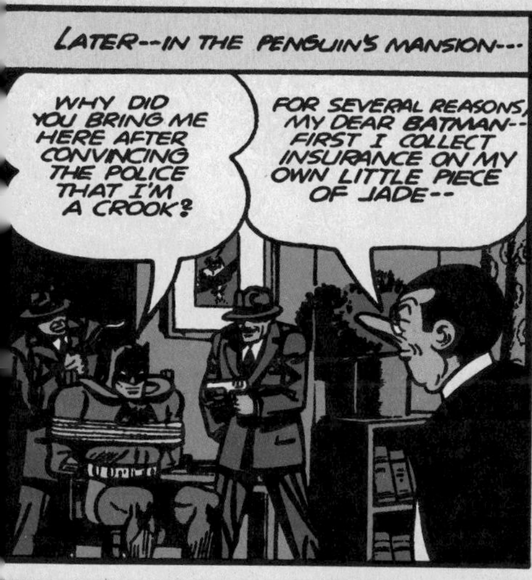

AT THE HOME OF BRUCE WAYNE, DICK GRAYSON HAS HEARD THE POLICE RADIO CALLS DENOUNCING THE BATMAN-DICK GOES INTO ACTION AS ROBIN THE BOY WONDER-

THE RESOURCEFUL BATMAN TAPS HIS FOOT IN MORSE CODE INFORMING ROBIN OF HIS WHEREABOUTS!

AND ANOTHER PERSON IS ALSO WORRIED--AND BROKEN--- COMMISSIONER GORDON--
THE BATMAN-- TURNED CRIMINAL- I CAN'T BELIEVE IT! WHY DID HE DO IT--WHY?

SOON AFTER---THE PENGUIN'S HOUSE ON THE CORNER OF LINCOLN AVENUE-
WHO RANG THE BELL?
IT'S A TELEGRAM MESSENGER!

AND HERE'S YOUR MESSAGE!
SSSPPLLFF!

ROBIN DASHES INSIDE THE HOUSE--BUT FINDS THE ODDS AGAINST HIM ARE MANY---
STOP THIS KID-HE WORKS WITH THE BATMAN!
I'LL STOP HIM-- FER GOOD!

GOSH! I'M GETTING POPULAR-- ER--NICE HEADWORK, BOYS!
OUCH!
GOT YOU-- OOOUH!

AS IF RELEASED BY A GIANT SPRING--ROBIN'S AGILE BODY CRASHES AGAINST THE HEAVILY LADEN TABLE---
GOT IT! NICE WORK, ROBIN!
OOOPS! HOW CLUMSY OF ME- DON'T CUT YOURSELF, BATMAN- GOT IT!

AS ROBIN WHIRLS TO MEET THE CHARGING THUGS--BATMAN HURLS HIS BOUND BODY--AND THE CHAIR TO WHICH HE IS ATTACHED--TO THE FLOOR-
I'VE GOT TO CUT THESE CORDS-- AND QUICKLY!

JAGGED BITS OF BROKEN GLASS SEVER THE BATMAN'S BONDS---AS ROBIN BRAVELY TACKLES BOTH THUGS—
ULP!
GOTTA CUT THIS KID DOWN BEFORE THE BATMAN FREES HIMSELF!
MUST HURRY--AH! THE STRANDS ARE PARTING!

THE BATMAN, FREED, LEAPS AT THE STRUGGLING GROUP IN TIME—
OHHH!
HOLD 'IM WHILE I KNOCK OUT HIS TEETH!
BETTER COUNT YOUR OWN TEETH--

--BECAUSE YOU WON'T HAVE THEM FOR LONG!

BUT VICTORY TURNS TO DEFEAT AS THE OILY VOICE OF THE PENGUIN CUTS THRU THE SOUNDS OF BATTLE.
ALL RIGHT, GENTLEMEN-- PLEASE STAND AT EASE!
TAKE IT EASY, ROBIN-- HIS UMBRELLAS ARE MORE DANGEROUS THAN GUNS!

THE PENGUIN'S HAND REACHES FOR HIS PHONE--
HMM---GLAD TO SEE YOU ACTING SENSIBLE, BATMAN--UH-- HELLO, OPERATOR, GIVE ME THE POLICE!-- THIS IS MR. BONIFACE- I'VE GOT THE BATMAN AT MY HOME---NO, DON'T THANK ME--

C'MON, ROBIN-- THIS IS ONE TIME STRATEGIC RETREAT IS SMARTER THAN COMPLETE DEFEAT! LET'S GO!
I'M RIGHT BEHIND YOU!
10

THEY'RE GETTIN' AWAY!
STOP THEM!

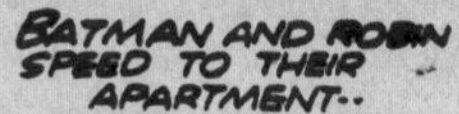

IN THE HEART OF THE BOWERY... WHERE HUMBLE FLOP-HOUSES RUB SHOULDERS WITH TALL, STATELY BUILDINGS THAT HOUSE UNTOLD WEALTH, HERE IS WHERE THE GREAT DIAMOND EXCHANGES MAKE THEIR OFFICES!

MEANWHILE IN THE STREET---

THERE THEY ARE- I RECOGNIZE THEIR SHADOWS!

FOR A BLIND MAN---YOU SEE PRETTY GOOD!

IN THE DARKENED ALLEYWAY, THE BLIND MAN AND THE URCHIN RIP OFF THEIR OUTER CLOTHES, AND ARE REVEALED AS THE BATMAN AND ROBIN-
WE'LL HAVE TO WORK FAST, ROBIN!
HERE I COME!

THE BATMAN AND ROBIN MOVE UPWARD UNTIL THEY REACH THE LEVEL OF THE LIGHTED WINDOW!
CHARMING BITS OF GLASS. THEIR SPARKLES SPELL OUR FORTUNES!
WE WON'T HAVE TIME TO OPEN THE WINDOW-- OR THEY'LL SPOT US!

IT'S THE BATMAN!
--AND WE SPELL MISFORTUNE!

THIS IS FOR FRAMING MY PAL!
AND THIS THROWN IN FOR INTEREST!

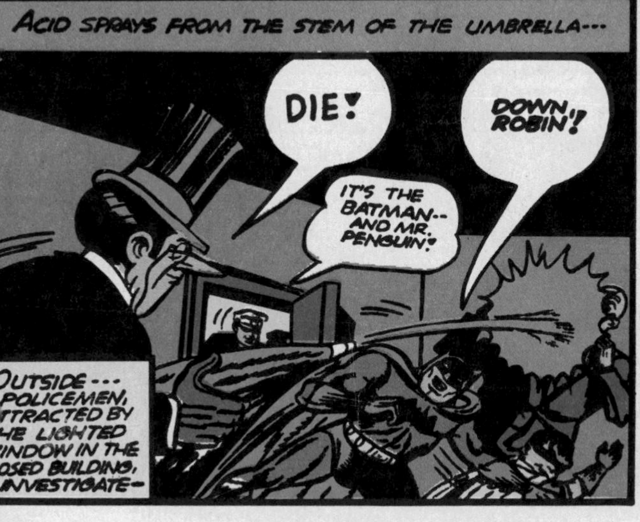
AS THE BATTLE RAGES- THE PENGUIN LEVELS HIS DEADLY UMBRELLA!
AMUSE YOURSELF, FOOLS, FOR SOON YOU--
ACID SPRAYS FROM THE STEM OF THE UMBRELLA---
DIE!
DOWN, ROBIN!
IT'S THE BATMAN-- AND MR. PENGUIN!
OUTSIDE--- POLICEMEN, ATTRACTED BY THE LIGHTED WINDOW IN THE CLOSED BUILDING, INVESTIGATE-

TAKING ADVANTAGE OF THE MOMENTARY CONFUSION-- THE PENGUIN MAKES A BREAK FOR FREEDOM---
YOU'LL NEVER GET ME, AND I'VE STILL GOT THE JEWELS- HEE! HEE!
12

RACING TO THE STREET BELOW--- THE PENGUIN CLATTERS UP THE STAIRS OF THE ELEVATED STATION.
WE'VE GOT HIM CORNERED, BATMAN!

WHAT'S YOUR HURRY? THERE'S STILL SOME UNFINISHED BUSINESS!
I'LL CROSS THE TRACKS AND-- --- UGH!

THE PENGUIN DRO HIS UMBRELLA AS THE BATMAN FIST THUNDER AGAINST HIS JA

GATHERING HIS STRENGTH IN ONE LAST EFFORT, THE PENGUIN WRESTLES BATMAN TO THE TRACKS--AS A TRAIN ROARS INTO THE STATION---
BATMAN! LOOK OUT! A TRAIN'S COMING!
AS THE METAL MONSTER ROARS DOWN UPON THE WRESTLING COMBATANTS-- AN UPTOWN EXPRESS THUNDERS TOWARDS THEM FROM THE OPPOSITE DIRECTION---

TEARING HIMSELF LOOSE FROM THE BATMAN'S GRIP--THE PENGUIN LEAPS FOR THE PASSING EXPRESS TRA
NOBODY CAN CATCH THE PENGUIN! HEE-HEE!
--AND THE OTHER STRING OF CARS PASS OVER THE BATMAN'S BO

AS THE LOCAL PULLS OUT OF THE STATION--
BATMAN! GOLLY--- B-BUT I WAS WORRIED!
I JUST LAY FLAT, ROBIN, AND THE CARS PASSED OVER ME--ER-- I WILL ADMIT, THOUGH, THAT I DIDN'T EXACTLY ENJOY THE SENSATION!
13

LATER, IN COMMISSIONER GORDON'S OFFICE--
ER---COUGH--- WE'RE SORRY WE SUSPECTED YOU, BATMAN, BUT OF COURSE I FELT ALL THE TIME THAT YOU WERE INNOCENT!
I KNOW THAT, GORDON, BUT THE MOST IMPORTANT THING IS THAT WE MISSED UP ON THE PENGUIN--YET SOME HOW I FEEL WE'LL MEET HIM AGAIN!
YES---PERHA SOME DAY T PATHS OF TH BATMAN AN THE W CROSS AGA
The End-

BATMAN
WITH
ROBIN
THE BOY WONDER
THE CATWOMAN IS BACK!
©1950 NATIONAL COMICS PUBLICATIONS, INC.
YES, ONCE AGAIN THE PRINCESS OF PLUNDER RETURNS TO BARE HER CLAWS AT BATMAN AND ROBIN AS SHE PLANS CRIMES AS SMOOTH AS A CAT'S FUR! BUT THEN -- SOMETHING HAPPENS! AND EXACTLY WHAT THAT IS WILL ASTOUND YOU AS MUCH AS IT DID THE DYNAMIC DUO! FOR, BEHIND THE DARK, GLITTERING EYES OF THE CATWOMAN ARE MYSTERY AND THE ASTONISHING ANSWER TO...
"THE SECRET LIFE OF THE CATWOMAN"
BY BOB KANE
NO NO NO NO
NO
NO NO NO NO NO NO NO NO

SOMEWHERE ON THE OUTSKIRTS OF GOTHAM CITY, AS HARD-FACED MEN LOOK EXPECTANTLY AT A MASKED FIGURE...
HA-HA.. ANOTHER HEADLINE ABOUT US! SO FAR WE'RE DOING FINE, BOYS ... BUT FOR THE OTHER ROBBERIES I'VE PLANNED, I'M GOING TO NEED A PARTNER!
GOT ANYBODY IN MIND, MISTER X?
GOTHAM NEWS
MR. X MOB ROBS CITY BANK!
NEW GANG CZAR'S THIRD HAUL THIS WEEK

YES-- THE CLEVEREST, MOST DANGEROUS-- AND MOST BEAUTIFUL LADY OF CRIME IN THE COUNTRY-- THE CATWOMAN!
CATWOMAN? BUT SHE'S IN JAIL!

THEN WE'LL GET HER OUT! YES, I KNOW JUST HOW TO DO IT...AND ONCE CATWOMAN IS FREE, NOTHING WILL STOP US! WE'LL EMBARK ON A CRIME WAVE THE LIKES OF WHICH GOTHAM CITY HAS NEVER BEFORE SEEN!
XX
SLAM!

NEXT DAY, IN THE HOME OF POLICE COMMISSIONER GORDON...
CATWOMAN ESCAPES THROUGH DYNAMITED PRISON WALL!
GOOD GRIEF, BATMAN! LOOK AT THAT HEADLINE ON THE TELEVISION SCREEN! CATWOMAN'S OUT TO COMMIT MORE CRIMES!
NOT IF WE CAN HELP IT... RIGHT, ROBIN?
RIGHT, BATMAN!

WHILE ELSEWHERE, IN A SPEEDING CAR--THAT PRINCESS OF PLUNDER--THE CATWOMAN!
SO YOUR BOSS PLANNED MY JAIL-BREAK, EH? BUT WHY?
HE NEEDS YOU FOR A DEAL, CATWOMAN! NOW I GOTTA BLINDFOLD YOU! MISTER X'S PLACE HAS TO BE KEPT SECRET--EVEN FROM YOU!

SOON, CRIME QUEEN MEETS CRIME KING!
MISTER X, I PRESUME!
CORRECT, CATWOMAN... LET'S GET DOWN TO BUSINESS! I'VE GOT MANY JOBS LINED UP FOR MY MOB. BUT IN ORDER TO WORK THEM, THE BOYS MIGHT HAVE TO KILL GUARDS OR WATCHMEN THAT, I DON'T WANT... I DON'T EVER WANT A MURDER RAP HANGING OVER MY HEAD!

CATWOMAN, YOU ALWAYS ROB WITHOUT KILLING, BY USING YOUR KNOWLEDGE OF CATS! SO HERE'S MY OFFER -- YOU DO THE JOBS FOR ME, AND WE'LL SHARE THE LOOT! IF YOU REFUSE, I'LL DO THE JOBS ANYWAY! WHAT DO YOU SAY?

OKAY--WE'RE PARTNERS!
GOOD! DIPPER, HERE, WILL TELL YOU OF THE FIRST PLACE TO BE ROBBED! BY THE TIME WE'RE THROUGH, WE'LL HAVE COMMISSIONER GORDON GOING AROUND IN CIRCLES!

LATER, AS THE CATWOMAN AND DIPPER DISCUSS ROBBERY PLANS IN A CRIMINAL HANGOUT...
HYA, DIPPER OL' PAL! DID-DIDJA TALK TO MISTER X ABOUT ME JOINING HIS MOB, HUH?
BEAT IT, MOUSEY! MISTER X DON'T WANT YOU AROUND! HE LIKES GUYS WITH NERVE! IF THE COPS EVER LOOKED AT YOU, YOU'D FAINT!

AW, PLEASE, DIPPER. I'LL DO ANYTHING TO JOIN THE MOB! UGH! DON'T SHOVE!
HE'S ALWAYS AROUND, CATWOMAN! A REGULAR PEST! HE'S JUST LIKE HIS NAME -- MOUSEY!
CAREFUL, MOUSEY, OR I'LL SEND THIS CAT AFTER YOU! HA-HA!
SPLAT
MEOWRR-

LATER, IN THE CAT-WOMAN'S EERIE LAIR...
(YAWN) I HATE TO LEAVE THIS WARM FIRE AND MY PRETTY PETS-- BUT IT'S TIME I LOOKED OVER THE FIRST PLACE I'M TO ROB! (YAWN)
MEOWRRR
PURR-RR
PURR-RR

BUT AS SHE STEPS OUT INTO THE NIGHT...
YOUR HUNCH WAS RIGHT, BATMAN! HER HIDEOUT IS SOMEWHERE AROUND HERE! LET'S GO!
LOOK, ROBIN! IT'S THE CATWOMAN!

STEALTHILY, THE MASKED CRIME-BUSTERS CLOSE IN--BUT SUDDENLY...
AH... I'VE BEEN EXPECTING YOU! MEET MY RED PERSIAN ... A CAT NOTED FOR A FIERY TEMPER THAT MATCHES ITS COLOR! BEING COOPED UP HAS MADE IT VERY IRRITATED! HA-HA!
ROBIN! WATCH OUT!
RRRRR

WHILE ROBIN PARRIES THE CLAWING CAT, BATMAN PURSUES THE FELINE FELON PAST A CONDEMNED BUILDING, WHERE...
OHH! A SECTION OF THE WALL IS TOPPLING! BATMAN WILL BE KILLED! I'LL BE ABLE TO ESCAPE NOW! I'LL BE FREE!
WARNING BEWARE OF FALLING BRICKS

BUT WAIT! FOR A SPLIT INSTANT, THE CATWOMAN HESITATES, THEN, LIKE A STREAK OF SABLE LIGHTNING, SHE LEAPS TO SAVE BATMAN!
GET BACK! BA... UHH!
WHAT..?
CRASH

MOMENTS LATER...
I SAW THAT, BATMAN! SHE RISKED HER LIFE TO SAVE YOU! I DON'T UNDERSTAND IT... SOMETIMES SHE ACTS LIKE THE EXACT OPPOSITE!
SHE'S STILL UNCONSCIOUS! WE'D BETTER RACE HER TO THE BAT-CAVE... SHE NEEDS EMERGENCY TREATMENT--FAST!

PRESENTLY, IN THEIR SECRET BAT-CAVE...
SHE'S COMING TO!
LISTEN! WHAT'S SHE SAYING?
FASTEN YOUR SAFETY BELTS! IF WE REMAIN CALM THE PILOT WILL GET US DOWN SAFELY!
FASTEN YOUR SAFETY BELTS

THEN, AS HER EYES SNAP OPEN...
WH-WHERE AM I? WHERE ARE THE PASSENGERS? DID WE LAND SAFELY? WH-WHO ARE YOU?
CATWOMAN, YOU KNOW PERFECTLY WELL THAT WE'RE BATMAN AND ROBIN!

OH, YES... I'VE READ ABOUT YOU! BUT WHY DID YOU CALL ME "CATWOMAN"? I'M SELINA KYLE... STEWARDESS WITH SPEED AIRLINES, AND--OHH--WHY AM I WEARING THIS STRANGE COSTUME?... AND WHY IS YOUR CALENDAR ALL WRONG?.. IT WON'T BE 1950 FOR YEARS!
1950
OCTOBER

I'M ALL MIXED UP! ALL I'M SURE OF IS THAT I FELL OUT THE DOOR JUST AS THE PLANE CRASHED... I HIT MY HEAD AGAINST A BRANCH AND BLACKED OUT!
IF WHAT YOU SAY IS TRUE, THERE CAN BE ONLY ONE EXPLANATION --AMNESIA! THAT BLOW FROM THE BRANCH MUST HAVE CAUSED IT--AND NOW, THIS SECOND BLOW TO YOUR HEAD HAS RESTORED YOUR MEMORY!

TO TEST HIS THEORY, BATMAN PROJECTS MICRO-FILM SLIDES, COLLECTED FROM NEWSREELS OF PAST CRIME CASES...
THIS IS FROM THE CASE CALLED "NINE LIVES HAS THE CATWOMAN"! REMEMBER IT?
NO! BUT THAT GIRL... IT'S ME! I--I DON'T UNDERSTAND...

AND AS A PICTURE HISTORY OF THE CATWOMAN'S CRIMES IS SCREENED--"THE DUPED DOMESTICS", "THE CLAWS OF THE CATWOMAN", "THE LADY ROGUES"...
NO! NO! DON'T SHOW ME ANY MORE! NOW I UNDERSTAND ...WHILE I HAD AMNESIA, I BECAME A CRIMINAL! OHH.. HOW HORRIBLE... HORRIBLE...
I'M SORRY, SELINA, BUT YOU HAD TO KNOW THE TRUTH!

ONLY ONE THING STILL PUZZLES ME--YOUR OBSESSION FOR CAT CRIMES!
MY DAD ONCE OWNED A PET SHOP! I LEARNED ALL ABOUT CATS FROM HIM! I GUESS, SUBCONSCIOUSLY, I REMEMBERED ABOUT CATS EVEN WHILE HAVING AMNESIA!

WE'D BETTER GO TO COMMISSIONER GORDON WITH YOUR STORY! TO KEEP THE BATCAVE'S LOCATION A SECRET, WE'LL HAVE TO BLINDFOLD YOU, SELINA!
BLINDFOLD? THAT WORD--SO FAMILIAR--SOMETHING IMPORTANT! WAIT--I REMEMBER! DIPPER--THE SECRET MEETING PLACE--MISTER X!
MISTER X?!
YES, AS IT OFTEN HAPPENS, IN AMNESIA CASES, A WORD STRIKES A CHORD, AND MEMORY BECOMES COMPLETE!

THIS MAN IS DANGEROUS! HE'S ALWAYS WANTED TO JOIN MR. X'S GANG! NOW, HE'LL SURELY TELL MR. X ABOUT ME -- AS A BRIBE!

IN THAT CASE, WE MUST LOCK HIM UP! OFFICER, CHARGE HIM WITH CARRYING A CONCEALED WEAPO... NOBODY'S TO SEE HIM TILL THIS CASE IS FINISHED!

HUH? I'LL GET YOU FOR THIS, CAT-WOMAN!

BUT IS HE? FOR AS SOON AS THE FURTIVE LITTLE CROOK IS ALONE IN HIS CELL...

HA, HA... LUCKY THOSE COPPERS DIDN'T FIND THIS FILE HIDDEN IN MY SHOE! ONCE I GET OUT, IT'LL BE BYE-BYE CATWOMAN!

EACH RASP OF THE FILE IS LIKE THE TICK O A CLOCK... AND WITH EACH PASSING MOMENT, DEATH LOOMS CLOSER FOR SELINA KYLE -- ALIAS THE CATWOMAN!

THAT NIGHT, IN THE HALLWAY OF A FAMED RECORDING FIRM, SECRET OPERATIVE **CATWOMAN** EMBARKS ON HER UNDERCOVER ASSIGNMENT...

REMEMBER THE STORY OF "**BELLING THE CAT**"? I'VE DONE JUST THAT: THE COLLAR'S MECHANISM WILL KEEP THIS BELL RINGING CONSTANTLY: NOW GET SET...

AND AS THE BELLED CAT IS RELEASED INTO A RECORDING STUDIO...

SOMEWHERE THE MOON IS... **EEEK!**

OMYGOSH! WE'VE GOT TO CATCH THAT CAT BEFORE HER BELL RUINS RECORDS IN THE OTHER STUDIOS, TOO! COME ON-- **EVERYBODY!**

DING DI-NG DING DING DING

THEN, WHILE EVERYONE CHASES AFTER THE JANGLING CAT...

NICE WORK, **CATWOMAN**... THERE AIN'T A PERSON IN SIGHT! WE'LL GET A NICE HAUL HERE, SINCE ALL MASTER RECORDS ARE MADE OF **GOLD PLATE.**

THE SCOUNDRELS! DURING MY AMNESIA, I'D HAVE GLORIED IN THIS ROBBERY! NOW IT JUST SICKENS ME!

MASTER RECORD ROOM KEEP OUT!

LATER, ON A LONELY ROAD...

HERE'S YOUR SHARE, **CATWOMAN**... AND THIS PAPER HAS THE NAME OF THE NEXT PLACE WE ROB!

BUT WAIT... I THOUGHT I WAS TO DEAL WITH **MISTER X PERSONALLY!**

SORRY... **MISTER X** GAVE ORDERS! YOU DON'T SEE HIM TILL **ALL** THE JOBS ARE DONE!

WILL MOUSEY ESCAPE IN TIME? WILL HE BE ABLE TO EXPOSE THE **CATWOMAN** TO CERTAIN DEATH?

LATER, ATOP THE WELL-GUARDED CASH REGISTER PLANT...
THE DOOR OPENS BY ELECTRICITY--WHEN A GUARD PUSHES DOWN THAT SWITCH LEVER! BUT HOW DO WE GET AT THE SWITCH? IT'S OVER 20 FEET DOWN--AND AT THE SIDE!
JUST WATCH THIS MECHANICAL MOUSE!
SILENTLY, THE CORD UNREELS UNTIL THE "MOUSE" ALMOST TOUCHES THE FLOOR..
IF THAT LEVER WASN'T SET SO FAR OVER, WE COULD DROP SOMETHIN' HEAVY ON IT, BUT... BUT... HEY, WHY THE CAT?
THIS CAT WILL OPEN THE DOOR FOR US!
AND AS THE CATWOMAN RELEASES THE LIVE ANIMAL...
SEE? SHE'S SPOTTED THAT FAKE MOUSE! AND THE ONLY WAY SHE CAN REACH IT IS BY FIRST LANDING ON THAT DOOR LEVER!
STEEL DOOR OF PLANT STARTS TO OPEN... 3
ELECTRIC FAN--1ST LANDING 1
DOOR LEVER GOES DOWN OPENING DOOR 2
PURSUIT OF TOY MOUSE 4
BEFORE THE GUARDS REALIZE IT, MISTER X'S MEN ARE THROUGH THE OPEN DOOR...
JUST RELAX, BUD... AND IT WON'T HURT A BIT!
CLUNK!
MEORRRRR
BUT AS THEY CROSS ANOTHER ROOM...
QUICK--ROBIN! SWING BACK TO THE CASH REGISTER!
LOOK!... UP THERE... IT'S BATMAN AND ROBIN! SAIL INTO 'EM, BOYS!
UH-UH!.. NO SAILING TODAY!
NO SALE

MISSED, BLAST 'EM! THEY KEEP HOPPING AROUND!
TIME FOR ME TO GO INTO ACTION!

MOMENTS LATER, A LENGTHENED CAT-O'-NINE-TAILS SNAPS OUT AT THE MASKED LAWMEN, AND...
HEY! CATWOMAN GOT 'EM FROM THE CATWALK! START SHOOTIN', BOYS!
NO! DON'T SHOOT! I WANT THEM ALIVE!

HUH? WHAT'S WHAT'S THE MATTER, CATWOMAN? GOIN' SOFT?
FOOLS! MY DEAL WITH MISTER X DIDN'T INCLUDE THE CAPTURE OF BATMAN AND ROBIN! I WANT A BONUS FOR THIS, AND I DON'T TALK BUSINESS TILL I SEE MISTER X IN PERSON!
OKAY! THIS IS IMPORTANT ENOUGH FOR ME TO CONTACT HIM!

YOUR PLAN'S WORKING, BATMAN! AT LAST, WE'RE GOING TO MEET MISTER X!
YES, ROBIN, BUT WE MUST REMAIN CAREFUL... LETTING OURSELVES BE "CAPTURED" IS ONLY HALF THE JOB! FROM NOW ON, ONE SLIPUP, AND WE'RE DEAD DUCKS!

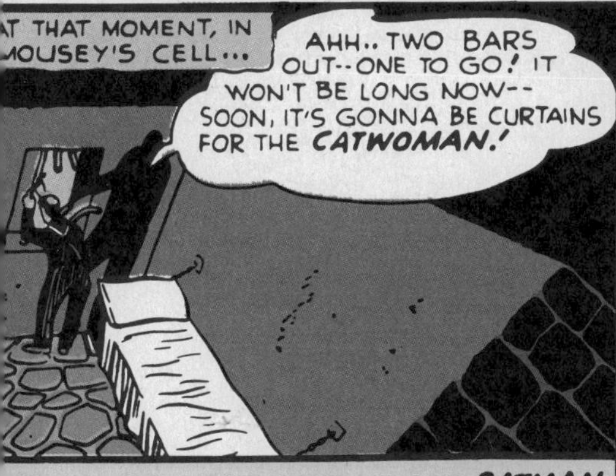
AT THAT MOMENT, IN MOUSEY'S CELL...
AHH.. TWO BARS OUT--ONE TO GO! IT WON'T BE LONG NOW--SOON, IT'S GONNA BE CURTAINS FOR THE CATWOMAN!
AND WILL IT ALSO BE CURTAINS FOR BATMAN AND ROBIN? FOR IF THE CATWOMAN DIES, THE PLAN TO RESCUE BATMAN AND ROBIN DIES WITH HER!

HOURS LATER, IN A DESERTED FARMHOUSE ON THE OUTSKIRTS OF GOTHAM CITY...
DIPPER EXPLAINED EVERYTHING, CATWOMAN! YOU DID A FINE JOB! BOYS, TAKE THEIR UTILITY BELTS AWAY--I'VE GOT PLANS FOR BATMAN AND ROBIN!
AND WE'VE GOT PLANS FOR YOU, TOO, MISTER X!

JUST THEN...
OH! MY CAT IS STILL ANGRY OVER THAT FAKE MOUSE! COME BACK, KITTY... YOU'RE HURTING THE NICE MAN!
HURTING HIM? I WONDER..?
ROWRRR

GET RID OF THIS LITTLE MONSTER!
WAIT! THAT SPINDLY OLD CHAIR! NOW I KNOW MY HUNCH IS RIGHT!

OKAY, JOE, AL--LOCK UP BATMAN AND ROBIN IN THAT OLD GRAIN MILL--AND PLANT A TIME BOMB THERE! THE ONLY WAY THEY'LL GET OUT IS BY BEING BLOWN OUT!
OH, DEAR... HOW WILL I SAVE THEM?

SOON, IN MISTER X'S MAKESHIFT PRISON...
UHH! THIS DOOR'S LOCKED SOLID! IT WON'T BUDGE!
AND THERE'S A TIME BOMB SET TO GO OFF ANY MINUTE! THE CATWOMAN HAD BETTER NOT FAIL US--OR WE'RE GONERS!

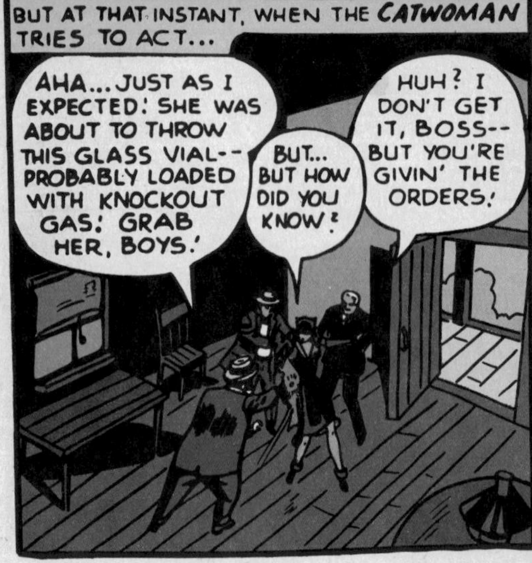
BUT AT THAT INSTANT, WHEN THE CATWOMAN TRIES TO ACT...
AHA...JUST AS I EXPECTED! SHE WAS ABOUT TO THROW THIS GLASS VIAL--PROBABLY LOADED WITH KNOCKOUT GAS! GRAB HER, BOYS!
BUT... BUT HOW DID YOU KNOW?
HUH? I DON'T GET IT, BOSS--BUT YOU'RE GIVIN' THE ORDERS!

MINUTES LATER...
TOO BAD, CATWOMAN... MOUSEY ESCAPED FROM JAIL AND LET ME IN ON YOUR WHOLE SCHEME! NOW, YOU'RE DOOMED! AFTER WE TIE YOU TO THIS TRACTOR, WE'LL SEND YOU HURTLING OVER THAT CLIFF! HA, HA!
WITH BOTH BATMAN, ROBIN AND THE CATWOMAN FACING DEATH, WHAT WILL HAPPEN NOW? HOW CAN THEY POSSIBLY BE SAVED?

MEANWHILE...
WE CAN'T RISK WAITING FOR THE CATWOMAN ANY LONGER! ROBIN, HELP ME PUSH THIS MILL STONE TO THE FLOOR! HURRY!
SURE... BUT I DON'T GET IT, BATMAN!
WHEN THE TWO MILL STONES LIE IN A LINE POINTING TO THE STRONG DOOR...
THERE! I'VE WEDGED THESE SACKS OF RICE BETWEEN THE DOOR AND THE FIRST STONE! GRAB THAT WATER HOSE, ROBIN AND START DRENCHING THE RICE BAGS!
GOSH, I HOPE YOU KNOW WHAT YOU'RE DOING ...I DON'T!
RICE SWELLS ENORMOUSLY WHEN IT'S WET! IT'S A KNOWN FACT THAT A WET CARGO OF RICE USED TO SMASH OPEN THE HULLS OF WOODEN SAILING SHIPS!
OH... I GET IT! YOU FIGURE THE WET RICE WILL EXPAND ENOUGH TO BURST DOWN THAT DOOR! IT'LL BE A NICE TRY, EVEN IF IT DOESN'T WORK!
SECONDS LATER...
OHH! THEY'RE DEAD! BATMAN AND ROBIN ARE DEAD! SOB
GOOD! NOW, DIPPER, START THE TRACTOR MOTOR! IT WILL TAKE THIS DOUBLE-CROSSER RIGHT OVER THE CLIFF!
DOUBLE-CROSSER? Y'MEAN SHE HELD OUT SOME LOOT? AND WHAT'S THAT CRACK YOU MADE ABOUT MOUSEY?
BOOM
AND AS THE TRACTOR GROWLS OMINOUSLY...
I'LL EXPLAIN THINGS LATER, BOYS! LET ME WATCH THIS FIRST!
RRR ROARR
BATMAN, WE'RE TOO LATE! THE CATWOMAN'S HEADED OVER THE CLIFF!
INSTANTLY, BATMAN WHIPS UP A DISCARDED, BROKEN WHEAT SCYTHE AND HISSES IT FORWARD LIKE A BOOMERANG...
SNAP

THEN, BEFORE THE STARTLED THUGS CAN TURN...
DIPPER HAS DROPPED! BATMAN--THERE GOES MISTER X.! HE'S GETTING AWAY!
BUT AS THE MASKED GANG CHIEF PASSES THE CATWOMAN...
THANKS FOR THE HAND, CATWOMAN! AHH--I HAD A HUNCH MISTER X WAS A SHORT MAN!
SHORT MAN?! WHY, MISTER X IS MOUSEY!!

I SEE... HE WORE A WOODEN FRAME TO MAKE HIM LOOK BIGGER!
I REALIZED MISTER X WAS ONLY MASQUERADING AS A BIG MAN BECAUSE HIS FLIMSY CHAIR DIDN'T CREAK OR BREAK UNDER HIS WEIGHT! HE DIDN'T YELL WHEN THE CAT WAS CLAWING HIS LEG, SO I GUESSED HE WAS WEARING WOODEN STILTS!
LATER, MOUSEY EXPLAINS THE REASON FOR HIS DISGUISE...
FIRST, IT WAS A GOOD COVERUP! THE COPS WOULD BE HUNTING FOR MISTER X, NOT A PUNK NAMED MOUSEY! YEAH... MY NAME... MOUSEY ... THAT WAS THE REAL REASON FOR EVERYTHING...

NO GANGSTERS WOULD TAKE ORDERS FROM A LITTLE GUY THEY CALL MOUSEY! IN THE UNDERWORLD, YOU HAVE TO BE IMPRESSIVE! SO, BY POSING AS A MYSTERY MAN --A BIG MAN-- I GOT MYSELF A GANG! MOUSEY, THE PUNK, BECAME MISTER X, THE BIG SHOT!
YES, MOUSEY, YOU'LL BE THE BIGGEST MAN IN PRISON!
AND SO, AT POLICE HEADQUARTERS!
THAT'S THAT! FROM NOW ON I'M PLAIN SELINA KYLE! THE CATWOMAN HAS RETIRED!
I WONDER! SOMEHOW, I THINK THE LAW WILL AGAIN NEED THE SERVICES OF CATWOMAN--POLICE OPERATIVE... AND IT MAY BE SOONER THAN YOU THINK!
THE END

Written by Edmond Hamilton/Art by Lew Sayre Schwartz & Charles Paris

SO THE PENGUIN DROPS OUT OF SIGHT, WHILE BATMAN AND ROBIN IN THEIR EVERYDAY IDENTITIES OF WEALTHY BRUCE WAYNE AND HIS YOUNG WARD DICK GRAYSON, GET A WELCOME REST...

CERTAINLY NOT! I INTEND MAKE A FORTUNE EXHIBIT-G MY LEGENDARY BIRDS, O I'LL NOT SHOW THEM OW AND SPOIL MY SHOW! M TAKING THEM TO MY EW COUNTRY-PLACE AVIARY!
AND WHAT'S IN THE CASE MARKED "MYSTERY BIRD"?
MYSTERY BIRD

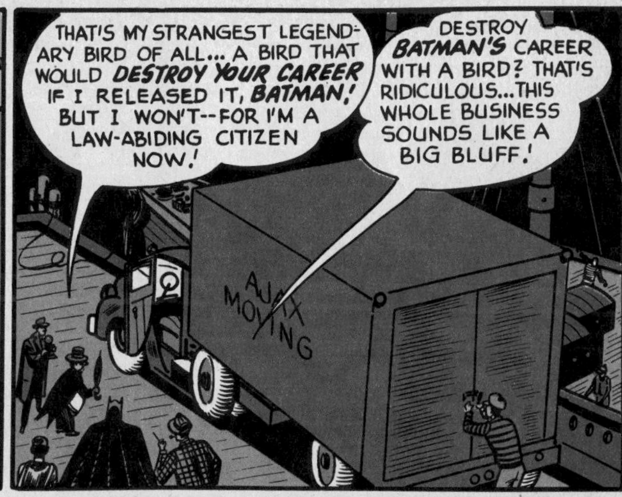
THAT'S MY STRANGEST LEGENDARY BIRD OF ALL... A BIRD THAT WOULD DESTROY YOUR CAREER IF I RELEASED IT, BATMAN! BUT I WON'T--FOR I'M A LAW-ABIDING CITIZEN NOW!
DESTROY BATMAN'S CAREER WITH A BIRD? THAT'S RIDICULOUS...THIS WHOLE BUSINESS SOUNDS LIKE A BIG BLUFF!
AJAX MOVING

UT THOUGH SKEPTICAL REPORTERS ONSIDER IT A BLUFF, BATMAN OES NOT DISMISS THE PENGUIN SO IGHTLY...
THIS EIRD LEGENDARY BIRD AY COVER UP SOME RIME HE'S HATCHING! E'LL GO TAKE A LOOK T HIS COUNTRY VIARY TONIGHT, ROBIN!
GOOD IDEA, BATMAN...I WON'T BELIEVE A THING UNTIL I SEE THOSE CREATURES WITH MY OWN EYES!

BUT THAT NIGHT, AS A STORM BUILDS OVER THE COUNTRYSIDE, THE CAPED CRIME-CRUSHERS FIND THE PENGUIN'S NEST BESET BY HUMAN BIRDS OF PREY!
FOR ONCE I'M GLAD TO SEE YOU, BATMAN! ENRAGED CROOKS HAVE JUST SET LOOSE MY FABULOUS BIRDS, BECAUSE I WAS UNWILLING TO RESUME MY LIFE OF CRIME WITH THEM.
WHAT--?

THERE THEY GO NOW!
THEY SIDESWIPED THE BATMOBILE, TO PREVENT US FROM FOLLOWING! ROBIN, USE THE POWER-HOIST TO PULL IT OUT WHILE I TAKE A LOOK AT THE PENGUIN'S CAGES.
WHROOM!

SOB THEY RELEASED THEM! MY FABULOUS BIRDS ARE GONE--AND THEY'RE DANGEROUS! THE WINGED LION, THE GIANT THUNDERBIRD, THE HUGE BASILISK--THEY'LL ENDANGER ALL GOTHAM CITY!
IF THEY REALLY EXIST!
BUT BATMAN'S SKEPTICISM IS DUE FOR A STUNNING SURPRISE ...

-- FOR WHEN HE RETURNS TO THE BATMOBILE...
BATMAN--IT'S INCREDIBLE! LISTEN TO THAT RADIO-FLASH FROM GOTHAM CITY!
WE REPEAT OUR WARNING...IMPOSSIBLE AS IT SOUNDS, A WINGED LION IS FLYING OVER GOTHAM CITY!
IT'S MY WINGED LION!
PEDESTRIANS ARE IN PANIC AS THIS STRANGE BIRD-LION WINGS ABOVE OUR STREETS!
WHY--WHY, IT'S A WINGED LION!
I STILL CAN'T BELIEVE IT, BUT WE'LL HAVE TO INVESTIGATE!
YES--AND HURRY! I MUST ROUND UP MY FABULOUS BIRDS BEFORE THEY WREAK TERROR THERE!
AND AS THE TRIO SPEEDS TOWARD GOTHAM CITY...
THANK GOODNESS THE MYSTERY BIRD'S CASE WAS IN THE HOUSE AND WASN'T NOTICED BY THOSE CRIMINALS! ONCE RELEASED, THAT CREATURE COULD BLAST YOUR CAREER, BATMAN!
HOW COULD A MYTHICAL BIRD DO THAT? IT JUST ISN'T POSSIBLE!
BULLETIN! THE WINGED LION SEEMS TO HAVE PASSED ON OVER THE CITY, BUT THERE'S A NEW ALARM!
LIGHTNING IS REPORTED STRIKING A STRANGE, GREAT BIRD PERCHED ON THE BILLINGS BUILDING!
IT'S MY THUNDERBIRD! INDIANS BELIEVED THE BIRD EXISTED, AND COULD DRAW STORM AND LIGHTNING TO ITSELF--AND NOW IT'S DRAWING DESTRUCTION HERE!
HOLD TIGHT... I'LL SWING AROUND TO THE BILLINGS BUILDING!
4
BUT AS THE BATMOBILE ROARS TO THE SCENE...
CRASH!
TOO LATE! LIGHTNING HAS ALREADY STRUCK, AND--AND THAT HUGE, WEIRD BIRD HAS KNOCKED DOWN THE LIGHTNING ROD!
RUN FOR YOUR LIVES! WE'VE BEEN INVADED FROM ANOTHER PLANET!
MY THUNDERBIRD--I MUST CATCH IT!

MINUTES LATER, INSIDE THE DAMAGED BUILDING...
IT FLEW AWAY BEFORE I COULD REACH IT!
THAT LIGHTNING BOLT IT DREW DESTROYED SOME OF MY VALUABLE ART OBJECTS! I CAN'T EVEN FIND THE FRAGMENTS!
HMMM... I WONDER?...
SEARCH THE PENGUIN, ROBIN! PERHAPS THOSE VALUABLE OBJECTS WEREN'T DESTROYED BY LIGHTNING AFTER ALL!
THERE'S NOTHING ON HIM, BATMAN-- BUT IT'S A CURIOUS CO-INCIDENCE THAT THE THINGS DISAPPEARED WHILE HE WAS HERE... TOO CURIOUS!
AT THAT MOMENT, A NEW ALARM SPURS THE DYNAMIC DUO INTO ACTION...
LOOK--ON THE NEXT BLOCK! THE GOTHAM CITY BANK IS ON FIRE!
A FIRE? MY PHOENIX LOVES FIRE AND WILL GO THERE! I MUST TRY TO RECAPTURE IT!
WE'LL GO ALONG, TOO! I DON'T TRUST YOU ALONE, PENGUIN--EVEN IN A BURNING BANK! BUT FIRST, WE MUST GET OUR ASBESTOS SUITS FROM THE BAT-MOBILE!
AND SOON, THREE ASBESTOS-ARMORED FORMS CRASH INTO THE FLAMING BANK...
THERE IT IS-- MY BEAUTIFUL PHOENIX! BE VERY CAREFUL, BATMAN ... I DON'T WANT IT TO TAKE FRIGHT!
THAT WALL--IT'S FALLING!
JUMP, ROBIN-- THIS WAY!
CRASH!
THE PENGUIN COULD HAVE PUSHED IT, TO MAKE IT FALL AND DELAY US! COME ON--HE'S BACK BY THE TELLERS' CAGES!
WHEW THAT WAS CLOSE!
MY PHOENIX! YOU ALARMED IT, AND IT FLEW AWAY!
HOLD IT, PENGUIN!
BUT YOU'RE NOT GOING TO FLY AWAY TILL WE LOOK INTO THIS!
BANK
5

SHORTLY, OUTSIDE...
YES, A LOT OF CASH WAS LOST IN THE FIRE!
I DIDN'T TAKE IT! YOU SEARCHED ME AGAIN, DIDN'T YOU?
I DID, PENGUIN, BUT I'M STILL NOT SATISFIED! I'M ARRESTING YOU ON SUSPICION OF ROBBERY!

AWHILE LATER, AT POLICE HEADQUARTERS...
BUT THESE FABULOUS BIRDS HAVE BEEN SEEN BY THE WHOLE CITY, BATMAN! THEY'RE REAL!
MAYBE, COMMISSIONER GORDON--BUT UNTIL WE CATCH THEM, I WANT THIS BIRD KEPT IN A CAGE!
HA, HA... MY HENCHMEN WILL SEE THA MY BASILISK GETS ME OUT BATMAN WILL LOSE HIS WITS TRYING TO SOLVE THE SECRET OF MY BIRDS!

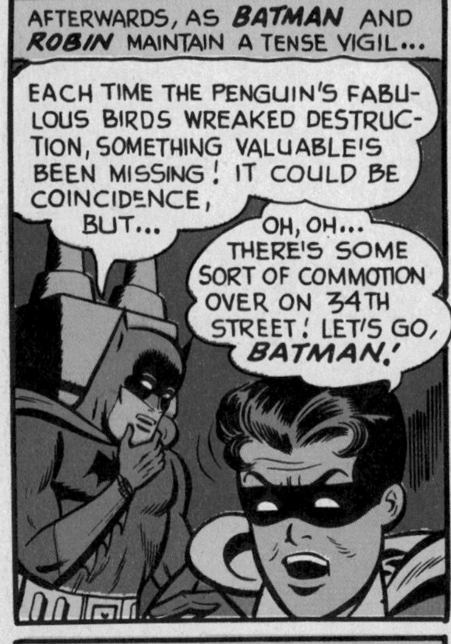
AFTERWARDS, AS BATMAN AND ROBIN MAINTAIN A TENSE VIGIL...
EACH TIME THE PENGUIN'S FABULOUS BIRDS WREAKED DESTRUCTION, SOMETHING VALUABLE'S BEEN MISSING! IT COULD BE COINCIDENCE, BUT...
OH, OH... THERE'S SOME SORT OF COMMOTION OVER ON 34TH STREET! LET'S GO, BATMAN!

IT'S MORE THAN MERE COMMOTION THAT GREETS THE CAPED CRIME-BUSTERS AS THEY REACH 34TH STREET...
THAT HORRIBLE MONSTER... ITS EYES ARE FREEZING ME! I CAN'T MOVE!
IT'S THE LEGENDARY BASILISK--THE GIANT BIRD WHOSE EYES CAN FREEZE A MAN!

AND AS A HORROR OUT OF ANCIENT TRADITION STALKS THE STREETS, FRANTIC REPORTS REACH HEADQUARTERS...
TERRIBLE BIRD ON 34TH STREET--MANY PEOPLE ALREADY FROZEN BY ITS STARE! OFFICER MANTON TRIED TO FACE IT BUT WAS FROZEN TOO...
IT'S MY ESCAPED BASILISK! I CAN CATCH IT--LET ME OUT BEFORE IT STRIKES DOWN MORE PEOPLE!

PENGUIN, IF YOU CAN HANDLE THAT HORRIBLE BIRD, CATCH IT AT ONCE! NO ONE ELSE CAN FACE IT!
I DID WRONG TO BRING MY FABULOUS FOWL TO GOTHAM CIT BUT I'LL RECAPTU THEM, COMMISSIONE

MEANWHILE, TWO BIRDLIKE HUMAN FIGURES HAVE ALREADY FLASHED DOWN TO BATTLE A BIRD OF DREAD...
BATMAN! THOSE EYES... THOSE AWFUL EYES...
I'M FROZEN-- CAN'T--MOVE...
ME--ME TOO...
FEARFUL EYES INDEED MEET THE GAZE OF THE TWO CRIME-FIGHTERS!
IT'S GETTING ME--THAT TERRIBLE GAZE...
BUT--BUT THAT MAN BESIDE THE BIRD WAS AFFECTED TOO! NOW I UNDERSTAND! ROBIN--YOUR UTILITY BELT--DO AS I'M DOING!
JUST THEN, AT A NEARBY JEWELRY SHOP...
STOP THIEF! BATMAN, STOP HIM!
HAT SHOPPE
BATMAN'S FROZEN BY MY BASILISK, I FEAR, AND CAN'T HELP YOU!
WRONG, PENGUIN! WHEN MAN ALONGSIDE THE ASILISK WAS FROZEN, I REALIZED WAS NOT THE BIRD'S STARE UT DEADLY GAS IT EXHALED AT DID THE FREEZING! SO OBIN AND I SIMPLY USED NOSE-PLUGS FROM OUR TILITY BELTS TO PROTECT US!
BUT MY BASILISK ISN'T THROUGH YET!
IT CAN STILL BE DEADLY, YOU SEE!
HE USED IT TO KNOCK OUT THAT BUS DRIVER-- AND THE BUS IS RUNNING WILD! QUICK, ROBIN--THE BATMOBILE!
BUS STOP
AVE
7

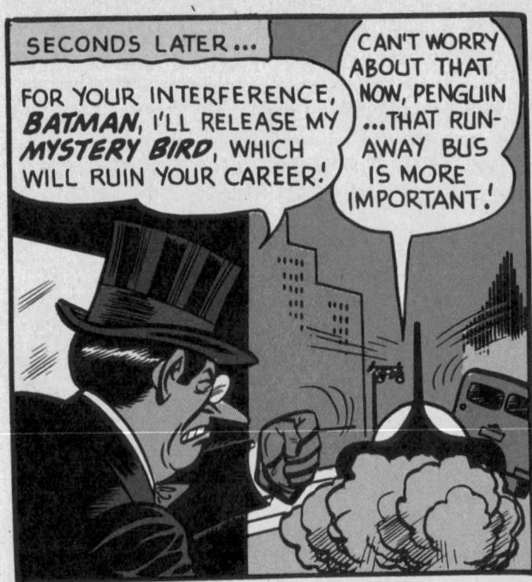
SECONDS LATER...
FOR YOUR INTERFERENCE, BATMAN, I'LL RELEASE MY MYSTERY BIRD, WHICH WILL RUIN YOUR CAREER!
CAN'T WORRY ABOUT THAT NOW, PENGUIN ...THAT RUN-AWAY BUS IS MORE IMPORTANT!

I CAN STOP THE BUS NOW, BATMAN, BUT I'M AFRAID THE PENGUIN FLEW THE COOP!
EVEN IN MID-AIR, YOU WOULD MAKE PUNS!
ACME
TRANSIT CO.
943

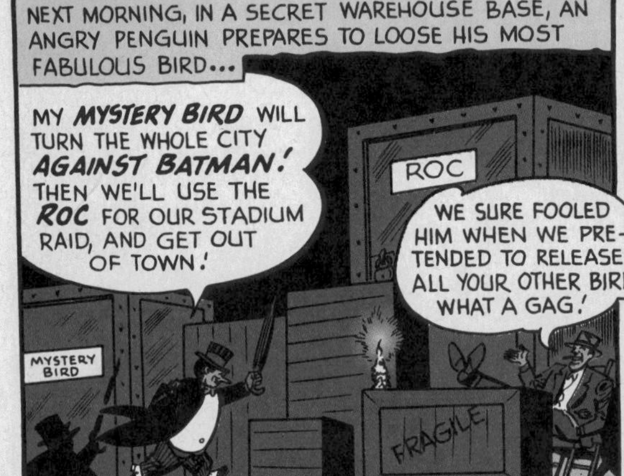
NEXT MORNING, IN A SECRET WAREHOUSE BASE, AN ANGRY PENGUIN PREPARES TO LOOSE HIS MOST FABULOUS BIRD...
MY MYSTERY BIRD WILL TURN THE WHOLE CITY AGAINST BATMAN! THEN WE'LL USE THE ROC FOR OUR STADIUM RAID, AND GET OUT OF TOWN!
WE SURE FOOLED HIM WHEN WE PRE-TENDED TO RELEASE ALL YOUR OTHER BIRDS! WHAT A GAG!
ROC
MYSTERY BIRD
FRAGILE

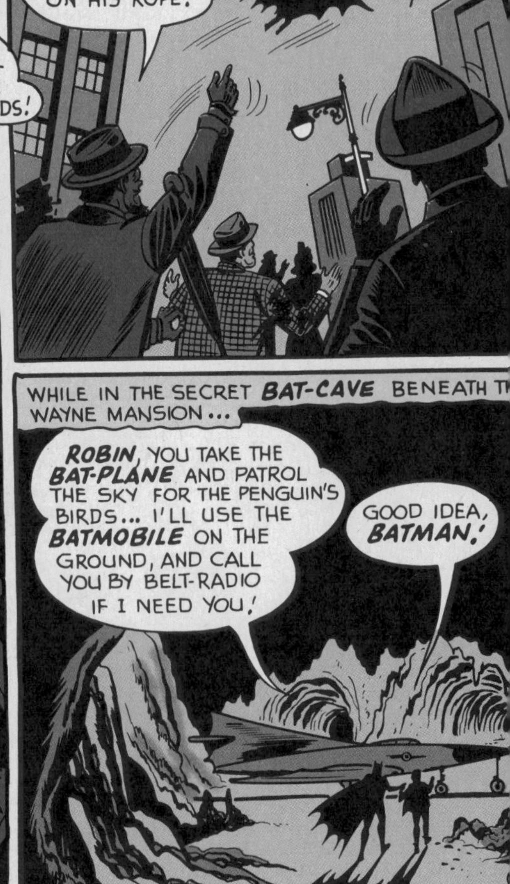
A LITTLE LATER...
LOOK--THERE'S BATMAN! HE MUST BE SWINGING DOWN ON HIS ROPE!
GEE--HE LOOKS LIKE HE'S FLYING!

WAIT A MINUTE-- HE IS FLYING! THAT'S NOT BATMAN... IT'S SOME SORT OF BATLIKE CREATURE... A MAN-BAT!
IT'S GHASTLY! RUN!

WHILE IN THE SECRET BAT-CAVE BENEATH T
WAYNE MANSION...
ROBIN, YOU TAKE THE BAT-PLANE AND PATROL THE SKY FOR THE PENGUIN'S BIRDS... I'LL USE THE BATMOBILE ON THE GROUND, AND CALL YOU BY BELT-RADIO IF I NEED YOU!
GOOD IDEA, BATMAN!

UT BATMAN, FOR THE FIRST TIME, SOON FINDS THE
EOPLE OF GOTHAM CITY FLEEING FROM HIM IN TERROR!
RUN! IT'S THAT
AWFUL MAN-BAT!
GET AWAY!
MAN-BAT? SO THAT'S THE MYSTERY BIRD THE PENGUIN THREATENED ME WITH? IT COULD DESTROY MY CAREER, BY MAKING PEOPLE AFRAID OF ME WHEREVER I APPEAR!
AT THAT INSTANT, FROM HIGH IN THE SKY, COMES A TENSE CALL BY BELT-RADIO...
BATMAN, THERE'S A WEIRD MAN-LIKE BIRD FLYING OVER 9TH AVENUE!
I'LL STOP THAT MAN-BAT! YOU SWOOP DOWN AND LAND ON THE TERMINAL ROOF!

MMEDIATELY, BATMAN RACES TO THE
OP OF A TALL SKYSCRAPER, AND...
SMACK!
THE ONLY WAY TO STOP THIS THING IS BY FORCING IT DOWN TO THE GROUND!

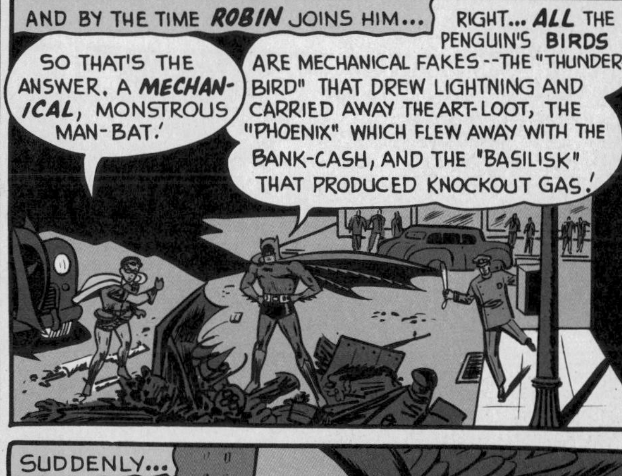
AND BY THE TIME ROBIN JOINS HIM...
SO THAT'S THE ANSWER. A MECHANICAL, MONSTROUS MAN-BAT!
RIGHT... ALL THE PENGUIN'S BIRDS ARE MECHANICAL FAKES--THE "THUNDER-BIRD" THAT DREW LIGHTNING AND CARRIED AWAY THE ART-LOOT, THE "PHOENIX" WHICH FLEW AWAY WITH THE BANK-CASH, AND THE "BASILISK" THAT PRODUCED KNOCKOUT GAS!

INSTEAD OF BEING AWAY HUNTING FABULOUS BIRDS, HE WAS BUILDING HOSE FAKES! I KNEW THIS BECAUSE WHEN A REAL BIRD IS RELEASED FROM CAPTIVITY, IT ALWAYS FLIES HOME... BUT THESE "BIRDS" WENT STRAIGHT TO THE CITY AND BEGAN WREAKING HAVOC!

SUDDENLY...
LOOK! THAT COLOSSAL BIRD SCREAMING OVERHEAD! IT MUST BE...
SCREECH!
SCREECH!
SCREECH!
THE PENGUIN'S FAKE ROC! QUICK--BACK TO THE BAT-PLANE!
9

NEXT MINUTE, OVER GOTHAM FOOTBALL STADIUM...
THAT MONSTER BIRD--IT'S SWOOPING DOWN ON US!
SCREEEEECH!
WATCH OUT!
HA, HA... THEY CAN'T SEE THE HELICOPTER BLADES FROM BENEATH, AND THE SIREN-SCREECHES DROWN OUT OUR MOTOR NOISE! IN THIS PANIC, WE CAN LAND AND GRAB ALL THE BOX-OFFICE RECEIPTS!
NO, PENGUIN-- LOOK ABOVE US! THE BAT-PLANE!
ROBIN, DROP THIS METAL MOORING-LINE IN THEIR PROPELLOR AS WE GO OVER THEM!
HURRAY! THE BAT-PLANE ... IT'S DIVING, ON THE ROC!
PENGUIN! WE'RE GOING DOWN! IN THE STADIUM, WE CAN'T GET AWAY!
IT'S THAT DRATTED BATMAN! I THOUGHT MY MAN-BAT GAG WOULD KEEP HIM TOO BUSY TO INTERFERE!
10
AND SO, AFTER A SWIFT ROUNDUP...
POOR PENGUIN... THIS LATEST SCHEME OF HIS REALLY LAID AN EGG, DIDN'T IT?
OH-H... BAD ENOUGH, I'M GOING BACK TO JAIL... DO I HAVE TO LISTEN TO THAT BRAT'S HORRIBLE PUNS, TOO
The END

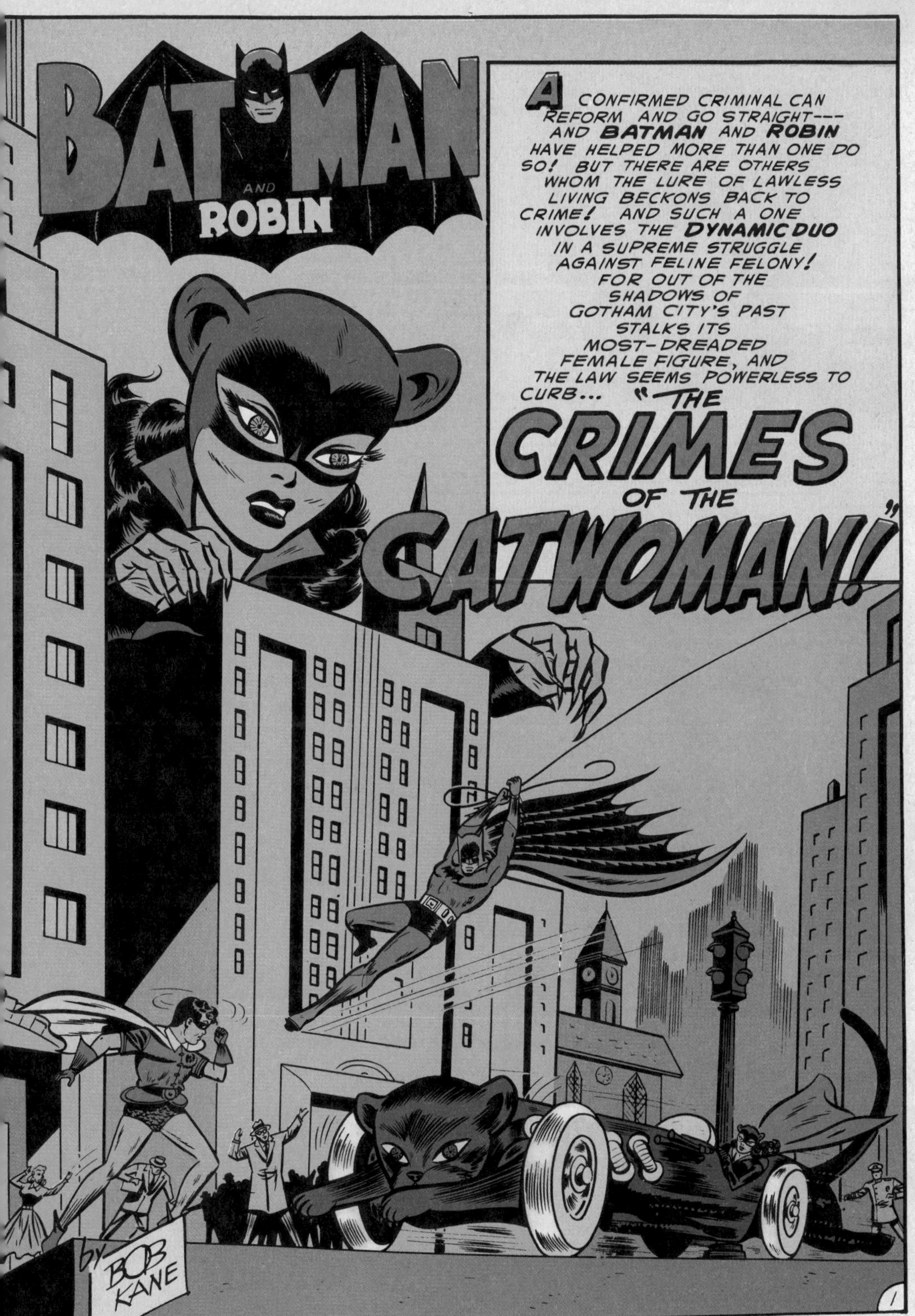

Written by Edmond Hamilton/Art by Lew Sayre Schwartz & Charles Paris/Lettering by Pat Gordon

IN THE EDITORIAL OFFICE OF THE "GOTHAM GAZETTE"...

CHIEF, THERE JUST ISN'T ANY BIG STORY RIGHT NOW! **BATMAN** AND **ROBIN** HAVE CLEANED UP CRIME SO WELL THERE ARE NO SENSATIONS!

HM, I'VE GOT IT... WE'LL RUN A FEATURE SERIES ON **BATMAN'S** GREATEST CASES! IT'LL BE A NATURAL!

THE EDITOR'S INSPIRATION IS TO HAVE FAR-REACHING, OMINOUS RESULTS! FOR, AS THE GREAT FEATS OF **BATMAN** AND **ROBIN** ARE RETOL

Gotham Gazette

BATMAN TRIUMPHS

THE CONQUEST

THE CATWOMAN

...THE FIRST OF THE FEATURES HAS A STRANGE EFFECT ON THE GIRL PROPRIETOR OF A SMALL PET-SHOP!

SO **BATMAN** IS NOW BOASTING OF HOW HE CONQUERED ME! WHEN I **WAS** THE **CATWOMAN**, BEFORE I REFORMED, HE HAD LITTLE TO BOAST OF! I OUTWITTED HIM OFTEN, EVEN THOUGH HE FINALLY CAPTURED ME!

BATMAN TRIUMPHS

YES, SELINA KYLE, GIRL SHOP-KEEPER, WAS ONCE THE DREADED **CATWOMAN!** AND THERE ARE THOSE IN THE UNDERWORLD WHO REMEMBE THAT, AND TAUNT HER!

HOW DO YOU LIKE YOUR PUBLICITY, **CATWOMAN**?

HA, HA! DON'T CALL HER THAT--- SHE'S REFORMED, SINCE **BATMAN** NIPPE HER CLAWS!

WHEN I WAS **CATWOMAN** CHEAP CROOKS LIKE YOU WOULDN HAVE DARED COME NEAR ME!

THANKS, BATMAN, FOR PROTECTING ME! DID YOU COME TO GLOAT OVER YOUR PAST VICTORY OVER CATWOMAN?
SELINA, I CAME TO TELL YOU I HAD NOTHING TO DO WITH THAT NEWSPAPER SERIES! I'D NEVER HAVE PERMITTED IT, FOR I KNOW YOU WANT TO FORGET ALL ABOUT YOUR CATWOMAN PAST!
DO I? I WONDER! THEY SAY A LEOPARD NEVER CHANGES ITS SPOTS---AND A LEOPARD IS A MEMBER OF THE CAT FAMILY!
DON'T TALK LIKE THAT! UNLESS YOU FORGET YOUR FORMER LIFE AS CATWOMAN, THERE'S NO FUTURE FOR YOU, EVER!

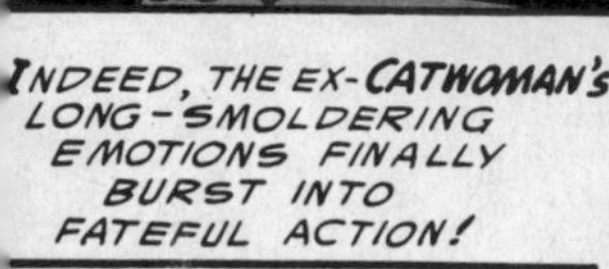
ATER, AS HE AND ROBIN RIVE HOMEWARD, A WORRIED ATMAN VOICES HIS ANXIETY!
SHE MISSES THE OLD EXCITEMENT, THE DARING THAT MADE HER SO DREADED IN CRIME! AND I'M AFRAID THIS PUBLICITY MAY TURN HER BACK TO HER OLD LIFE!
YOU'RE REALLY WORRIED ABOUT HER, AREN'T YOU? OR MAYBE I SHOULDN'T SAY THAT!

INDEED, THE EX-CATWOMAN'S LONG-SMOLDERING EMOTIONS FINALLY BURST INTO FATEFUL ACTION!
O ONE LAUGHED AT ME WHEN I WORE THIS! AND 'LL WEAR IT AGAIN! I'LL STUN GOTHAM CITY WITH UCH CAT-CRIMES THAT THEY'LL NEVER DICULE CATWOMAN AGAIN!

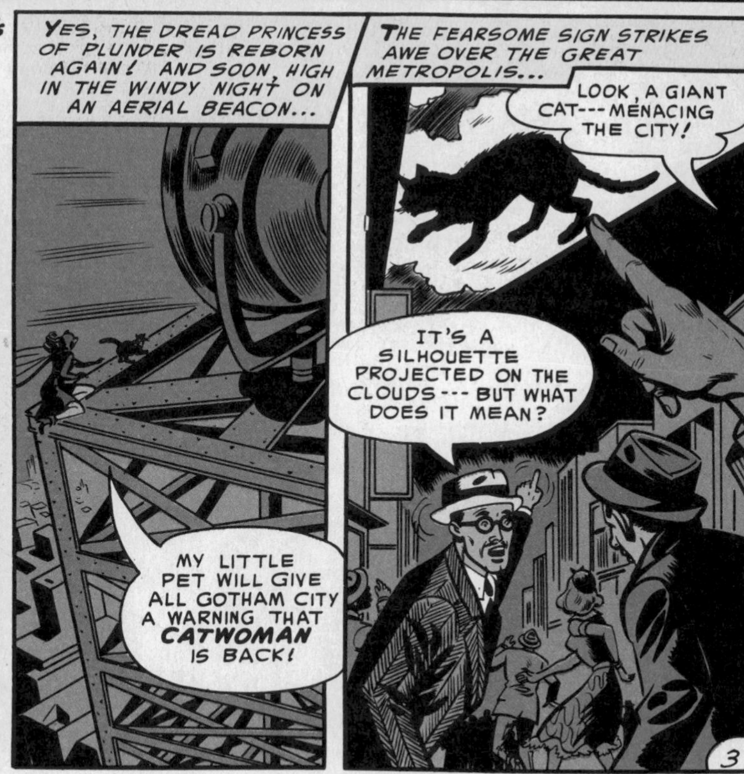
YES, THE DREAD PRINCESS OF PLUNDER IS REBORN AGAIN! AND SOON, HIGH IN THE WINDY NIGHT ON AN AERIAL BEACON...
MY LITTLE PET WILL GIVE ALL GOTHAM CITY A WARNING THAT CATWOMAN IS BACK!
THE FEARSOME SIGN STRIKES AWE OVER THE GREAT METROPOLIS...
LOOK, A GIANT CAT---MENACING THE CITY!
IT'S A SILHOUETTE PROJECTED ON THE CLOUDS---BUT WHAT DOES IT MEAN?
3

TO BRUCE WAYNE AND HIS WARD, DICK GRAYSON, WHO ARE SECRETLY BATMAN AND ROBIN, THE BOY WONDER, THAT CRYPTIC SYMBOL MEANS BUT ONE THING!
THAT SIGN CAN ONLY MEAN THE CATWOMAN IS ON THE PROWL AGAIN!
HOW COULD SHE DO IT? I'VE DONE EVERYTHING TO KEEP HER AWAY FROM CRIME! TOO LATE NOW --- SHE'S CHOSEN HER PATH, AND WE HAVE TO STOP HER AT ANY COST!
IN THE BATCAVE BENEATH BRUCE WAYNE'S MANSION, A SWIF SWITCH OF COSTUME--- AND THE THE BATPLANE SOARS INTO TH NIGHT!
ROBIN, THE MAIL-HELICOPTER IS CARRYING A SHIPMENT OF VALUABLE IRIDIUM TONIGHT! I THINK WE'D BETTER WATCH IT! ANYWAY!
RIGHT IT'S THE KIND OF BAIT CATWOMAN WOULD STRIKE AT!
THEY THINK THEIR MAIL-HELICOPTER IS SAFE WHEN IT'S CROSSING THE CITY TO THE AIRPORT, BUT THEY DON'T REALIZE---
...THAT MY CAT-APULT CAN GET ME TO IT FAST---
CATWOMAN! WHAT--- HOW---
...AND THAT MY CAT-OF-NINE-TAILS CAN BIND THE PILOT TO HIS SEAT IN ONE WHIP OF THE LASH! NOW TO LAND ON A ROOF AND ESCAPE WITH THE IRIDIUM!
BUT KEEN EYES HAVE SEEN, AND DOWN FRO THE SKY HURTLES A DARK-WINGED NEMESI SUPPORTED BY A SLENDER SILKEN CORD!
THAT MAIL-HELICOPTER WOULDN'T LAND ON THAT ROO IF ALL WAS WELL--- THERE ISN'T ROOM TO LAND THE BATPLANE THERE, BUT I CAN MANAGE THIS SHOR DROP WITH MY SILKEN CORD!

AND HIGH ABOVE THE CITY, THE TWO GREAT ANTAGONISTS ONCE AGAIN CONFRONT EACH OTHER!
LEFT THE PILOT ED AND THE MOTOR'S RUNNING-- I KNOW YOU'LL MAKE SURE HE'S SAFE BEFORE YOU COME AFTER ME, BATMAN!
BUT YOU CAN'T ESCAPE FROM THIS ROOF! YOU MIGHT AS WELL SURRENDER, SELINA!
BUT AS BATMAN HASTILY STOPS THE HELICOPTER MOTOR, THE FELINE FELON HAS SWIFTLY FLUNG A ROPE TO THE NEXT ROOFTOP IN INTRICATE PATTERN!
I'M CATWOMAN NOW! AND A CAT'S-CRADLE MAKES A GOOD BRIDGE FOR ME, DON'T YOU THINK?
I'M FOLLOWING YOU FROM HERE ON!
I COULD HAVE WAITED TILL YOU WERE ON IT AND THEN DONE THIS, BATMAN... BUT THAT WOULD BE TOO CATTY A TRICK!
STILL THIS MANIA FOR CAT-CRIME TRICKS! YOU MAY ESCAPE BY USING ONE THIS TIME, BUT THEY'LL BRING YOU TO YOUR DOOM!
OON, ACROSS A STARTLED CITY PREADS THE SINISTER NEWS...
Daily Times
ATWOMAN DARING MAIL ROBBERY
COMES BACK
EXTRA
AND IN THE SHADOWY UNDERWORLD THERE IS NEW RESPECT FOR THE CATWOMAN!
SHE WAS TOO MUCH FOR BATMAN, ALL RIGHT! IF I COULD GET INTO HER GANG, I'D SURE DO IT!
THE RUMOR IS THAT SHE'S FITTED UP A NEW HIDEOUT--- A NEW CATACOMB!
ES, THE PRINCESS OF PLUNDER AGAIN HAS A SECRET LAIR WITH THE FELINE FURNISHINGS SHE LOVES!
HIS NEW CATACOMB EVEN SPLASHIER THAN YOUR OLD NE, CATWOMAN!
YES, AND MY NEW KITTY CAR IS EVEN MORE POWERFUL! NOW I'LL MAKE GOTHAM CITY DREAD THE VERY NAME OF CAT--- AND THIS IS HOW WE'LL START!
5

MEANWHILE, A GRIM BATMAN PREPARES FOR A DEADLY DUEL! IN POLICE COMMISSIONER GORDON'S OFFICE...
BATMAN, YOU SEEMED SO INTERESTED IN THIS GIRL, THE WAY YOU TRIED TO GET HER TO GO STRAIGHT--- PERHAPS YOU'D RATHER STAY OUT OF THIS CATWOMAN CASE?
NO, I TRIED TO HELP HER, BUT SHE CHOSE TO RETURN TO CRIME! I MUST BRING HER TO JUSTICE!
BUT HOW CAN WE TELL WHERE SHE'LL STRIKE NEXT?
SHE ALWAYS SPECIALIZES IN CAT CRIMES. NOW LOOK AT THESE TWO ITEMS--- ONE ABOUT GUY VANEY, THE LION-TAMER AT THE GOTHAM GARDEN CIRCUS! THE OTHER ABOUT HORACE BRAHAM, MILLIONAIRE COLLECTOR OF CAT'S-EYE JEWELS!
I GET IT--- A LION-TAMER IS A "CAT" MAN, IN SHOW SLANG!
YES, AND THAT'S WHY I'M GOING TO GOTHAM GARDEN! ROBIN, YOU WARN BRAHAM TO GET HIS CAT'S-EYE JEWEL COLLECTION TO SOME SAFE PLACE!
SOON, BENEATH THE GREAT ROOF OF GOTHAM GARDEN AS A CAPACITY CROWD WATCHES A BREATH-TAKING LION ACT!
MEEEOOW
THOSE LION-SNARLS MAKE ECHOES FROM THE CEILING THAT SOUND LIKE CAT-SNARLS!
THOSE AREN'T ECHOES --- THEY SOUND LIKE REAL CAT-CRIES! CATWOMAN MUST BE USING CATS UP THERE IN SOME CRIME-PLAN!
SWIFTLY, UNSUSPECTED BY THE AUDIENCE, THE BATMAN CLIMBS HIGH INTO THE NETWORK OF GIRDERS THAT SUPPORT THE ROOF!
I THOUGHT SHE MIGHT USE REAL CATS, AND BROUGHT CATNIP IN MY UTILITY-BELT TO DIVERT THEM IN CASE --- BUT WHAT'S THIS?
MEEOWWW
MEEOWW
MEEOWW
THEY'RE NOT CATS BUT CATBIRDS --- BIRDS THAT UTTER A REALISTIC CAT-LIKE CALL! SHE TURNED THEM LOOSE SO THEY'D LEAD A FALSE TRAIL UP HERE!

ATMAN HAS GUESSED RIGHT, BUT TOO LATE! FOR UNDERNEATH THE STAGE, WHERE THE AIR-CONDITIONING MACHINERY THROBS AWAY...
HOOKING A GAS-TANK TO THE AIR-CONDITIONING SYSTEM IS A SMART GAG, CATWOMAN--- BUT IT ISN'T A CAT-CRIME!
OH, YES, IT IS ---
...FOR THAT GAS PUTS EVERYONE HERE INTO A CAT-ALEPTIC SLEEP, LONG ENOUGH FOR US TO GRAB THE BOX-OFFICE RECEIPTS!
AND IT'LL BE A CAT-ASTROPHE FOR THE MANAGEMENT! HAW, HAW!
THE GREAT GOTHAM GARDEN HAS NEVER SEEN A MORE DARING ACROBATIC ACT THAN THE VAST, FLYING SWING THAT BATMAN MAKES AS HE BEGINS TO BLACK OUT!
ON THE GIRDERS ABOVE, BATMAN FIGHTS TO ACT AS INSIDIOUS FUMES OVERPOWER HIM!
GAS--- (COUGH) DIDN'T FORESEE THAT---ONLY CHANCE IS TO SWING DOWN INTO THAT OFFICE AHEAD OF THEM --- (COUGH)
BATMAN! HE'S GETTING AHEAD OF US!
THE GAS MUST HAVE HIM ALMOST OUT! HURRY!
INSTINCTIVELY, THE DAZED BATMAN USES HIS LAST STRENGTH TO THWART THE CRIMINALS!
HE MANAGED TO LOCK THE SAFE--- IT'LL TAKE TIME TO OPEN IT!
AND WE HAVEN'T GOT TIME NOW! HE TOUCHED THE ALARM-BUTTON, BLAST HIM!
AND AS THE CAPED CRIME-CRUSHER SINKS SENSELESS, DEATH HOVERS CLOSE TO HIM!
BUT IT'LL ONLY TAKE A SECOND TO FIX HIM FOR GOOD, BEFORE WE GET OUT OF HERE!
NO, DON'T SHOOT! I COULDN'T BEAR TO SEE HIM KILLED! I--- MEAN, WE'LL TAKE HIM ALONG--- AS A HOSTAGE!
7

NOT TOO LATE TO SAVE THE BOX-OFFICE FUND THERE--- YOU LOCKED THE SAFE IN TIME! BUT TOO LATE TO SAVE YOURSELF!

SO YOU BROUGHT ME HERE, INSTEA OF LETTING YOUR THUGS MURDER ME--- WHY?

AT THE MANSION OF THE MILLIONAIRE COLLECTOR

IF CATWOMAN IS AFTER MY CAT'S-EYE COLLECTION, I'LL BE SAFEST WITH IT ON MY YACHT ANCHORED IN MID-RIVER!

WE'LL KEEP AN EYE ON YOUR YACHT, AS SOON AS I CONTACT AND PICK UP BATMAN!

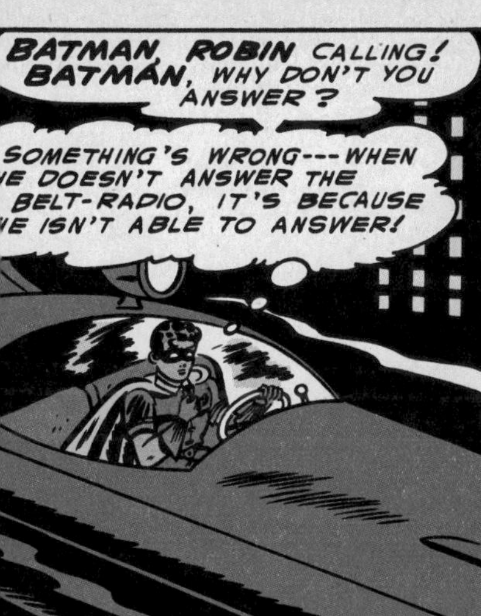

ND AS THE SHARP, FELINE CLAWS TEAR AT THE CORDS, NE BY ONE THE STRANDS PART!

THAT DID IT --- NOW TO GET OUT OF HERE AND CALL ROBIN!

MEEOW

SOON...
I CALLED COMMISSIONER GORDON--- HE SAID THE PEOPLE AT GOTHAM GARDEN SOON RECOVERED FROM THE KNOCKOUT GAS, AND THAT YOU'D PREVENTED THE ROBBERY THERE!
BUT CATWOMAN'S CATBIRD TRICK WAS ALMOST TOO MUCH FOR ME!
THOSE ANGRY CROOKS WOULD SURELY HAVE KILLED YOU IF SHE HADN'T INTERVENED, BATMAN! IT'S STRANGE, HER FEELING TOWARD YOU!
NO USE TALKING ABOUT THAT--- SHE'S GOT TO BE STOPPED! I ONL HOPE WE'RE NOT TOO LATE AT BRAHAM'S YACHT!
HORACE BRAHAM FEELS PERFECTLY SAFE--- ALTHOUGH A BIT BORED!
YOU CREWMEN KEEP A LOOKOUT FOR ANY BOAT THAT TRIES TO APPROACH US!
YES, MR. BRAHAM!
HA, HA--- CATS DON'T LIKE WATER AND CATWOMAN CAN'T BOTHER MY CAT'S-EYES HERE! I'LL DO A LITTLE FISHING UNTIL THE BATMAN GETS THIS FEMALE FELINE UNDER ARREST!
BUT A LITTLE WAY UPRIVER, CRYPTIC PREPARATIONS ARE BEING SWIFTLY MADE!
BRAHAM'S SUCH AN AVID ANGLER, I KNEW HE'D BE FISHING--- AND I'M GOING TO USE THAT FACT TO GET ABOARD HIS YACHT! YOU BE READY TO PICK ME UP WHEN I HAVE THE JEWELS!
WE'LL BE WATCHING!
AND A MOMENT LATER...
THERE SHE GOES AND BRAHAM HAS GOT A SURPRISE COMING

PRESENTLY...
'VE HOOKED A RECORD CATFISH--- HELP ME PULL T UP ON DECK!
YES, SIR!
A MOMENT LATER...
THAT DUMMY PLASTIC "CATFISH" MADE A GOOD WAY FOR CATWOMAN TO GET ON BOARD! I'LL TAKE THOSE CAT'S-EYE JEWELS NOW!
EANWHILE, AS THE BATMOBILE ROARS NTO THE SCENE...
THAT'S CATWOMAN N THE YACHT--- SHE GOT ABOARD SOMEHOW!
AND LOOK--- THAT LAUNCH IS STARTING DOWN TOWARD THE YACHT, TOO, AND THOSE ARE HER TWO ACCOMPLICES IN IT! HOLD TIGHT, ROBIN!
URLING THE BATMOBILE UT ONTO THE BRIDGE AS THE AUNCH PASSES UNDERNEATH...
THEY'RE RIGHT UNDERNEATH--- NOW!
JUST THOUGHT WE'D DROP IN ON YOU, BOYS!
NOT SO MUCH PUN, AND MORE PUNCH, ROBIN!
YOU MIGHT AS WELL SURRENDER, CATWOMAN--- THIS TIME YOU'RE TRAPPED!
IT SEEMS THAT YOU ESCAPED A TRAP, BATMAN--- AND SO CAN I!
11

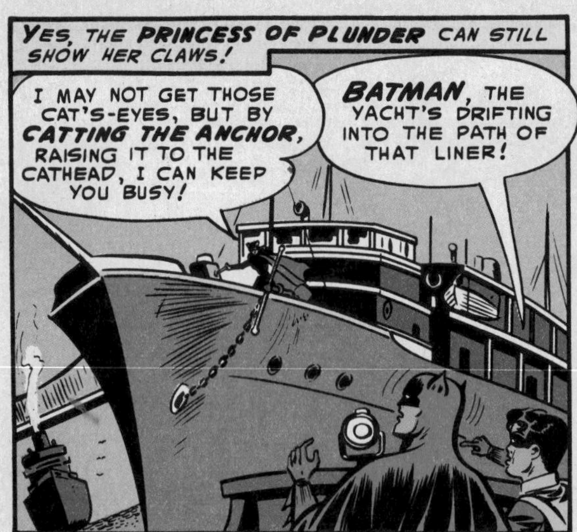

THE GRIM PURSUIT RACES OUT OF THE RIVER INT THE STORMY OUTER SEA!

BATMAN, LOOK--- THE WAVES WERE TOO MUCH FOR HER LITTLE CATBOAT--- IT WAS WRECKED ON THAT MARSHY SHORE!

WE'LL RUN IN THERE---WE MIGHT STILL BE IN TIME!

--- IT'S MORE LIKELY SHE USED ONE OF THESE HOLLOW CAT-TAIL REEDS TO BREATHE THROUGH, AND ESCAPED UNDERWATER UNSEEN!

LIVING, OR DEAD? ONLY TIME WILL TELL ABOUT THE CATWOMAN.

TH EN.

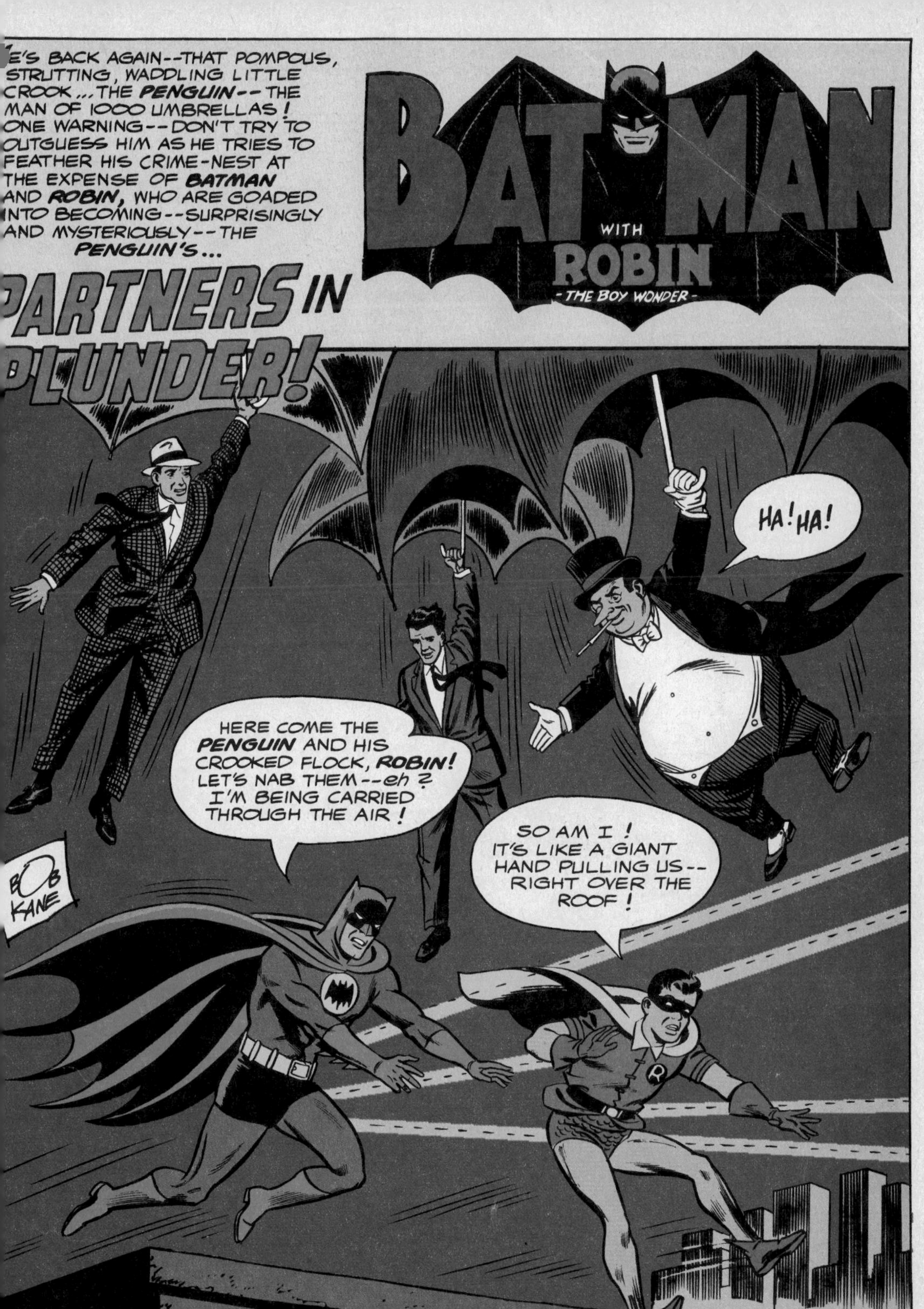

Written by France Eddie Herron/Art by Sheldon Moldoff & Joe Giella

AH... WHAT A BIRD-BRAIN I'VE BEEN! NO WONDER MY MIND'S A BARREN WILDERNESS! I NEED AN UMBRELLA FOR INSPIRATION!

SHORTLY, INSIDE THE STORE...
ONDER WHAT EVERYBODY'S DOING
ITH AN UMBRELLA ON A NICE DAY
IKE THIS... WEATHER REPORT
DIDN'T MENTION RAIN...

AND AT TEN SHARP...
HEY! MY UMBRELLA OPENED BY ITSELF!
SO DID MINE! WHAT'S GOIN' ON?
SNAP!
SNAP!
SNAP!

RACKLE!!
HELP! THESE UMBRELLAS ARE ACTING UP... SHOOTING OUT SMOKE, LIGHTNING--!
SALE
CALL THE POLICE!

HE POLICE ARRIVE--ON THE DOUBLE...
DON'T KNOW WHAT HAPPENED! EVERYBODY
AME IN WITH UMBRELLAS--THEN THAT WILD
CTION STARTED! NOPE--
OBODY TRIED TO ROB US...

SOON, COMMISSIONER GORDON IS ON THE HOT-LINE WITH BATMAN...
BETTER HOP OVER TO HEADQUARTERS, BATMAN! I THINK THE PENGUIN'S UP TO SOME NEW UMBRELLA TRICKS!
WE'LL BE RIGHT THERE, COMMISSIONER.
3

AT 10:15, IN FRONT OF A BANK ACROSS TOWN...
MAKING A DEPOSIT, SIR? THAT'S ALWAYS GOOD FOR A RAINY DAY--AND SO IS THIS FREE UMBRELLA! MY COMPLIMENTS!
UH-- THANK YOU!
GOTHAM BANK

AS THE BATMOBILE WENDS ITS WAY THROUGH THE STREETS-- THE HOT-LINE PHONE AGAIN...
BATMAN! A PATROLMAN SPOTTED ANOTHER MAN GIVING AWAY UMBRELLAS AT THE BANK ON JEFFERSON AND SEVENTH!
I GET YOU, COMMISSIONER! WE'LL GO STRAIGHT TO THE BANK!
FOR A BRIEF SPELL, THE FREE UMBRELLAS CARRIED INTO THE BANK SEEM HARMLESS ENOUGH--BUT, SUDDENLY...
SNAP!
SNAP!

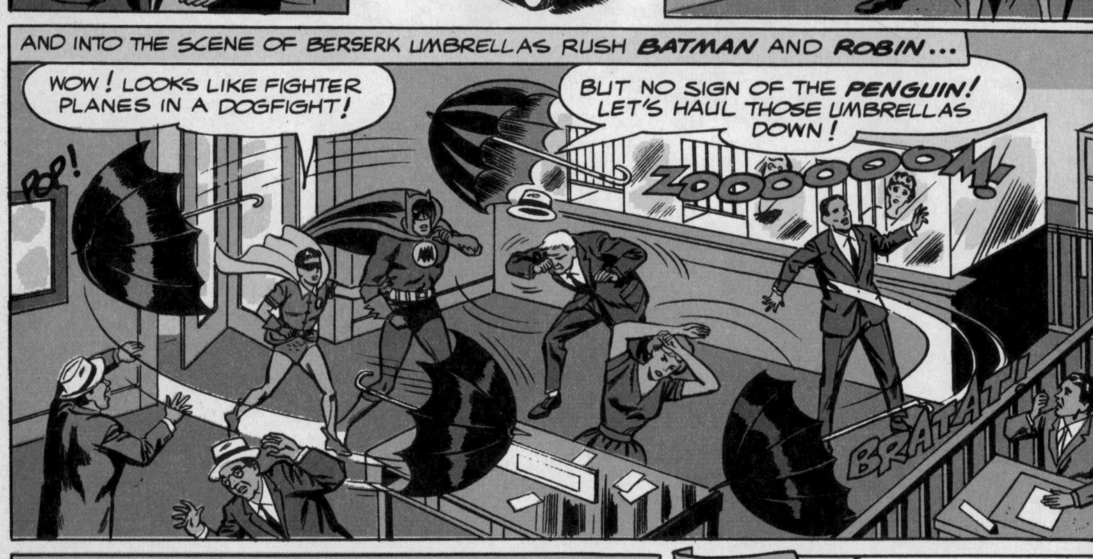
AND INTO THE SCENE OF BERSERK UMBRELLAS RUSH BATMAN AND ROBIN...
WOW! LOOKS LIKE FIGHTER PLANES IN A DOGFIGHT!
BUT NO SIGN OF THE PENGUIN! LET'S HAUL THOSE UMBRELLAS DOWN!
POP!
ZOOOOOOOM!
BRATATAT!

IN A WILD SCRAMBLE, THE GOTHAM CRIME-FIGHTERS TANGLE WITH THE STRANGEST "ENEMY" THEY'VE EVER FOUGHT--UMBRELLAS!
GOT TWO OF THEM--BUT IT'S LIKE WRESTLING WITH FLYING EELS!
I JUST PUT ANOTHER ONE OUT OF ACTION!

FINALLY...
WE KNOW THE PENGUIN'S BEHIND THIS, BUT...
BUT WHY? WHAT'S HE UP TO? WHAT'S HIS GAME THIS TIME?
WE'D BETTER HAVE A CHAT WITH THAT CAGEY LITTLE BIRD-- HE BRAZENLY LEFT HIS ADDRESS ON THE UMBRELLAS!

T THE PENGUIN'S UMBRELLA SHOP...
ATMAN NO DOUBT GOT WORD OF MY EWELRY STORE CAPER--THEN THE ONE T THE BANK! FROM THE BANK HE'LL OME HERE... BUT MY OTHER UMBRELLAS N ROUTE SHOULD GIVE HIM A STORMY TIME FIRST!
THE WADDLING LITTLE CROOK IS SO RIGHT!
KA-PATTA
KA-PATTA
LOOK OUT! MORE WILD UMBRELLAS! THEY MIGHT EXPLODE!
RUNAWAY UMBRELLAS! LET'S USE OUR ROPE BATARANGS!
THE BAT-ARANGS WHIRL TO THEIR MARK...
WE'RE SLOWING 'EM DOWN!
NOTHING ELSE SPECIAL ABOUT THESE UMBRELLAS! THEY WERE SIMPLY RIGGED TO ROLL ALONG LIKE JUGGERNAUT WHEELS! WHY?
BATMAN! OVER THERE! LOOK!
5

A GREAT SHADOW FALLS OVER GOTHAM SQUARE AS..
A HUGE UMBRELLA-- DRIFTING DOWNWARD-- IN REVERSE! IT'S LIKE A... FLYING SAUCER!
STAY BACK, EVERY-BODY!

WHEN THE MYSTERY-UMBRELLA LANDS...
NO HIDDEN GIMMICKS ON THIS ONE, EITHER! BUT WE'VE GOT ENOUGH TO SLAP THE PENGUIN BEHIND BARS... OBSTRUCTING TRAFFIC... DISTURBING THE PEACE--AND SO FORTH!
YES... WE CAN NAIL HIM BE- FORE HE PULLS HI BIG PAY- OFF... WHATEVE IT IS!
BUT ALREADY THE WILY KING OF UMBRELLAS AWAITS THE DARING DU
TEN-FIVE! BATMAN WILL BE HERE IN ONE MINUTE--SO DIS- APPEAR, HERBIE! I HOPE HE'S FIGURED UNUSUAL WAYS TO PROFI BY MY UMBRELLA GIMMICKS-- BECAUSE I HAVEN'T! Hmmm-- FIRST--TO SWITCH MY MONOCLE TO MY LEFT EYE...!

SPRING ISSUE
No. 1
BATMAN
10¢
No. 120
FEB.
Ten Cents
Detective COMICS
BATMAN and ROBIN give The Penguin the bird in "Fowl Play"

PARTNERS IN PLUNDER!-- PART 2
XACTLY IXTY ECONDS ASS AND HE CRIME-IGHTERS ENTER THE ENGUIN'S SHOP...
AH! BATMAN AND ROBIN! SUCH DISTINGUISHED CUSTOMERS! MAY I SHOW YOU MY WARES?
WE'RE NOT HERE TO BUY UMBRELLAS, PENGUIN--AND YOU KNOW IT! WE'RE "FLYING" YOU DOWN TO HEADQUARTERS!

E HAVE ENOUGH COUNTS GAINST YOU AND YOUR MBRELLAS TO PUT YOU ON ICE!
TUT-TUT, BATMAN! I HEARD THOSE WILD REPORTS ABOUT MY UMBRELLAS ON THE RADIO... I MEAN THE UMBRELLAS THAT HAD BEEN MINE!

YOU SEE, I MERELY SELL UMBRELLAS! WHAT HAPPENS TO THEM AFTER THEY LEAVE HERE IS NOT MY CONCERN, IN SHORT, YOU HAVEN'T A SCRAP OF EVIDENCE AGAINST ME!
AH! THEY'RE STARING AT MY WRONG-EYE MONOCLE! I KNEW IT WOULD GET THEM!

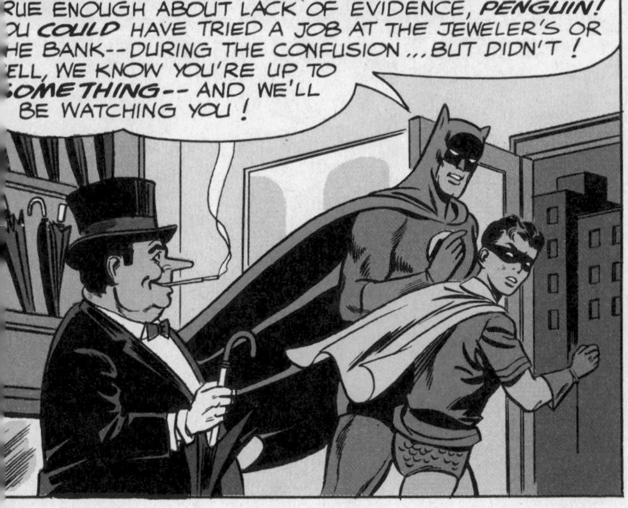
RUE ENOUGH ABOUT LACK OF EVIDENCE, PENGUIN! OU COULD HAVE TRIED A JOB AT THE JEWELER'S OR HE BANK--DURING THE CONFUSION... BUT DIDN'T! ELL, WE KNOW YOU'RE UP TO OMETHING-- AND WE'LL BE WATCHING YOU!

WHEN ONCE AGAIN IN THE BATMOBILE...
I'M CONVINCED THE PENGUIN'S BEHIND ALL THIS MYSTERY, AND THINGS HAVE GOT TO COME TO A HEAD, SOONER OR LATER!
AND WHAT ABOUT HIS MONOCLE? HE ALWAYS WORE IT IN HIS RIGHT EYE--BUT NOW IT'S IN HIS LEFT!
7

YES--THAT WAS CURIOUS! I WONDER IF THE MONOCLE HAS ANYTHING TO DO WITH THIS PUZZLER? IT'S SUCH A WHACKY CASE I CAN BELIEVE ANYTHING WILL HAPPEN!
LET'S JUST HOPE WE'RE ON HAND WHEN IT DOES!

MEANWHILE...
TELL ME, BOSS--WHY DID YOU MOVE YOUR MONOCLE TO THE OTHER EYE?
JUST STRATEGY, HERBIE! IT'S A LITTLE SOME-THING ELSE THAT'LL KEEP BATMAN GUESSING--KEEP HIM WORRIED! THAT'S THE ONLY REASON I DID IT! NOW--

I THINK TONIGHT WILL BE THE BIG NIGHT! SUMMON THE REST OF THE BOYS HERE AT ONCE! WE MUST WORK FAST--ON THE BIGGEST PLAN OF MY LIFE--AND THE BIGGEST UPSET BATMAN EVER GOT!

LATE THAT NIGHT, FROM THE PROWLING BATMOBILE, THE CRIME-FIGHTERS SEE A STRANGE AND FAS-CINATING GLOW ABOVE GOTHAM CITY...
THAT LOOKS LIKE THE AURORA BOREALIS!
STRANGE--IT USUALLY APPEARS FAR NORTH OF HERE--IT'S HARDLY EVER SEEN IN GOTHAM CITY!

SUDDENLY, THE BRILLIANT LIGHTS FADE, AND...
BATMAN--TWO UM-BRELLAS! THEY CAUSED THE MULTI-COLORED LIGHTS!
YES--NOW THE LIGHTS ARE GONE, AND THEY'RE COMING DOWN! ONE IS A "PARACHUTE" UMBRELLA--AND THE ONE SUSPENDED FROM IT HAS A SPARKLER ON IT! WHAT'S UP?

RACING TO WHERE THE STRANGE PAIR OF UMBRELLAS LANDED...
I DON'T SEE ANY OBVIOUS GIMMICKS IN THE UMBRELLAS-BUT LET'S TAKE A CLOSER LOOK! THE PENGUIN DOESN'T MAKE ANYTHING OBVIOUS!

HE RODS OF THIS ONE ARE OLLOW--NOT GIMMICKED VITH ANYTHING, AS FAR AS I CAN SEE!
SAME WITH THIS ONE! BUT SOMEHOW I CAN'T BELIEVE THE PENGUIN WOULD DROP TWO MEANING-LESS UMBRELLAS!

ISN'T THAT KIND OF A LOUD COLOR DESIGN?
THE SAME IDEA STRUCK ME! YOU KNOW--MAYBE THE COLORS ARE A CLUE TO THE PENGUIN'S PLOTTING! HE'D LIKE TO TAUNT US BY THROW-ING A CLUE TO HIS UP-COMING CRIME AT US, JUST TO SEE IF WE COULD TUMBLE TO IT!

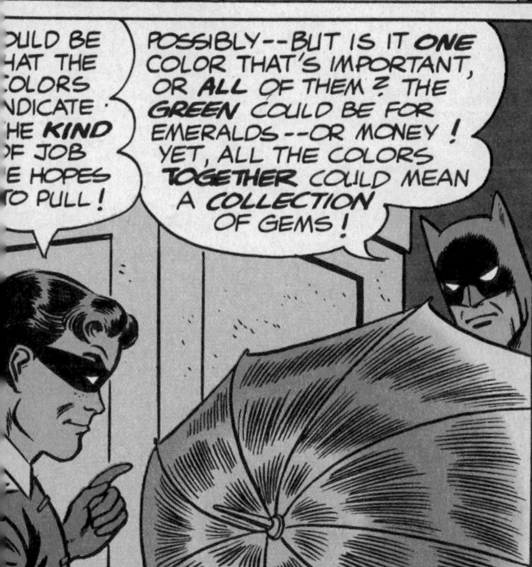
OULD BE HAT THE OLORS NDICATE HE KIND F JOB E HOPES O PULL!
POSSIBLY--BUT IS IT ONE COLOR THAT'S IMPORTANT, OR ALL OF THEM? THE GREEN COULD BE FOR EMERALDS--OR MONEY! YET, ALL THE COLORS TOGETHER COULD MEAN A COLLECTION OF GEMS!

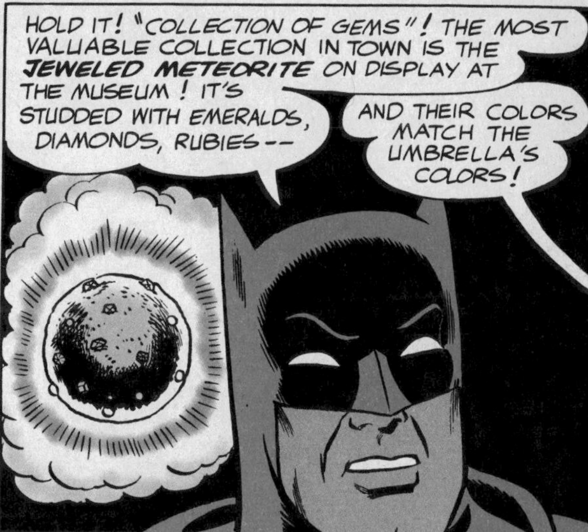
HOLD IT! "COLLECTION OF GEMS"! THE MOST VALUABLE COLLECTION IN TOWN IS THE JEWELED METEORITE ON DISPLAY AT THE MUSEUM! IT'S STUDDED WITH EMERALDS, DIAMONDS, RUBIES--
AND THEIR COLORS MATCH THE UMBRELLA'S COLORS!

UT EVEN AS BATMAN AND ROBIN VOICE THEIR EDUCTIONS--
HAT MUST BE T, BATMAN! HE PENGUIN'S LANNING TO STEAL HE JEWELED METEORITE!
HA! I TOLD YOU I'M AS WISE AS AN OWL! OUR TWO FRIENDS DON'T REALIZE THEY'RE TALKING INTO A TINY TRANSISTOR MICRO-PHONE, CONCEALED IN THE "PARACHUTE" UMBRELLA!

ONE HALF OF MY PREDICTION HAS COME TRUE--BATMAN HAS TOLD ME WHAT TO STEAL! NEXT, HE'LL TELL ME HOW TO DO IT! LISTEN...
9

BUT THE **PENGUIN** WILL HAVE HIS TROUBLES, **BATMAN!** THE METEORITE IS ON DISPLAY BEHIND A **BREAKPROOF** WINDOW --
AND GUARDS ARE CONSTANTLY ON DUTY IN THE ROOMS FLANKING THE DIS-PLAY ROOM, AS WELL AS IN THE CORRIDORS! **BUT--** THERE'S ONE WEAK SPOT...

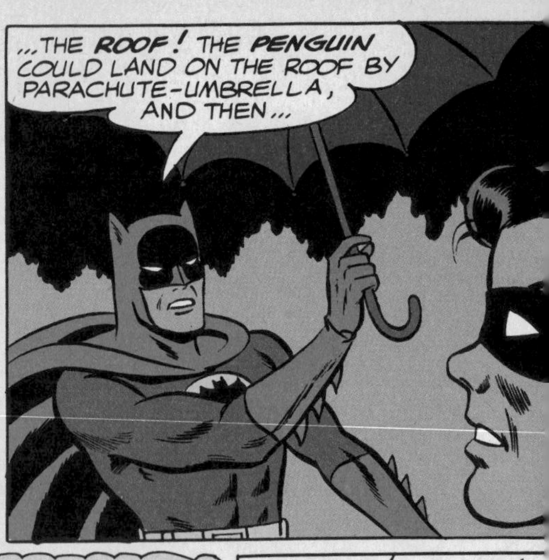
...THE **ROOF!** THE **PENGUIN** COULD LAND ON THE ROOF BY PARACHUTE-UMBRELLA, AND THEN...

"AFTER LANDING, HIS GANG COULD CUT THROUGH THE ROOM WITH AN ACETYLENE TORCH..."

"AND BY USING A TRICK UMBRELLA WITH AN **EXTENSION** CANE, HE COULD REACH FAR DOWN, HOOK THE JEWELED METEORITE..."

--AND BE OFF WITH HIS PRIZE BEFORE THE GUARDS KNEW WHAT HAPPENED!
SEE! **BATMAN** NOT ONLY SELECTED MY CRIME BUT **BLUE-PRINTED** IT FOR M I'LL USE HIS PLAN BUT WITH **OWN** SPECIA TOUCH!

LET'S GO! THE **PENGUIN** WILL STRIKE... RIGHT BEFORE **BATMAN'S** EYES, WHERE HE'LL BE WAITING ON THE ROOF! DON'T FORGET THE **PENGUIN-MAGNET,** HERBIE!
GOT IT, BOSS!

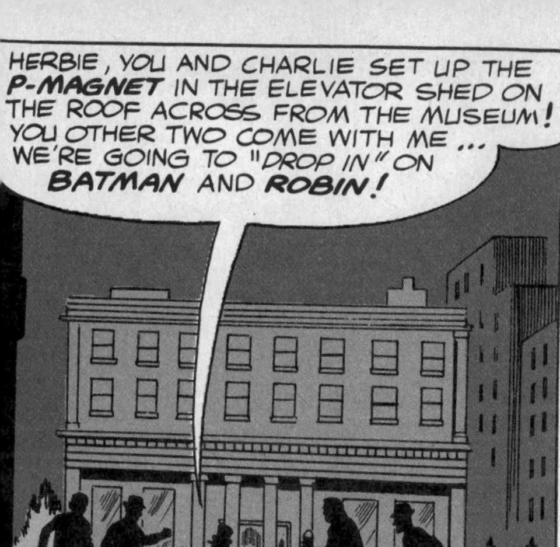
HERBIE, YOU AND CHARLIE SET UP THE P-MAGNET IN THE ELEVATOR SHED ON THE ROOF ACROSS FROM THE MUSEUM! YOU OTHER TWO COME WITH ME ... WE'RE GOING TO "DROP IN" ON BATMAN AND ROBIN!

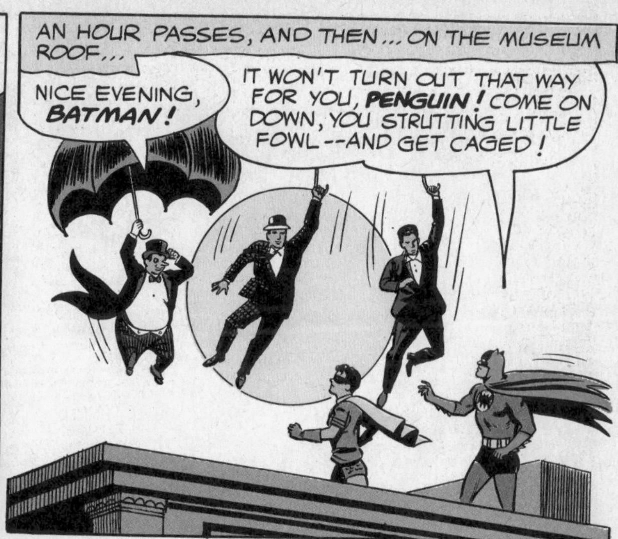
AN HOUR PASSES, AND THEN... ON THE MUSEUM ROOF...
NICE EVENING, BATMAN!
IT WON'T TURN OUT THAT WAY FOR YOU, PENGUIN! COME ON DOWN, YOU STRUTTING LITTLE FOWL--AND GET CAGED!

NAB THE PENGUIN, ROBIN-- I'LL GIVE THE OTHER TWO A ROUGH LANDING!

BUT--AS THE CRIME-FIGHTERS CHARGE FORWARD...
I C-CAN'T STOP! IT'S LIKE A G-GIANT HAND PULLING ME!
HA, HA!
SAME WITH ME! I'M STRAINING TO STOP-- BUT CAN'T!

WE'RE FLYING! HOW'S IT POSSIBLE--?!
YOUR "CHARM" IS MAGNETIC, BATMAN--HA, HA! YOUR BELT-BUCKLES WERE SUBJECTED TO A POWERFUL AND SPECIAL MAGNETIC FORCE WHEN YOU PICKED UP MY LAST TWO UMBRELLAS...
11

WE WERE ABLE TO TURN ON MY P-MAGNET AT ANY TIME, DRAWING YOU TO IT! IT'S INSIDE THE ELEVATOR SHED ACROSS YONDER ROOF!
THAT PESKY PENGUIN-- ONE STEP AHEAD OF US AGAIN!

STUCK--LIKE FLIES IN FLYPAPER!

JUST AS WE DEDUCED, THE PENGUIN'S USED AN ACETYLENE TORCH TO CUT THROUGH THE ROOF, AND MUST BE PULLING THE JEWELED METEORITE OUT BY NOW! WE'VE GOT TO GET LOOSE--BUT NOT WITH THOSE TWO WATCHING US LIKE HAWKS!

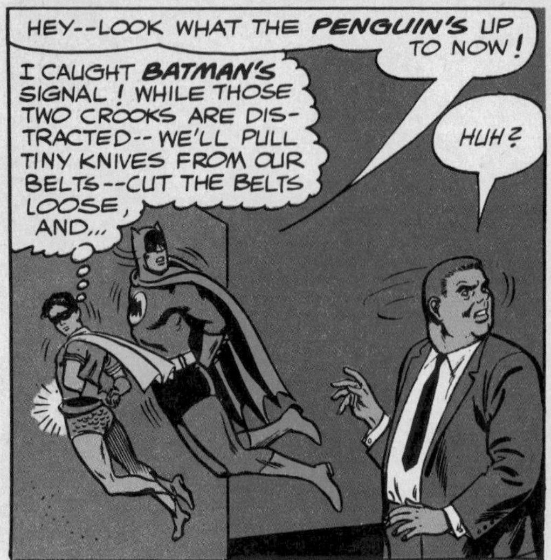
HEY--LOOK WHAT THE PENGUIN'S UP TO NOW!
I CAUGHT BATMAN'S SIGNAL! WHILE THOSE TWO CROOKS ARE DISTRACTED--WE'LL PULL TINY KNIVES FROM OUR BELTS--CUT THE BELTS LOOSE, AND...
HUH?

WITHIN MOMENTS, BATMAN AND ROBIN HAVE FREED THEMSELVES AND SLAMMED INTO THE TWO CROOKS...
WE'LL COOL OFF THESE TWO, ROBIN--THEN GET OUR BATROPES FROM THE BELTS AND RUFFLE THE PENGUIN'S FEATHERS!

THEN, AS THEY SWING TOWARD THE MUSEUM ROOF...
THE **PENGUIN'S** GOT THE METEORITE--AND IS ESCAPING WITH A **JET**-UMBRELLA!
GO AHEAD, BOSS-- WE'LL HOLD OFF **BATMAN** AN' THE KID!

BUT TO THE ASTONISHMENT OF THE CROOKS...
THIS **RING-AROUND-THE ROSY** TRICK SHOULD KEEP 'EM IN KNOTS FOR AWHILE, eh?
YES--YOU MIGHT SAY THEY'D LIKE TO GO SOMEWHERE-- BUT THEY'RE ALL "*TIED UP*"!

WITH THE LAST OF THE CROOKS TRUSSED UP...
IT SEEMS THERE'S NO WAY FOR US TO GO AFTER THE **PENGUIN**-- TILL YOU **WONDER** HOW THE TWO CROOKS WITH HIM WERE GOING TO GET AWAY...
OF COURSE! THEIR UMBRELLAS MUST **ALSO** BE JET-EQUIPPED!

AND THEN BEGINS AN ASTONISHING CHASE THROUGH NIGHT SKIES...
FROM NOW ON IT'S A QUESTION OF WHICH JET-UMBRELLA IS THE FASTEST--THE **PENGUIN'S**... OR ONE OF OURS!

HE JETTISONED THE METEORITE! I'LL GO AFTER IT, ROBIN! YOU STICK WITH THE PENGUIN!
HE'S STARTING TO PICK UP SPEED! BUT I KNOW HOW TO OVERCOME THAT...

ROBIN'S ROPE WHISTLES THROUGH THE AIR, AND...

SNARED HIM!
eh? WHAT'S THIS?

SOON...
LIKE A HOMING PIGEON, YOU'RE FLYING BACK TO WHERE YOU BELONG... A CAGE IN JAIL!

BAH!

LATER, AFTER THE JEWELED METEORITE IS RETRIEVED...
THE CASE IS BEATEN, PENGUIN-- EXCEPT FOR THE MYSTERY OF WHY YOU PULLED THE MONOCLE SWITCH! WE'RE TAKING IT ALONG FOR FURTHER STUDY!
HA! LET 'EM BAT THEIR BRAINS OUT! THEY'LL NEVER SOLVE THAT PART OF THE CASE.. WHICH GIVES THIS OLD BIRD SOMEWHAT OF A VICTORY!
?
The End

Detective Comics
12¢
An EXTRA-LONG BATMAN ADVENTURE... The CAT-MAN STRIKES BACK
GREAT SCOTT! BATWOMAN HAS JOINED FORCES WITH THE CAT-MAN AND BECOME THE CAT-WOMAN!
BATMAN
12¢
WHAT A WAR! The PENGUIN and his WEAPON-UMBRELLA ARMY AGAINST BATMAN and ROBIN!

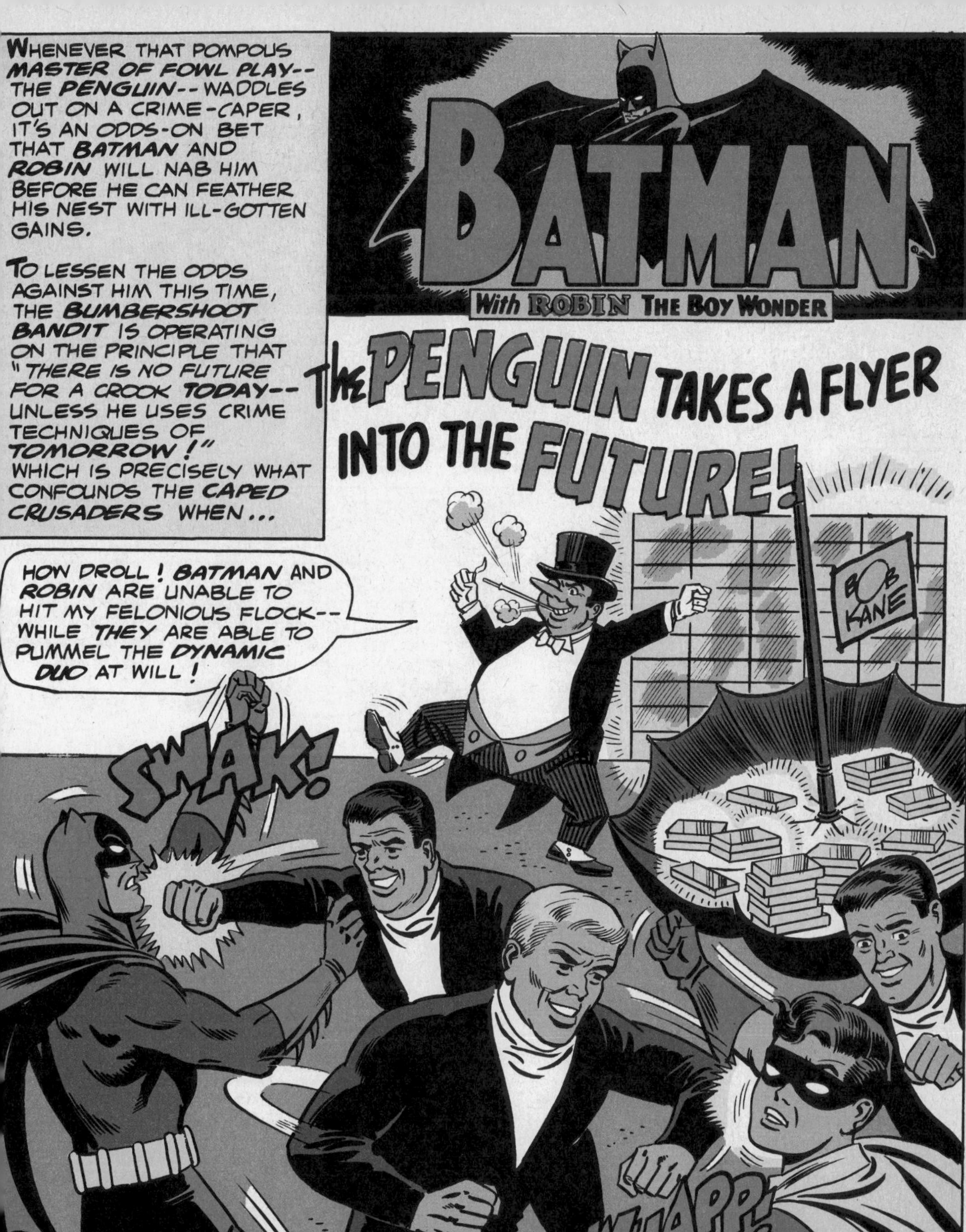

Written by Gardner Fox/Art by Chic Stone & Sid Greene

BUT IN A CERTAIN UNDERWORLD HANGOUT, FOUR GANGSTERS "COOL IT" IN STYLE...

AIR-CONDITIONED UNIFORMS!

PENGUIN, THIS IS THE GREATEST IDEA YOU'VE EVER HAD!

PFAH! GOOD, YES--BUT NOT GREAT! THE TIME IS COMING WHEN SUCH UNIFORMS WILL BE COMMONPLACE! TONIGHT--WHILE EVERYONE ELSE IS WILTING FROM THE HEAT--YOU'LL BE BREEZING THROUGH A CRIME-CAPER!

YES, HERE HE IS AGAIN--THE BIRDMAN BANDIT, THE MAN OF 1000 UMBRELLAS--THE PENGUIN HIMSELF, WADDLING ON TO MORE WICKEDNESS...

YES INDEED,--A COMFORTABLE CROOK IS AN EFFECTIVE CROOK! MOREOVER--AN ENERGETIC CROOK IS AN ENDURING CROOK, WELL ABLE TO STAND UP TO MEDDLING BUSYBODIES LIKE BATMAN AND ROBIN! COME ALONG TO MY NEXT SURPRISE...

FELLOW BIRD-BRAINS--MEET *CHEF PENGUIN*!
B-BUT, B-BOSS--YOU DIDN'T TELL US YOU HAD A TWIN BROTHER!

BOSH! WHAT YOU ARE SEEING IS MERELY A *ROBOT PENGUIN*! I'VE PROGRAMMED HIM TO BE THE WORLD'S GREATEST CHEF! AND HERE IS HIS CULINARY MASTERPIECE!

HUH? A BUNCH O' PILLS?
WHERE'S THE FOOD?
EGAD, YOU INDIGENT IGNORAMUSES! THESE PILLS *ARE* THE MEAL--ONE FOR EACH OF US! WHAT YOU ARE ABOUT TO DINE UPON IS THE FEAST OF THE FUTURE!

EACH OF THESE PILLS CONTAINS ALL THE CONCENTRATED FOOD ELEMENTS OF A *CHATEAUBRIAND STEAK--CAESAR'S SALAD--POTATO AND VEGETABLES*--AND *BAKED ALASKA*!

COME, COME--EAT HEARTY, MY FINE-FEATHERED FINKS! ENJOY THE FUTURE TODAY! WE HAVE A JOB TO DO THIS NIGHT!
I'D STILL RATHER DIG INTO A STEAK! BUT WHAT'S ALL THIS TALK ABOUT THE **FUTURE** YOU'RE SPOUTING?

I THOUGHT YOU'D NEVER ASK! YOU SEE BEFORE YOU A GENIUS WHO HAS COME TO GRIPS WITH THE FUTURE--AND OUT-THOUGHT IT! BY JOVE! I--THE *PENGUIN*, MASTER OF FOWL PLAY, HAVE AT LAST COME INTO MY OWN!
3

WE SHALL BE INVIGORATED--INCOMPARABLE--INVULNERABLE! THE DYNAMIC DUO SHALL GO DOWN BEFORE US LIKE PINS TO A BOWLING BALL IN THE HANDS OF AN EXPERT!

YA HEAR THAT, BALD EAGLE? THAT'S US TH' BOSS IS TALKIN' ABOUT!

INTO THE OFFICES OF THE INTER-NATIONAL GOLD COR-PORATION RACE THE MASKED MAN-HUNTER AND BOY WONDER...
THERE'S OUR ANSWER, BATMAN-- THAT WISE OLD BIRD THE PENGUIN!
AH! MY FOOTLOOSE AND FANCY-FREE FOES! HALT! YOU'VE GONE FAR ENOUGH!

NEXT INSTANT...
HUH--WHAT'S THIS? MY FEET FEEL SO HEAVY--I CAN'T EVEN MOVE THEM!
YUK! YUK! YOU'VE BEEN CAUGHT FLAT-FOOTED BY MY HEAVY GRAVITY BEAM!

A GRAVITY BEAM? BUT NOBODY'S EVER INVENTED SUCH A-- OOFF!
HOW DROLL! YOU CAN HARDLY MOVE-- YET YOU DENY THE TRUTH OF WHAT'S HAP-PENING TO YOU! HIT HIM AGAIN, SWIFTY!
THWOKK!

I'M SO HEAVY-FOOTED HE KEEPS BEATING ME TO THE PUNCH!
THUMP

ROBIN, TOO, FINDS HIMSELF DESPERATELY HANDICAPPED BY THE FUTURISTIC DEVICE OF THE BUMBERSHOOT BANDIT...
IF GRAVITY DIDN'T HOLD HIM, ROBIN WOULD BE FLYIN' CLEAR ACROSS THE ROOM!
SWOK!
5

OOF--CAN'T GET CLOSE ENOUGH TO LAY A HAND ON HIM!
HA, HA! THAT OL' GRAVITY BEAM'S GOT YA, ROBIN! YUH'RE SLOWER'N MOLASSES!
I WONDER WHY THE PENGUIN'S GANG IS NOT AFFECTED BY THE GRAVITY BEAM-- THE WAY WE ARE! COULD IT BE BECAUSE--
AS WE RAN IN--WE POUNDED OVER SOMETHING THAT GRATED UNDER OUR BOOTS! IF THOSE WERE IRON FILLINGS--
ROBIN--QUICKLY! GET OUT OF YOUR BOOTS! THE PENGUIN MUST HAVE CONCEALED A POWERFUL ELECTRIC MAGNET UNDER THE FLOOR--
JUST WHAT I WAS THINKING! THE MAGNETISM'S GRIPPING THE IRON FILINGS STUCK TO OUR BOOT SOLES AND HOLDING US TIGHT--JUST AS A REAL GRAVITY BEAM MIGHT DO!
WITHOUT OUR BOOTS-- WE'RE OUR FIGHTING SELVES AGAIN!
THWUKK!
NOW IT'S OUR TURN TO DISH OUT THE SOKS AND POWS!
EGAD! THOSE TWO HAVE THE CALCULATING MINDS OF A COUPLE OF COMPUTERS!
SSSWOOSH

THE WAY TO GET RID OF A WEED IS TO PULL IT OUT BY ITS ROOTS!
LOCK!
YOU MIGHT SAY WE'RE GOING TO "ROOT" FOR YOU, PENGUIN!
THUMP!

PFAH! MUST I BE SUBJECTED TO SUCH PUTRID PUNS? MUST I ENDURE THESE EAR-GRATING PLAYS ON WORDS? THE GOLD I MEAN TO TAKE FROM THIS PLACE IS HARDLY WORTH IT!

YOU SAID IT, PENGUIN!
WOULD YOU SETTLE FOR A PUNCH INSTEAD OF A PUN?
AWNK!

HOW'S THAT FOR A SAFE DEPOSIT, PENGUIN?
EGAD... ET TU, BATMAN?
ZWOPP!

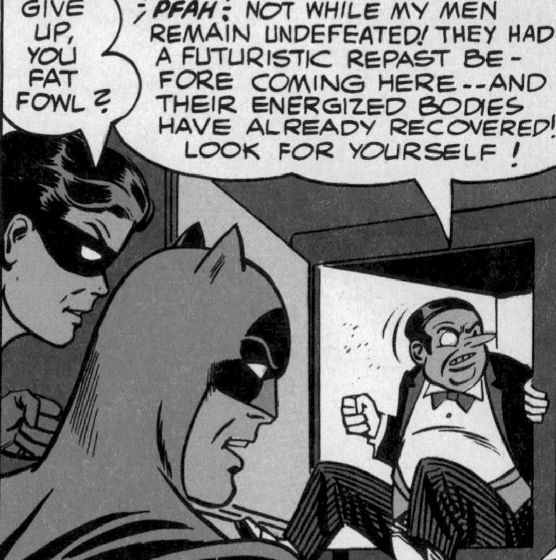
GIVE UP, YOU FAT FOWL?
PFAH! NOT WHILE MY MEN REMAIN UNDEFEATED! THEY HAD A FUTURISTIC REPAST BE-FORE COMING HERE--AND THEIR ENERGIZED BODIES HAVE ALREADY RECOVERED! LOOK FOR YOURSELF!
7

AH, THOSE SOUNDS ARE MUSIC TO MY EARS! HIT 'EM AGAIN-- HARDER, HARDER!
WHUPPP!
WHAPPP!

I CAN'T WAIT UNTIL B AND R BEGIN TO FIGHT BACK AGAIN! ANOTHER FUTURE-SURPRISE AWAITS THEM!
ZOKK!
WHAKK!

DEC. NO. 197
12¢
BATMAN
HAVE IT YOUR OWN WAY, BATGIRL!
YOU'LL TAKE BATMAN TO YOUR CATACOMBS OVER MY DEAD BODY, CATWOMAN!
"CATWOMAN SETS HER CLAWS FOR BATMAN!"
12¢
MAR. NO. 210
BATMAN
IT'S ALL OVER, BATMAN! YOU JUST LOST THE BATTLE OF THE SEXES!
BATMAN FIGHTS THE LEGION OF FELINE FURIES!

The PENGUIN TAKES A FLYER--INTO THE FUTURE!

PART 2

SWEPT OFF THEIR FEET BY THE UNEXPECTED ONSLAUGHT, **BATMAN** AND **ROBIN** RECOVER SWIFTLY--SEND FLYING FISTS AT THEIR FOES...

HERE I GO AGAIN--WITH A SECOND HELPING OF PUNCH PUDDING!

THOSE CROOKS MUST BE SO STUNNED AT OUR OWN RAPID RECOVERY, THEY'RE NOT EVEN MAKING A MOVE TO STOP US!

WHY SHOULD THEY? THEY KNOW YOU CAN'T LAY A HAND ON THEM!

YOU'RE FIGHTING OUTA YOUR LEAGUE, BATMAN! ALL YOU CAN DO IS STRIKE OUT-- WHILE WE MAKE THE HITS!
GRUMMP!

ONLY ONE ANSWER! SOME STRANGE FORCE IS DEFLECTING MY FIST AWAY FROM ITS TARGET!
ANOTHER OF MY FUTURISTIC GIMMICKS, BATMAN! I CALL IT MY FIST-FENDER-OFF! I BETTER EXPLAIN IT TO YOU WHILE YOU'RE STILL CONSCIOUS!
JUST AS FUTURE SPACESHIPS WILL HAVE METEOR BUMPERS--TO WARD OFF METEORS THAT FLY THROUGH SPACE--SO I HAVE EQUIPPED MY MEN WITH DEVICES TO FEND OFF YOUR FLYING FISTS!
MY FELONIOUS FLOCK IS THUS PROTECTED EVEN FROM THE BOMBASTIC BLOWS OF SUCH CRIME-KILLJOYS AS YOU TWO!
HEY, FELLA--YOU KNOW WHEN A SPANKING IS LIKE A HAT? WHEN IT'S FELT... OOOPS! I MISSED AGAIN!

SHADES OF JOE MILLER'S JOKEBOOK! MUST I EVER-LASTINGLY LISTEN TO SUCH CLAP-TRAP? HURRY IT UP! KNOCK THEM BOTH OUT SO I WON'T HAVE TO ENDURE THOSE AWFUL JOKES ANY LONGER!
BAPPP!

WHILE BATMAN'S FISTS KEEP MISSING, HIS WITS KEEP CLICKING...
FOR ALL PENGUIN'S BOASTS, I CAN'T BELIEVE HE'S COME UP WITH A "FIST-FENDER-OFF"! IT'S GOT TO BE A TRICK-- TO MAKE IT APPEAR THAT WAY!
SOCK!
ROBIN, TOO, IS ALERT TO WHAT GOES ON AROUND HIM...
MAYBE I'M TELEGRAPHING MY PUNCHES! THAT WOULD MEAN THE MAN I'M FIGHTING KNOWS WHERE I'M GOING TO HIT! BUT SUPPOSE I FAKE A PUNCH?? I'LL FEINT A RIGHT AND STRIKE FAST WITH MY LEFT...
ZOK!
THE DYNAMIC DUO ACTS AS ONE...
THE CROOK THINKS I'M GOING TO HIT HIM WITH A RIGHT FIST BUT...
...I'LL SOCK HIM WITH A LIGHTNING LEFT JAB!
LWUPP!
THWAK!
AS HE FOLLOWS THROUGH, BATMAN'S CHEEK COMES CLOSE TO THE BANDIT'S UNIFORM AND...
SO THAT'S IT! THEIR UNIFORMS ARE EQUIPPED TO RELEASE AIR UNDER HIGH PRESSURE AT CERTAIN POINTS! WHEN THE CROOK SEES WHERE MY PUNCH IS AIMED, HE SENDS OUT A CONCENTRATED BLAST OF AIR TO HIT MY FIST AND BRUSH IT ASIDE!
KRAK!
11

NOW THAT WE'VE SOLVED THE SECRET OF THEIR "INVULNERABILITY"...
SOK!

...WE MISS WITH ONE-- AND CONNECT WITH THE OTHER!
THWAKK!

AS THE LAST OF HIS CROOKED FLOCK IS GROUNDED, THE BUMBER-SHOOT BUCCANEER WADDLES OFF...
WHUKK!!
BOPP!
ODZOOKS! CAN NOTHING STOP THOSE FLYING FISTED DO-GOODERS?

WE'RE TOO LATE! THERE HE GOES ON HIS JET-UMBRELLA!
YES, BOY WONDER! IT'S TIME I FLEW THIS CON-FOUNDED "COUP"... WITH ALL THE GOLD I CAN CARRY IN MY UMBRELLA CANOPY!

AS HE RACES ACROSS THE NIGHT SKY, BITTER REALIZATION COMES TO THE PENGUIN...
MY BIRD-BRAIN GANG WAS INCAPABLE OF THINKING AS FAST AS BATMAN AND ROBIN! I'LL HAVE TO DEVISE SOME NEW MEANS OF HANDLING THOSE TWO!

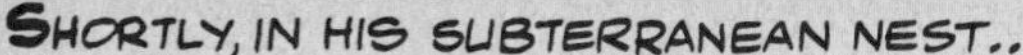
SHORTLY, IN HIS SUBTERRANEAN NEST...

AH--YES! I HAVE IT! JUST AS I CREATED A ROBOT PENGUIN, I SHALL MAKE ROBOT UMBRELLAS--ROBOTRELLAS--TO STEAL AND DO BATTLE FOR ME!

BY CONTROLLING THEIR EVERY MOVE WITH MY OWN BRAIN, I WILL BE IN COMPLETE COMMAND AT ALL TIMES! NOW--TO WORK, TO WORK!

BACK IN GOTHAM CITY, AFTER THEY HAVE TAKEN THEIR PRISONERS TO JAIL, THE DYNAMIC DUO HEADS HOMEWARD..
PENGUIN SURE TOOK A FLYER--INTO THE FUTURE! I WONDER WHAT STUNTS HE'LL WHIP UP FOR US NEXT TIME WE MEET?
NO ONE KNOWS WHAT TOMORROW WILL BRING, ROBIN! WE MUST BE ON GUARD AT ALL TIMES!

SOME NIGHTS LATER, SILENT SHAPES JET SMOOTHLY THROUGH THE AIR...
MUFFLERS PREVENT MY ROBBER-ROBOTRELLAS FROM MAKING ANY NOISE!
JEWELRY
ACE JEWELERS

TINY LASER BEAMS MELT THE GLASS WINDOWS WITHOUT SETTING OFF THE BURGLAR ALARMS, PERMITTING MY BUMBERSHOOT BANDITS TO ENTER!

FROM HIS UNDERGROUND NEST, THE PENGUIN GLOATS AS...
AFTER USING CONCEALED MAGNETS IN THEIR HANDLES TO OPEN SAFE DOORS, I REMOTE-CONTROL MY PLUNDERING PARASOLS TO CHOOSE MY LOOT FOR ME!
13

BY SCANNING EACH JEWEL WITH A JEWELER'S EYE-PIECE, THEY WILL SELECT ONLY THE FINEST STONES FOR MY ENJOYMENT!

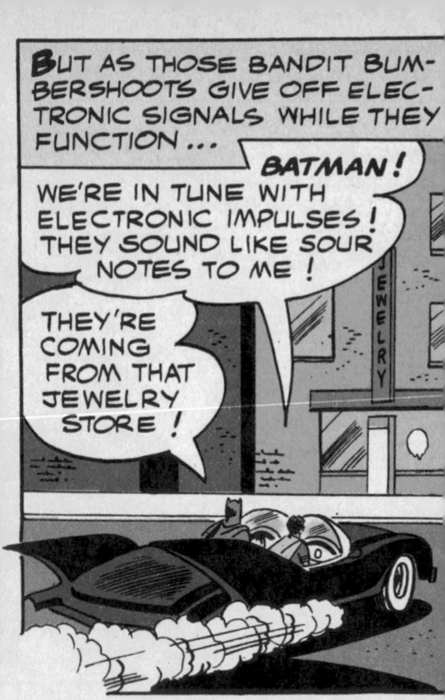
BUT AS THOSE BANDIT BUMBERSHOOTS GIVE OFF ELECTRONIC SIGNALS WHILE THEY FUNCTION...
BATMAN! WE'RE IN TUNE WITH ELECTRONIC IMPULSES! THEY SOUND LIKE SOUR NOTES TO ME!
THEY'RE COMING FROM THAT JEWELRY STORE!
JEWELRY

BATMAN-- LOOK! JET-UMBRELLAS--
--WHICH SPELL OUT PENGUIN! BUT WHERE'S THE EMPEROR BIRD?

NO SIGN OF OUR MAN OF A THOUSAND UMBRELLAS! HE MUST BE ROBOT-CONTROLLING THEM FROM HIS HIDE-OUT!

FRAMED IN THEIR BAT-NOCULARS THEY SEE A CARAVAN OF WEALTH AS THE JEWELS GLOW WITH INCANDESCENT COLORS...
INTO THE BATMOBILE, ROBIN! THOSE UMBRELLAS WILL LEAD US TO OUR PREY!

FOR A COUPLE OF MINUTES THEY KEEP THE ROBOTRELLAS IN SIGHT UNTIL...
THEY'RE GETTING OUT OF RANGE-- MOVING FASTER AND FASTER!
LOOKS LIKE THE PENGUIN'S GETTING AWAY WITH HIS SKYWAY ROBBERY!

JUST FOR **THIS** TIME, **ROBIN**! WHEN HE STRIKES AGAIN, WE'LL HAVE THE SCIENTIFIC SOLUTION TO HIS ROBBERIES-BY-UMBRELLAS-- **BAT-RELLAS**!
WE'LL BEAT HIM AT HIS OWN GAME, *eh*?

SOON **COWLED CRUSADER** AND **BOY WONDER** ARE HARD AT WORK IN THE **BAT-CAVE**...
WHERE CAN **ALFRED** BE? I SENT HIM FOR THOSE SPECIAL TRANSISTORS WE NEED FOR THIS JOB!

THE CONCEALED **BAT-DOOR** OPENS--AND A GUST OF WIND USHERS ALFRED THE BUTLER AND A SPRAY OF RAIN INTO THE **BATCAVE**...
HERE I AM, SIR! I DIDN'T WANT TO AROUSE AUNT HARRIET'S SUSPICIONS, SO I CAME IN BY THE HILLSIDE ENTRANCE!

WHAT A TERRIBLE NIGHT IT IS! A GOOD THING I HAD MY TRUSTY UMBRELLA ALONG!
SAY--THAT BUMBERSHOOT OF YOURS GIVES ME AN IDEA, ALFRED! YOU MAY COME IN USEFUL IN OUR NEXT TRY FOR THE **PENGUIN**!

FAR FROM THE **BAT-CAVE**, ELATION SURGES THROUGH THE POUTER-PIGEON CHEST OF THE **BIRDMAN BANDIT** AS HE HOLDS UP A HANDFUL OF HIS LOOT..
EGAD! I'M A GENIUS'S GENIUS! MY **ROBOTRELLAS** ARE THE PERFECT THIEVES!

HEIGH-HO! ORDINARILY I WOULD NEVER REPEAT THE SAME METHOD OF COMMITTING A CRIME -- BUT THIS METHOD IS SO SPECTACULAR, SO SAFE, THAT I SHALL MAKE AN EXCEPTION IN THIS CASE --FOR THE **DYNAMIC DUO'S** BENEFIT!
15

I CAN'T RESIST THE SATISFACTION OF SEEING THEM FAIL AGAIN!
LIGHT ME UP, ROBOT-PENGUIN!

I'LL GIVE THEM A WEEK TO THINK UP SOME COUNTER-MOVE AGAINST ME!
IF YOU WILL PERMIT ME TO SAY SO, SIR--YOU'RE THE MOST SUPERLATIVE SCALAWAG OF ALL TIME!
TUSH, TUSH! YOU'LL SPOIL ME! THOUGH WHAT YOU SAY IS TRUE ENOUGH!

TO CONTINUE--YOU'RE ABSOLUTELY TOPS, PENGUIN! THE ACME OF ABILITY, THE PRINCE OF PLUNDERERS, THE KING OF KNAVES!
EXCELLENTLY PHRASED--EVEN IF I DID PUT YOUR SPEAKING SPOOL INSIDE YOU!

PRECISELY ONE WEEK LATER...
THERE THEY ARE! THIS TIME AS BANK-BANDITS!
RELEASE BAT-RELLAS ROBIN!

LIKE INTERCEPTOR MISSILES, THE BAT-RELLAS HURTLE SKYWARD...
ZWIP!
ZWOOSH!

FROM THEIR SKY-HIGH VANTAGE POINT, THE BAT-RELLAS SEND OUT ELECTRONIC BEEPS TO THE BATMOBILE BELOW...
CLICK
CLICK
CLICK
CLICKETY

MANY MILES OUTSIDE GOTHAM CITY THE ROBOTRELLAS DROP DOWN ONTO AN EMPTY FIELD...
THE ROBOT UMBRELLAS ARE GETTING RID OF THEIR LOOT !

WHERE HIS LOOT IS, CAN THE PENGUIN BE FAR BEHIND?

IN HIS UNDERGROUND HIDEAWAY, THE BUMBERSHOOT BUCCANEER GLOATS WITH EVIL SATISFACTION...
NO, BATMAN! I AM CLOSE BY, READY TO TURN MY FIGHTING FORCES INTO-- DYNAMIC DUO DEATH-DEALERS!

AND THEN-- THEIR CANOPIES WHIRLING MADLY, APPEAR THE FIGHTING FORCES OF THE MAN OF 1000 UMBRELLAS!...
Whoa! UMBRELLA ATTACK HEADED OUR WAY!
BRACE YOURSELF, ROBIN! THIS MAY BE THE TOUGHEST FIGHT OF OUR LIVES!

YEOW! TWO OF THEM TEAMING UP AGAINST ME!

USING THIS MACE-UMBRELLA-- TO PULL ME FREE OF THE NECK-GRABBING ONE!
17

SHIELDS?! BUT SURELY BATMAN AND ROBIN COULDN'T HAVE BEEN FORESIGHTED ENOUGH TO EQUIP THEMSELVES WITH SUCH PROTECTIVE DEVICES!

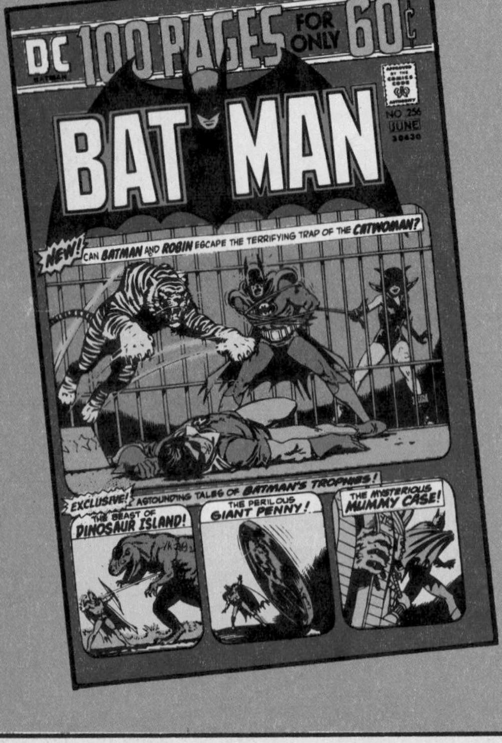

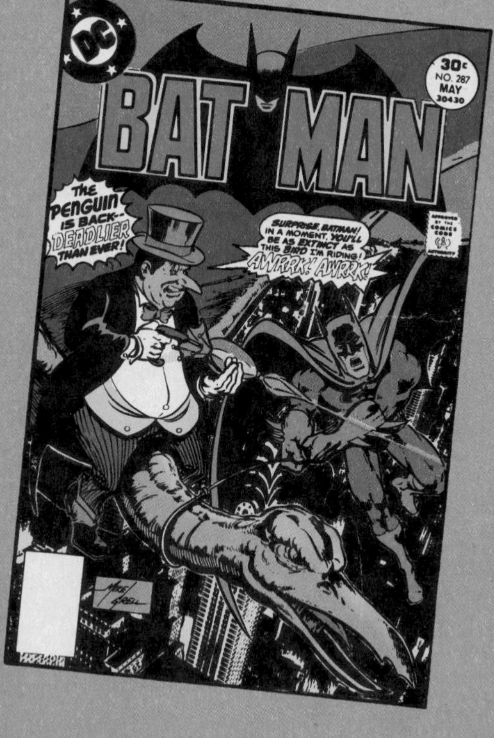

the PENGUIN TAKES A FLYER--INTO THE FUTURE!

PART 3

FROM THE BATMOBILE WHEELS, BATMAN AND ROBIN YANK OFF METAL HUB-CAPS THAT SERVE AS SUITABLE SHIELDS!...

THIS'LL BLUNT THIS BUZZSAW-RELLA!

WE'LL HAVE TO FIGHT OUR WAY PAST HIS WEAPON-UMBRELLAS TO GET AT THE PENGUIN!

SO INTENT ARE THEY ON THEIR DESPERATE STRUGGLE FOR SURVIVAL THAT THEY FAIL TO SEE TWO NET-BRELLAS SWOOPING DOWN ON THEM ...
BY KNOCKING 'EM OFF TWO AT A TIME, THE PENGUIN WILL SOON RUN OUT OF UMBRELLAS!
I MANEUVERED THOSE THINGS INTO POSITION--AND DUCKED JUST IN TIME!
THE FLYING NET-BRELLAS DROP DOWN--CABLES LENGTHEN TO GATHER IN THEIR PREY...
YIII! THAT WAS A NET LOSS--FOR US!
THAT'S IT, ROBIN! NO MATTER WHAT THE DANGER--DON'T LOSE YOUR SENSE OF HUMOR!
TWISTED INSIDE THE NETTING OF METALLIC CABLES, THE TRAPPED DUO IS FLOWN TO THE PENGUIN'S NEST...
OH, HAPPY HOUR! OH, DELIGHTFUL DAY! YOU ARE MY PRISONERS AT LAST, BATMAN AND ROBIN! NOW YOU SHALL PAY THE PENALTY LONG OVERDUE YOU!
THE GAME'S NOT OVER TILL THE LAST OUT, PENGUIN--AND THAT'S WHAT WE'LL DO NEXT--GET OUT!
GRIPPING THE NET STRANDS, THE TERRIFIC TWOSOME SWINGS THEM TOGETHER SO THAT THE UMBRELLAS ARE DRIVEN FORWARD INTO THE WICKED WADDLER!..
THIS WILL LOOSEN THE NETS JUST ENOUGH FOR ROBIN AND MYSELF TO FREE OURSELVES OF THIS GRIP!

SURRENDER, PENGUIN!
WE'VE GOT A JAIL-CAGE ALL READY FOR YOU!
TUT-TUT! DID YOU FORGET I AM MASTER OF THE FUTURE? OBSERVE--!
HUH? THE PENGUIN-- FLYING !?
NOT EVEN A REAL PENGUIN-BIRD CAN DO THAT!
A DEMONSTRATION OF MY MIND-OVER-MATTER CONTROL OF OBJECTS SHOULD CONVINCE YOU OF THE FUTILITY OF RESISTING ME!
HURLING FURNITURE AT US?!
ACTING WITH INSTANTANEOUS TEAMWORK--THE DYNAMIC DUO GRIPS CHAIR-ARMS AND TABLE-LEGS AND...
AS CHAIR-MAN I VOTE THAT WE TABLE THIS DISCUSSION UNTIL PENGUIN TAKES THE FLOOR, BATMAN!
I TOLD YOU I HAD MASTERED GRAVITY! I AM NO LONGER EARTH-BOUND! NOW YOU SURRENDER TO ME BEFORE I USE MY FUTURISTIC ABILITIES TO DESTROY YOU BOTH!
AS THE THROWN CHAIR AND TABLE THUD INTO THE CEILING-HIGH PENGUIN...
HOLY DECEPTION! THAT'S A ROBOT PENGUIN!
BARROOM!
WE'VE BEEN TRICKED AGAIN, ROBIN!
21

AS WE KNEW, PENGUIN HAD NO GRAVITY CONTROL -- NOR MIND-OVER-MATTER ABILITY! HE WORKED THOSE TRICKS BY CUNNINGLY PLANTED MAGNETS!
THE REAL PENGUIN WAS OUT OF OUR REACH ALL THE TIME! I WONDER WHERE HE IS?

BUT SEARCH AS THEY WILL, THE CAPED CRIME-FIGHTERS CANNOT LOCATE THEIR QUARRY! FINALLY, WHEN THEY GLUMLY RETURN TO THE BATMOBILE...
ALFRED! YOU CAUGHT THE PENGUIN!
YOUR TRICK OF USING ALFRED PAID OFF, BATMAN!

INDEED IT DID, MASTER ROBIN! WHEN YOU LEFT ME HIDDEN IN THE BATMOBILE TRUNK AND I SAW YOU NETTED AND CARRIED OFF--I ALMOST GAVE CHASE--BUT YOU HAD TOLD ME TO WATCH THE LOOT--SO IN DUE TIME WHEN I SAW THE GROUND OPENING AND THE LOOT DROPPED DOWN INTO IT I LEAPED AFTER IT!

"I RAINED DOWN ON THE PENGUIN ALONG WITH HIS STOLEN MONEY..."
EGAD! WHAT'S THIS? I'VE CAUGHT A BUTLER ALONG WITH MY BANKNOTES...

"BEFORE THE FOWL BANDIT COULD MOVE AGAINST ME, I BASHED HIM WITH MY TRUSTY UMBRELLA..."
THAT WILL LAY YOU OUT WHILE I TAKE YOU AND YOUR ILL-GOTTEN GAINS TO THE BATMOBILE!

EVIDENTLY HE HAD TWO UNDERGROUND HIDEOUTS! ONE FROM WHICH HE CONTROLLED HIS UMBRELLAS AND HIS ROBOT OTHER SELF, THE OTHER WHERE HE HAD US BROUGHT!
I IMAGINE HE EQUIPPED HIS ROBOTS WITH TELEVISION CAMERAS TO SEE AND HEA WHAT WAS GOIN ON--SO HE COULD UTILIZE THEM MOST EFFECTIVELY WELL, PENGUIN'S FLYER HAS LED HIM BACK TO PRISON!

SOMEWHAT LATER, IN THE BUMBERSHOOT BANDIT'S CELL...
YOU WON'T HANDLE AN UMBRELLA FOR A LONG WHILE IN THERE, PENGUIN!
ARE YOU THE PENGUIN? IT'S A GREAT HONOR TO BE YOUR CELL MATE!

INDEED, MY GOOD MAN? YES, I RATHER IMAGINE IT IS! WHAT IS YOUR NAME!
BROLLY--
BROLLY!? WHY--THAT'S THE ENGLISH SLANG WORD FOR AN UMBRELLA!
327056

SO BATMAN AND ROBIN THINK I CAN'T COME IN CONTACT WITH AN "UMBRELLA" IN HERE, DO THEY? WELL-- THIS BROLLY CHARACTER IS AN "UMBRELLA" THAT WILL PROVE OF INESTIMABLE AID IN ENABLING ME TO ESCAPE FROM THIS NEFARIOUS NEST OF PENAL SERVITUDE!
The End

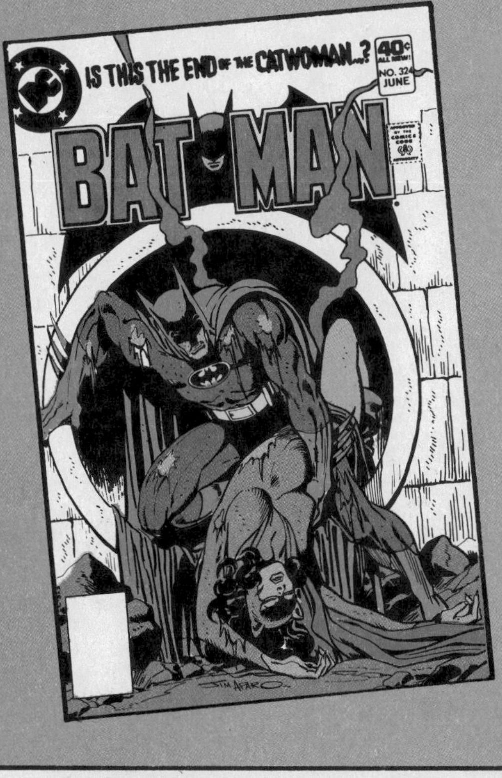

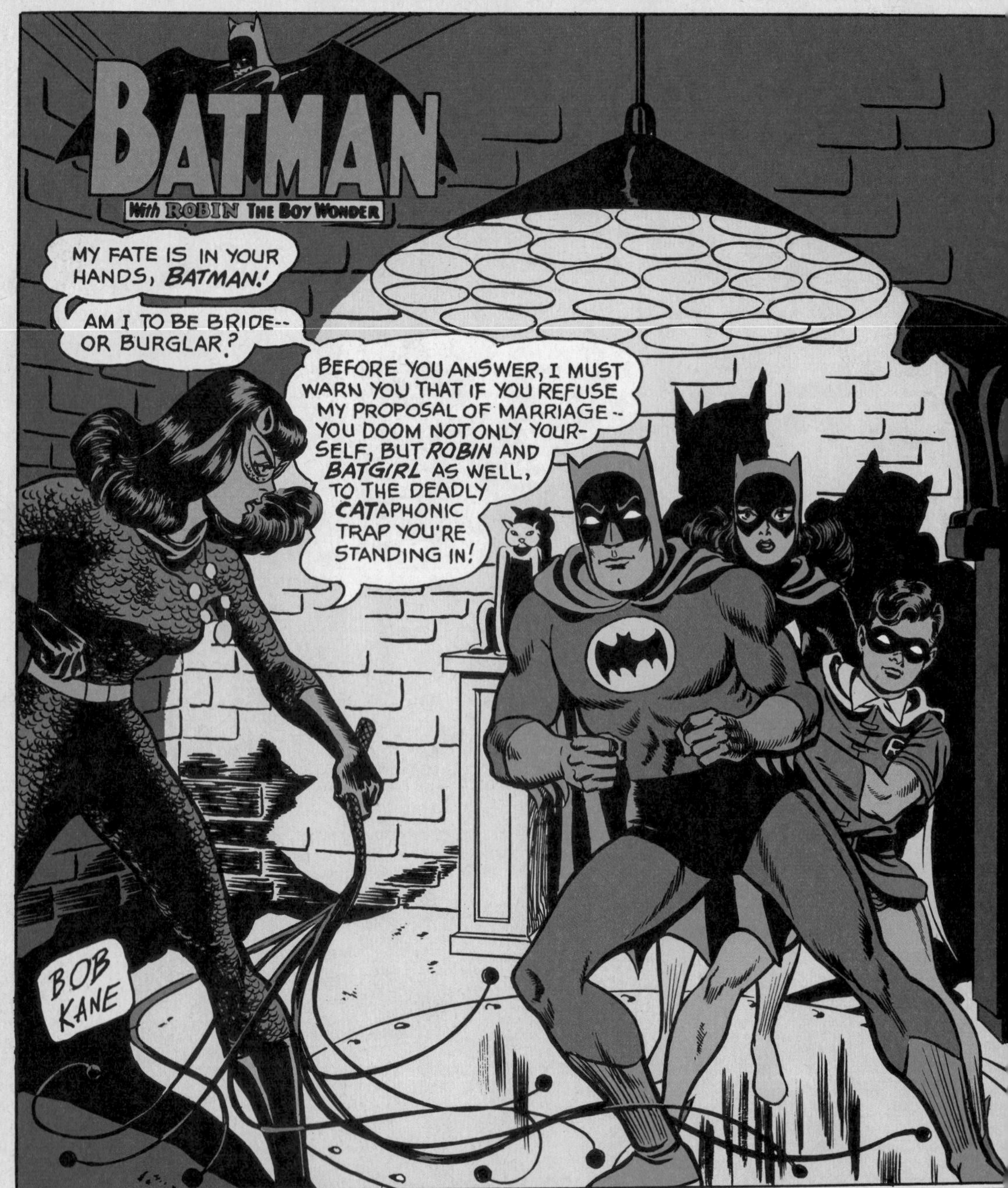
BATMAN
With ROBIN THE BOY WONDER
MY FATE IS IN YOUR HANDS, BATMAN!
AM I TO BE BRIDE-- OR BURGLAR?
BEFORE YOU ANSWER, I MUST WARN YOU THAT IF YOU REFUSE MY PROPOSAL OF MARRIAGE--YOU DOOM NOT ONLY YOURSELF, BUT ROBIN AND BATGIRL AS WELL, TO THE DEADLY CATAPHONIC TRAP YOU'RE STANDING IN!
BOB KANE
WHAT A DESIGNING WOMAN WAS-- CATWOMAN! SHE HAD DESIGNS ON SNARING BATMAN FOR HER MATE-- EVEN IF IT MEANT ABANDONING HER ROLE AS THE PRINCESS OF PLUNDER! IF THE WORST CAME TO PASS AND HE TURNED HER DOWN, SHE'D MANAGE TO SURVIVE WITHOUT BATMAN--WHILE MAKING SURE HE DIDN'T LIVE AT ALL!
"CATWOMAN Sets Her Claws for BATMAN!"

THIS IS THE KITTY CAR-- CHALLENGING THE BATMOBILE ON A NIGHTLY QUEST FOR CRIMINAL ACTIVITIES IN GOTHAM CITY...
BATMAN-- YOU'RE ABOUT TO BE "TAKEN".!
THESE ARE THE CAT'S WHISKERS-- DELICATE FILAMENTS ATTUNED TO CRIMINAL ACTIVITY...
AH! VILLAINY AFOOT-- IN THE WINERY!
GOTHAM WINERY INC.
AND THIS IS CATWOMAN-- THE CRIME CRUSADER-- AT THE WHEEL!...
THEY'RE AFTER ITS PAYROLL--BUT THEY'RE GOING TO LATCH ON TO MY CLAWS!
BATMAN-- THIS IS THE BEGINNING... OF YOUR END!...
YES--THIS IS THAT FELINE FEMALE --LONG A CATASTROPHIC THREAT TO LAW AND ORDER--NOW TURNED CROOK CATCHER EXTRAORDINARY!...
AS FOR BATGIRL-- SHE'S HAD IT!
THERE'S A NEW TOP CAT IN TOWN!
SHOCK WAVES RUN FROM THE LEATHER THONGS OF THE CAT-O'-NINE-TAILS AS...
GET YOUR GRUBBY FINGERS OFF THAT CASH!
YIIII!
?
WHO'S THAT?!
SWWIIIP!
2

CATWOMAN--?!
BUT YOU'RE A CROOK--LIKE US!
NO LONGER! I'VE REFORMED! THE "NOW LOOK" CATWOMAN HAS JOINED THE OTHER SIDE!
IN THAT CASE--WE'RE GONNA BRING YOUR NEW CAREER TO A SUDDEN STOP!
YEAH--WITH A COUPLE OF BULLET HOLES IN YOUR CAT'S HIDE!
BAH! YOU'RE NOT MEN--YOU'RE MICE!
AS THONGS STRETCH TO CURL ABOUT AN OVERHANGING CHANDELIER--CATWOMAN TUGS...
AND I USE TRAPS TO CATCH MICE!
KAA-RAASH!
AS THE THIRD CROOK TAKES TO HIS HEELS...
THERE'LL BE NO CHICKENING OUT WHILE I'M AROUND!
ZWAKK
TWOW!
THIS'LL PUT YOU IN A CATABATIC TRANCE!
ZWAK!
NOW TO CROSS PATHS WITH BATMAN--SHOW HIM MY NIGHT'S CATCH-
--AND AT THE SAME TIME SHOW UP BATGIRL!

SHIPS MAY PASS IN THE NIGHT UNSEEN AND UNHEARD--BUT NOT THE KITTY CAR AND BATMOBILE...
GREETINGS, CAPED CRUSADERS! BAGGED ANYTHING YET?
IT'S CATWOMAN--AND SHE'S CAPTURED THE PARKER BROTHERS!
WE'VE BEEN AFTER THAT GANG FOR WEEKS!
MIGHT BE A GOOD IDEA TO ASK HER ROBIN!
WHAT'S SHE UP TO, BATMAN--MASQUERADING IN THAT NEW UNIFORM?
YOU'RE NOW LOOKING AT THE NOW LOOK CATWOMAN--MY CRIMINAL PAST IS BEHIND ME--MY FUTURE IS TO JAIL ALL THE THIEVES I CAN LAY MY CAT-O'-NINE TAILS ON!
YOU'VE REFORMED BEFORE, CATWOMAN--BUT IT NEVER LASTED LONG!
YOU SHALL SEE FOR YOURSELF, YOU DOUBTING ROBIN--BEGINNING WITH THIS HAUL AT A WINERY WHERE I WENT CAT-WILD
IT'S A PURR-FECT DEMONSTRATION THAT ANYTHING BATGIRL CAN DO, I CAN DO--BETTER!
TA-TA! I'LL BE SEEING YOU IN THE MORNING PAPERS!
THIS NIGHT'S WORK WILL CATAPULT ME INTO THE HEADLINES!
WHAT SNEAKY GAME IS SHE PLAYING?
4

I CAN'T FIGURE OUT WHETHER SHE'S TRYING TO SHOW *US* UP -- OR *BATGIRL* --
--OR *BOTH*!
AT LEAST SHE'S "REFORMED" IN ONE WAY! IN THE PAST, HER CRIMINAL ACTIVITIES USED TO INVOLVE A "CAT" IN SOME WAY OR OTHER! BUT THERE'S NO "CAT" IN *GOTHAM WINERY*!
NOT SO, *ROBIN*! I HAPPEN TO KNOW THE *GOTHAM WINERY* USES *CATAWBA* GRAPES TO MAKE ITS WINES!
SO MAYBE SHE *DOES* HAVE A CAT-TRICK HIDDEN BEHIND HER CAT-MASK! WE'LL JUST HAVE TO POSSESS THE PATIENCE OF A CAT-- TO LEARN WHAT IT IS!

THE FOLLOWING NIGHT THE *BAT-MOBILE* DETECTION GEAR LOCATES A ROBBERY AT A SILK HANDKERCHIEF FACTORY...
NO SIGN OF OUR RIVAL--OR *BATGIRL*!
THAT SUITS ME FINE! NABBING CROOKS IS *MAN'S* WORK!
SILK FACTORY LTD.

OUT OF THE NEXT ROOM STORM FOUR HEAVILY MUSCLED THUGS-- TO RAIN BLOWS ON THE UNSUSPECTING BATMAN...
THE BOSS HELD US IN RESERVE--JUST FOR AN OPPORTUNITY LIKE THIS!
SOCK!
FROM THE SIDE, THE TEEN TITAN EXPLODES INTO ACTION...
HERE I COME LIKE A BOLT FROM THE BLUE--
A BOLT OF BLUE SILK, THAT IS!
THEY'RE TOO HEAVY TO FLIP OFF...
GNNFFF!
GOOD BOY, ROBIN!
NOW I CAN THROW THESE CROOKS OFF-- GET TO MY FEET--

NOW THAT I'VE GOT MY FEET ON SOLID GROUND --
SWOTT!

I CAN SET MYSELF FOR A SOLID LEFT HOOK...
ZMAK!

... AND A RIGHT UPPERCUT!
GYAAGH!
ZZOOCK!

MEANWHILE, THE BOY WONDER FINDS THREE THUGS A BIT MORE THAN HE CAN HANDLE...
GANGING UP ON ME--
NEED SOME MANEUVERING ROOM--!

BUT IN DUCKING AWAY FROM A ROUNDHOUSE PUNCH...
WHUNK!

SUDDENLY OUT OF THE SHADOWS OF THE HANDKER-CHIEF FACTORY, WHIPS THE BATROPE...
THAT WAS GOOD NOOSE, BATMAN...
SOON AS I CLEAR MY HEAD-- I'LL PITCH IN...

UT AS THE MASKED MAN-HUNTER AULS IN IS CATCH...
THEY-- RUSHED ME--!

EXT MOMENT SIX GUNS LIFT AS SIX INGERS CURL ABOUT HALF A OZEN TRIGGERS...
OBVIOUSLY, BATMAN AND ROBIN CAN USE A HELPING HAND!

ICHES FROM HE EARS OF HE SEXTET OF UNMEN, TINY OMBS ATTACHED O THE THONGS F THE CAT-O-INE TAILS ETONATE WITH DEAFEN-NG FURY...
BOOM!
CRACK!
EEEEY! IT'S LIKE MY HEAD WAS BUSTIN' OPEN!
BLAPP!
BLAM!
WHOPP!
CRACK!

QUICK, ROBIN-- BEFORE THEY RE-COVER FROM THAT NOISE BOMBARDMENT!
FOR ONCE IN MY LIFE--I'M ACTUALLY HAPPY TO SEE YOU, CATWOMAN!
8

BLESS YOU FOR THOSE KIND WORDS, ROBIN!
JUST FOR THAT I'LL FETCH OUT MY CAT-COMPACT AND...
DUST OFF THOSE CROOKS FOR YOU!
MMMPPFFF!
KOFF!
KOFF!
ULP! HOW COME THEY WERE AFFECTED BY THAT POWDER AND I WASN'T, CATWOMAN?
WHY, ROBIN! YOU DON'T THINK I'D HARM EITHER YOU OR BATMAN? MY CAT-POWDER WORKS ONLY AGAINST THIEVES--NOT CRIME CRUSADERS!
AND SPEAKING OF BATMAN-- PARDON ME, ROBIN!
MY CATARANG WILL LIGHTEN YOUR BURDEN, BATMAN SWEETIE!
DO I DETECT A NOTE OF AFFECTION IN CATWOMAN'S VOICE?
COULD BATGIRL DO THAT, BATMAN?
THERE'S THAT CONCERN OVER BATGIRL AGAIN!
WHONK!
WHEN THE SMOKE OF BATTLE CLEARS.
BATGIRL HAS HAD HER DAY-- AND NIGHT, BATMAN!
COULD SHE HAVE HELPED YOU--AS I DID?
9

IF YOU WANT A FELINE FRIEND TO HELP YOU PLAY CAT-AND-MOUSE WITH ANY MORE ROBBERS-- REMEMBER CATWOMAN!

YOU DEFINITELY ARE IN NEED OF--A WOMAN'S TOUCH!
WHY IS SHE MAKING THOSE CATTY REMARKS ABOUT BATGIRL?

AS THE FELINE FURY DRIVES OFF...
ONE THING'S FOR SURE-- WE COULDN'T HAVE DONE AS WELL AS WE DID WITHOUT HER!
THERE'S NOTHING ABOUT A "CAT" IN A SILK HANDKERCHIEF FACTORY! PERHAPS SHE'S REFORMED PERMANENTLY!

HAS CATWOMAN REALLY ABANDONED HER CAT-MOTIVE? THIS BURNING THOUGHT SEARS THE MIND OF BARBARA (BATGIRL) GORDON NEXT DAY IN THE LIBRARY OF WHICH SHE IS BOSS-LADY...
I SEEM TO REMEMBER SOMETHING ABOUT SILK HANDKERCHIEFS...A PARTICULAR WORD THAT MY PHOTOGRAPHIC MEMORY TELLS ME MAY FIT IN...

ALONE IN HER OFFICE, SHE TURNS ON THE RADIO, FOR BABS GORDON HAS TRAINED HERSELF TO READ A BOOK AND SIMULTANEOUSLY ABSORB WHAT IS BEING SAID TO HER...
IF ROBIN COULD SEE ME NOW, HE'D SAY THAT SINCE I HAVE A PHOTOGRAPHIC MEMORY, I OUGHT TO WEAR A FILMY DRESS WHEN I USE IT...
CLICK

OUR REPORTER ON THE SPOT INFORMS US THAT LAST NIGHT WHEN BATMAN MADE HIS REPORT TO THE POLICE, HE TOLD THEM THAT CATWOMAN AGAIN REMARKED -- "ANYTHING BATGIRL CAN DO, I CAN DO--BETTER!"
AH--HERE'S THAT WORD--
PULICAT!
Pulicat

A PULICAT IS A SILK BANDANA OR HANDKERCHIEF! IT DERIVES ITS NAME FROM LAKE PULICAT IN MADRAS, INDIA, WHERE IT IS MANUFACTURED--WHAT'S THAT?
CATWOMAN MENTIONING BATGIRL?

THE INFERENCE WAS THAT CATWOMAN WAS MOCKING BATGIRL...
WAS SHE NOW? MAYBE I'D JUST BETTER SEE FOR MYSELF, NEXT TIME SHE GOES PROWLING IN THAT KITTY CAR OF HERS!
SHE'S ROUSED MY FEMININE CURIOSITY-- AS WELL AS MY FEMININE INTUITION!
AND THAT SAME INTUITION TELLS ME CATWOMAN WILL STRIKE AT THE GOTHAM WAX MUSEUM-- WHERE A BIER OF A FAR EASTERN MAHARAJAH IS ON LOAN FROM HIS NATIVE COUNTRY!
ESPECIALLY SINCE A BIER IS ALSO KNOWN AS A-- CATAFALQUE!
Daily Gotham
CATW
THERE ARE TREASURE CHESTS OF REAL EMERALDS, REAL DIAMONDS, REAL PEARLS AT THAT CATAFALQUE, TO LEND THE WAX FIGURE AN AIR OF REALITY AS IT LIES IN STATE!
IF CROOKS MAKE A TRY FOR THOSE JEWELS-- CATWOMAN IS BOUND TO MAKE A TRY FOR THE CROOKS!
INSIDE HER PRIVATE CLOSET, FINGERS PULL DOWN THE ROLL-RIM OF A BERET, FORMING A COWL...
NEITHER OF THEM IS GOING TO GET WHAT THEY WANT...
...BECAUSE I'M GOING TO SHOW UP...
...FOR A SHOWDOWN WITH CATWOMAN...
REVERSING HER SKIRT, SHE TURNS IT INTO A CAPE...
SHE ROLLS UP HER BOOT-FLAPS...
HER SPECIALLY DESIGNED HANDBAG BECOMES HER WEAPONS-POUCH...
...AS BATGIRL!

THAT NIGHT SHE SPEEDS CROSSTOWN ON HER *BATBIKE...*

FIRST ISSUE FEATURING 8 PAGE EXTRA STORY! NEMESIS... A DYNAMIC NEW SERIES! 50¢ ALL NEW! NO. 166 SEPT.
the BRAVE and the BOLD
STARRING BATMAN AND BLACK CANARY
"The RETURN of the PENGUIN"
PLUS WILL NEMESIS BALANCE THE SCALES OF JUSTICE--WITH HIS LIFE?

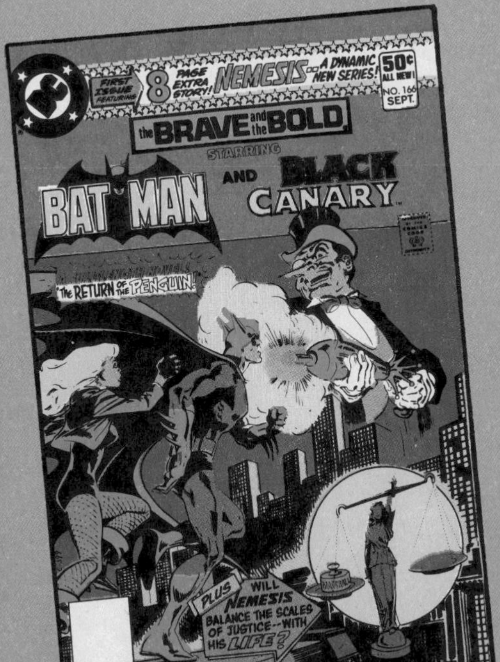

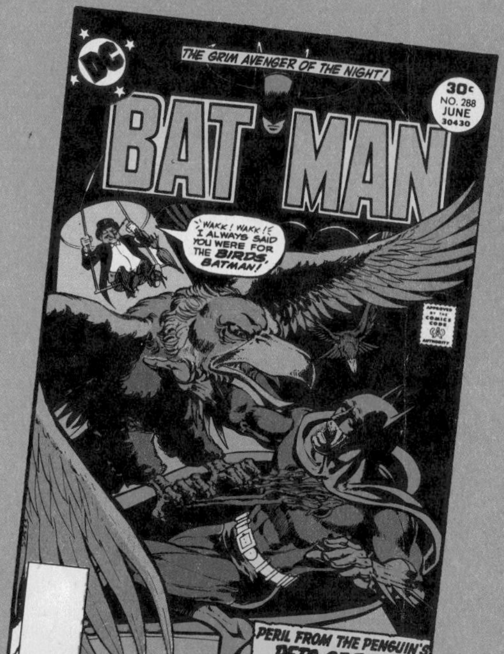

THE GRIM AVENGER OF THE NIGHT!
30¢ NO. 288 JUNE 30430
BATMAN
WAKK! WAKK! I ALWAYS SAID YOU WERE FOR THE BIRDS, BATMAN!
PERIL FROM THE PENGUIN'S PETS OF PREY!

YOU CAN HAVE FIRST CRACK AT THOSE CROOKS, BATGIRL!
I'VE ALREADY CONVINCED BATMAN I'M A BETTER FIGHTER THAN YOU--SO AFTER YOU FAIL MISERABLY AT CAPTURING THOSE CROOKS, I'LL CONVINCE YOU, TOO!
TALK IS CHEAP...
WHAT COUNTS IS ACTION-- OOPS!
MY CHOP MISSED HIS NECK-- LANDED ON HIS SHOULDER INSTEAD!
MY TURN NOW, BATGIRL!
BETTER SWITCH TO A JUDO DEFENSE AGAINST THAT BILLY-ARMED THUG...
JUST AS SOON AS YOU ADMIT HOW INEPT YOU ARE, BATGIRL--I'LL TAKE OVER!
WHA--?! INSTEAD OF GETTING MY LEVERAGE GRIP UNDER HIS ARM, MY HAND WENT OVER IT!
IT'S A MYSTERY TO ME WHY YOU HAVEN'T GOTTEN YOURSELF KILLED BEFORE THIS, IF YOU CAN'T DO ANY BETTER THAN THAT!

AGAIN THE DOMINOED DAREDOLL IS OFF TARGET...
WHUMP!
HURLED MYSELF AT HIS LEGS--
AND ENDED UP AGAINST THIS CATAFALQUE POST?!
SUDDENLY THE CAT-O'-NINE TAILS LOOPS ACROSS THE ROOM...
THWAAK!
MUSTN'T HIT A LADY, BOYS -- ESPECIALLY WHEN SHE'S DOWN!
REALLY! WHAT DID BATMAN EVER SEE IN YOU IN THE FIRST PLACE, BATGIRL?
YOU'VE MADE A MISHMASH OF THIS!
SHE'S RIGHT! I COULDN'T DO ANYTHING RIGHT--
BONK!
LET ME SHOW YOU HOW IT'S DONE, GIRLIE!
THE IDEA IS TO HIT THE CROOKS--LIKE SO!--AND KNOCK THEM OUT!
THEN ALL YOU HAVE TO DO IS TURN THEM OVER TO THE POLICE!
THWAK!
IN POLICE HEADQUARTERS, SOON AFTERWARD...
BATMAN! I'M GLAD YOU'RE HERE!
I'VE BEEN ASKING ALL ALONG IF BATGIRL COULD DO WHAT I COULD--AND NOW I HAVE THE PROOF POSITIVE!
GO ON, BATGIRL! TELL BATMAN WHAT HAPPENED!
14

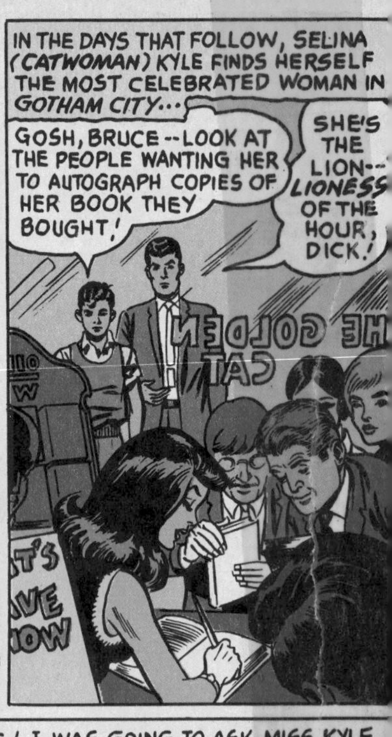

THE GOLDEN CAT RESTAURANT HAS NEVER BEEN SO CROWDED . . .

...SO I THOUGHT, MISS KYLE, THAT IF YOU WOULD ATTEND THE AFFAIR, IT'D BE A SELLOUT!

SORRY, MR. WAYNE. IN MY NEW ROLE OF CROOK CATCHER--I HAVE NO TIME FOR SUCH THINGS.

OH, SELINA--CATWOMAN! ONLY YOU REALIZED YOU WERE IN THE PRESENCE OF YOUR BELOVED BATMAN

YES, INDEED! CATWOMAN'S NIGHTS ARE FULLY OCCUPIED AS SHE BATTLES THE LAWLESS FROM DUSK TO DAWN...

BATGIRL TEAMED UP WITH BATMAN TO MAKE HIM FALL FOR HER--BUT NOW SHE'S OUT OF THE PICTURE!

AND STILL BATMAN HASN'T TOLD ME HE LOVES ME! WHAT'S THE MATTER WITH HIM, ANYHOW?

HEN SHE MEETS THE CAPED CRUSADER, HE THROWS DISCRETION TO THE WIND, ND...
MADE UP YOUR MIND YET, BATMAN?
WHEN ARE YOU GOING TO ASK ME TO JOIN YOU IN CROOK-CATCHING--AND IN WEDLOCK?
I'M QUITE SATISFIED WITH THE WAY THINGS ARE RIGHT NOW, CATWOMAN!
HOW DO YOU LIKE THAT! HE'S ALOOF--AND I'M IN LOVE!
HERE I GO AND ELIMINATE BATGIRL--AND ALL HE CAN SAY IS--HE'S SATISFIED!
WELL, HE MAY BE SATISFIED--BUT I'M NOT!
OOOH! THAT MAN MAKES ME SO MAD--I FEEL LIKE GOING BACK TO CAT-CRIMES AGAIN!
BUT I'LL GIVE HIM ONE MORE CHANCE!
SINCE I'M A WOMAN IN LOVE--I'D RATHER BE WITH THE MAN I LOVE!
IF HE WON'T MAKE THE FIRST MOVE--I'VE GOT TO STOP BEING COY--I'LL ASK BATMAN TO MARRY ME!
IF HE REFUSES--AHH, BUT HE WON'T REFUSE, NOT WHEN CONFRONTED WITH THE CHOICE I'M GOING TO GIVE HIM!
IN THE BATCAVE, THE FOLLOWING NIGHT..
I DON'T WANT TO SOUND EGOTISTICAL, ROBIN--BUT I'VE COME TO THE CONCLUSION THAT CATWOMAN IS IN LOVE WITH ME!
OF COURSE SHE IS! EVERYBODY KNOWS THAT--BUT YOU!
THE QUESTION IS--WHAT'RE YOU GOING TO DO ABOUT IT?
MAKE A CERTAIN PRECAUTIONARY MOVE BEFORE GOING OUT TONIGHT--AND SO ARE YOU!
ME? BUT SHE'S NOT IN LOVE WITH ME!
PERHAPS NOT! NEVERTHELESS, WE'LL BOTH TAKE THAT CERTAIN PRECAUTION!
16

THE CRIME-PATROL BEGINS WITH THE BATMOBILE HEADING FOR A RARE COIN EMPORIUM! ALSO CONVERGING ON THAT SAME COIN CHATEAU ARE THE KITTY CAR-- AND THE BATBIKE...
THE COLLECTION OF RARE DUCATS--SILVER COINS ISSUED IN 1140 BY THE DUKE OF APULIA--MAY TEMPT SOME CROOKS INTO STRIKING FOR THEM!
STARTLED FACES LIFT FROM PILES OF COSTLY COINS AS...
BATMAN AND ROBIN!
WITH CATWOMAN--
AN' BATGIRL TOO!
WHAT ARE YOU DOING HERE, BATGIRL? I THOUGHT YOU'D LEARNED YOUR LESSON!
I THOUGHT I HAD, TOO--UNTIL MY PHOTOGRAPHIC MEMORY RECALLED A CERTAIN WORD--
CATOPTRICS--THAT BRANCH OF OPTICS WHICH DEALS WITH THE REFLECTION OF LIGHT!
THE BAUBLE YOU KEPT SWINGING DISTORTED THE LIGHT--AND MY VISION--JUST ENOUGH--TO THROW MY TIMING OFF!
TO HER INTENSE SURPRISE, THE MASKED MAIDEN DISCOVERS THAT CATWOMAN IS NOT EVEN LISTENING...
SINCE I KNEW YOU'D CAUSED ME TO LOOK BAD I DECIDED TO COME OUT TONIGHT. I GOT A FIX ON YOUR KITTY CAR AND--
SWOTT!
BATMAN--LOOK OUT!

NOW THAT CAT'S REALLY SHOWING HER CLAWS!
BUT SHE ISN'T GOING TO GET AWAY WITH IT!
THUNK!
I'M TAKING YOU TO MY CATACOMBS, BATMAN!
YOU'LL TAKE BATMAN TO YOUR CATACOMBS OVER MY DEAD BODY, CATWOMAN!
HAVE IT YOUR OWN WAY, BATGIRL!
NEXT INSTANT...
OHHH! I'M BEGINNING TO CATCH WISE! ALL THOSE "CRIMINALS" YOU CAUGHT--WERE YOUR OWN MEN! NO WONDER THEY ONLY ROBBED PLACES WITH A "CAT" TIE-IN!
GNNG!
ND LATER, IN THE CATACOMBS, AFTER SENDING HER MEN INTO THE NEXT ROOM...
I CAN'T RESIST SEEING WHAT BATMAN REALLY LOOKS LIKE!
I DON'T WANT MY BOYS AROUND--FOR NONE BUT I MUST SEE BATMAN'S UN-MASKED FACE! WHEN HE MARRIES ME, HE'LL HAVE NO SECRETS FROM ME--SO I'LL JUST JUMP THE MARRIAGE CEREMONY A LITTLE!
BUT AS THAT COWL PEELS BACK...
EH?!
WHAT A MAN! HE OUTSMARTED ME--BY PAINTING HIS FACE IN THE SEMBLANCE OF HIS OWN MASK!
WELL, AT LEAST I CAN HAVE THE SATISFACTION OF SEEING WHAT ROBIN AND BATGIRL REALLY LOOK LIKE!
18

ONCE MORE THE *PRINCESS OF PLUNDER* STARES IN ANGRY DISMAY...

THEY'RE PAINT-MASKED TOO.!

I'D TRY TO REMOVE THAT PAINT--BUT IF THEY WERE ALL SO FORE-SIGHTED TO TAKE SUCH PRE-CAUTIONS, I'M SURE SOME SPECIAL CHEMICAL IS NEEDED TO GET RID OF IT!

SUMMONING HER MEN FROM THE NEXT ROOM, THE *FELINE FELON* SNAPS HER ORDERS...

PICK THEM UP! PUT THEM IN THE TRAP I'VE ARRANGED FOR THEM.!

AND DON'T FORGET TO REMOVE THEIR UTILITY BELTS--AND WEAPONS-BAG!

SHORTLY...

GOOD! I SEE YOU CAME TO FIRST, *BATMAN*!

WE HAVE MATTERS TO TALK OVER, YOU AND I.! YOU SEE, I REFORMED FOR YOU--BUT YOU HAVEN'T REWARDED ME BY PROPOSING TO ME!

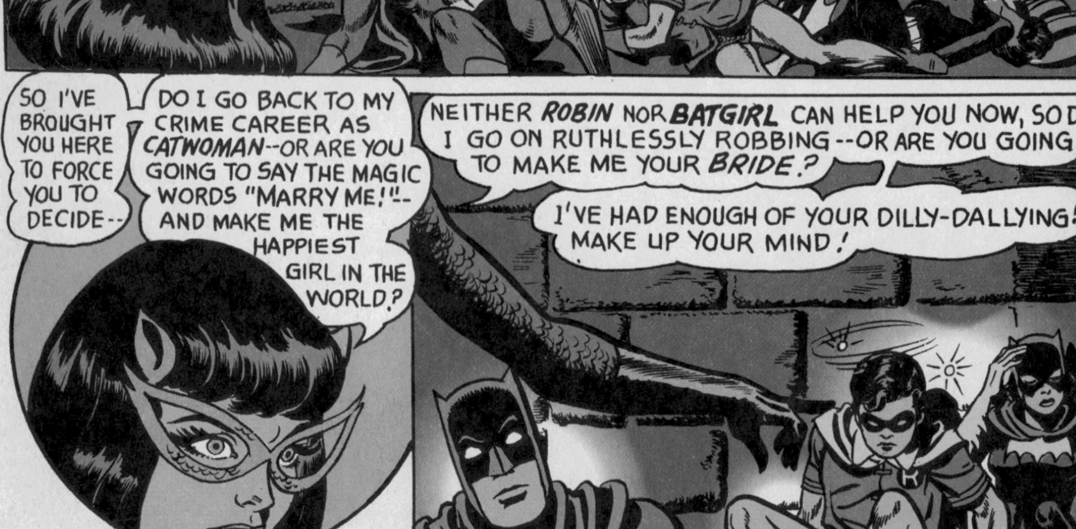

WITH A GRIM SMILE THE CAPED CRIME-FIGHTER HURLS HIMSELF FORWARD...
REALLY, NOW, CATWOMAN! YOU DON'T EXPECT ME TO STAND HERE AND LET YOU THREATEN ME LIKE THIS?
CAREFUL, BATMAN-- I WARN YOU!

UDDENLY, MYSTERIOUSLY, THE IR IS RENT BY AN ANGRY CAT-NARL AS THE MASKED-MAN-UNTER STIFFENS IN AGONY...
MEEE-OWWRRRR
OHHH! THAT SOUND-- STABBING INTO MY BODY-- MY BRAIN--LIKE SHARP HOT KNIVES!
IF YOU CAN'T STAND IT, BATMAN--GET BACK ON THAT METAL DISC!

PANTING AND SWEATING WITH THE STRAIN OF TORTURED NERVES, BATMAN DROPS INTO THE SAFETY ZONE OF THE SOUND-TRAP...
YOU CAN'T ESCAPE MY CATAPHONIC TRAP! THOSE CAT SNARLS FORM AN INVISIBLE CAT'S CRADLE OF SOUND WAVES--BOUNDING BACK AND FORTH LIKE STRINGS CHILDREN PUT ON THEIR FINGERS--WHICH GO RIGHT THROUGH YOUR BODY TO THE BRAIN'S CONTROL CENTER!
NOW--GIVE ME YOUR ANSWER! AM I TO BE-- BRIDE OR BURGLAR?
THE ANSWER IS--NO!
ON YOUR HEAD BE IT!
I'LL LEAVE YOU HERE-- TORTURED BY THE KNOWL-EDGE I'M GOING OUT TO ROB THE WORLD'S MOST FABULOUS POKER GAME!
STARTING OUT WITH THE GAME'S "KITTY" OF COURSE!

HORTLY, AT A PLUSH PRIVATE CLUBROOM IN GOTHAM CITY...
THE RICHEST MEN IN THE WORLD--AND THE WEALTHIEST WOMAN!
I'LL TAKE NOT ONLY THE KITTY BUT THE POT OF CASH AND JEWELS!
SNAPPPP!
SINCE EACH OF THEM COMES TO THESE ANNUAL POKER GAMES WITH A MILLION DOLLARS-- I'VE MADE A REAL "KILLING"! I'M THE ONLY WINNER!
20

SOON, BACK IN THE CATACOMBS HIDEAWAY...
MEN, PUT MY FIVE MILLION HAUL BEFORE BATMAN--AND LET HIM EAT HIS HEART OUT!
YOU ARE THE ONE WHO'S RESPONSIBLE FOR THAT ROBBERY, BATMAN--YOU FORCED ME INTO IT!
AFTER HER CAT-CROOKS LEAVE...
ALL YOU HAVE TO DO IS CHANGE YOUR MIND--AND I'LL SEND BACK THE LOOT!
YOU CAN NEVER CHANGE YOUR SPOTS, CATWOMAN!
ONCE A CROOK--ALWAYS A CROOK WHERE YOU'RE CONCERNED!
BATGIRL COMING THROUGH MY SOUND-TRAP--?!
HOWEVER YOU MANAGED IT, I'LL QUICKLY CUT YOU DOWN!
GOING TO USE THAT CAT'S-EYE BAUBLE AGAIN TO DISTORT MY VISION-
MY KARATE-HAND IS QUICKER THAN YOUR CAT'S-EYE...
KRAAAKK!
AIEEE!
SOK!
SNAP!
YOU MEN IN THE NEXT ROOM--HELP! HELP!
WHUMMMPP!

BUT AS CATWOMAN'S REINFORCEMENTS ARRIVE--BATMAN AND ROBIN LEAP OUT OF THEIR TRAP TOO...
THAT WAS OUR SIGNAL FOR ACTION, ROBIN!
DO YOU HAVE THE FEELING THAT SIGNAL SHOULD HAVE BEEN-- A CAT-CALL?
PAPPP!
SOKK!
WHEN THE BATTLING IS OVER...
HOW DID YOU EVER GET OUT OF MY ESCAPE-PROOF SOUND-TRAP, BATMAN?
WITH THE HELP OF BATGIRL! SHE SIMPLY TALKED ME OUT OF IT!
"WHEN WE WERE ALONE, I ASKED HER TO REMOVE HER GLOVE AND SWING IT BACK AND FORTH WHILE I CONCENTRATED MY ATTENTION ON IT..."
IT ISN'T WORKING! I'M NOT BEING HYPNOTIZED!
I HAVE AN IDEA, BATMAN! I'VE READ A GREAT DEAL ABOUT HYPNOTISM, THOUGH I'VE NEVER PRACTICED IT!
BY SWINGING MY GLOVE GENTLY AGAINST THE TRAP'S SOUND-BARRIER--I'LL MAKE IT EMIT LOW SOUNDS--SOOTHING NOISES LIKE A SOFT PURR...
HYPNOTISTS INDUCE SLEEP BY SOFT WORDS-- OR SOUNDS--
MEEOOOWW MEOOOOWW
"SURE ENOUGH I FELL UNDER HER SPELL--AND JUST AS HYPNOTIZED PEOPLE FEEL NO SENSATION OF PAIN FROM A PIN-PRICK OR A MATCH FLAME HELD UNDER THEIR FINGERS--NEITHER DID I AS..."
WALK FORWARD, BATMAN! YOU WILL EXPERIENCE NO PAIN--
NOW STEP OVER TO THE CONTROLS AND SHUT OFF THE SOUND-TRAP!
ATTA GIRL-- YOU'RE DOING IT!
22

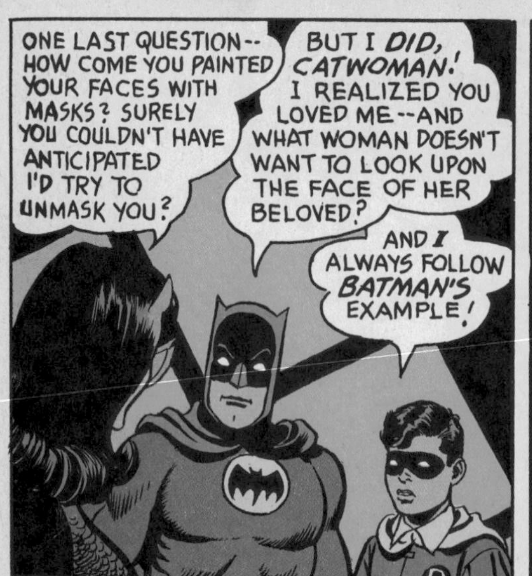

Detective Comics PRESENTS BATMAN
75¢ 559 FEB 86
CATWOMAN AND BATMAN VS Green Arrow AND BLACK CANARY
BECAUSE YOU DEMANDED IT!

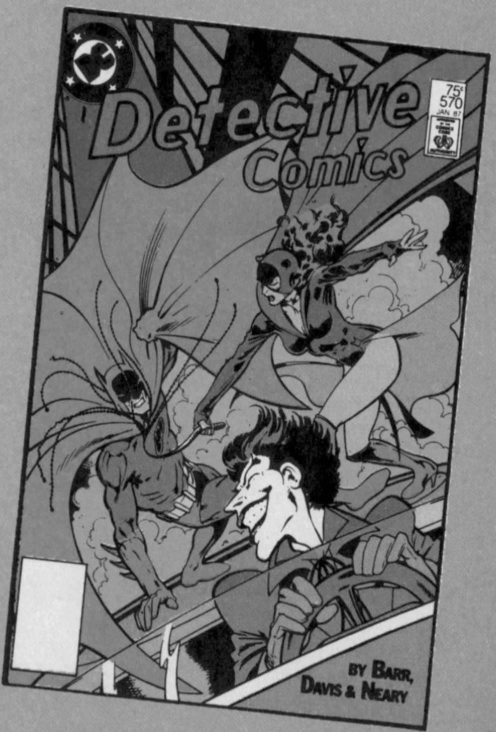

Detective Comics
75¢ 570 JAN 87
BY BARR, DAVIS & NEARY

AN OLD FOE RETURNS TO PLAGUE AND IMPERIL-- the BATMAN
OLD-FASHIONED BATMAN ACTION MADE MODERN BY--
DENNY O'NEIL — WRITER
IRV NOVICK & DICK GIORDANO — ARTISTS
JULIUS SCHWARTZ - EDITOR
IT IS QUIET IN THIS ROOM... THE STILLNESS BROKEN ONLY BY THE LABORED BREATHING OF THE TWO ENEMIES, THE SIGH OF THE LOVELY, VEILED WOMAN AND THE SLIGHT SNUFFLING OF THE BOY!
DANGER LIES BEHIND THIS MOMENT ...AND ALMOST CERTAIN DEATH-- AS THE BATMAN STRIVES TO CAGE THE MASTER OF FOUL PLAY!
"Hail Emperor PENGUIN!"

IT BEGINS THIS BRISK SPRING AFTERNOON AT THE CAMPUS OF HUDSON UNIVERSITY... WHERE KING PEEBLE IV, TWELVE-YEAR-OLD RULER OF THE KINGDOM OF SWAWAK, IS PAYING A VISIT...

YOUR MAJESTY, I'M DICK GRAYSON! THE COLLEGE PRESIDENT ASKED ME TO GIVE YOU THE GRAND TOUR!
YOU? A MERE CHILD? I SHOULD BE INSULTED!
I TRUST YOU ARE AT LEAST AN HONOR STUDENT!
FOR WHAT IT'S WORTH... I AM!

THIS IS A STATUE OF OUR FOUNDER! HE BUILT THE SCHOOL IN 1895 AND...
WHO CARES? I WANT TO SEE THE "MALT SHOP" WHERE THE "CATS AND CHICKS HANG OUT"-- JUST LIKE IN THE AMERICAN FILMS!

I AM INTERESTED IN "SOCK HOPS" AND "BEACH BLANKET BIKINI BINGO"!
ER... I'M AFRAID THE MOVIES GIVE A RATHER DISTORTED PICTURE OF OUR LIFE!
AS FOR BEACHES AND BIKINIS... IT'S A BIT EARLY IN THE YEAR!
BIT EARLY FOR SOMETHING ELSE--

--THOSE BIRDS... AND THEY'RE ACTING STRANGELY!
HOVERING OVER US... STARTING TO SWOOP--

--ATTACK!

I'M TAKING A CHANCE... SWITCHING IDENTITIES IN BROAD DAYLIGHT--

--BUT EVERYONE'S BUSY TRYING TO FEND OFF THOSE WINGED NASTIES --AND BESIDES, I NEED MY CAPE TO PROTECT MY EYES!
ODD... THEY'RE NOT GOING NEAR THE KING!
JUST GIVING THE MISERIES TO EVERYONE ELSE!

BRO-THER! IT'S LIKE FIGHTING A FEATHERSTORM FULL OF BROKEN GLASS!
CHUP.
CHUP.
HUH--? I HEAR AN ENGINE--
CHUP!

-- A HELICOPTER... LANDING AS THOUGH IT GOT A CUE-- WHICH I'M BETTING IT DID!
GOT TO GET THROUGH TO THE KING!

HE'S BEING KIDNAPED!
NO CHANCE OF REACHING HIM BEFORE THE 'COPTER LEAVES--
3

CHUP- CHUP- CHUP!
--BUT AT LEAST I CAN NAIL THIS SPECIMEN...

...HARD!

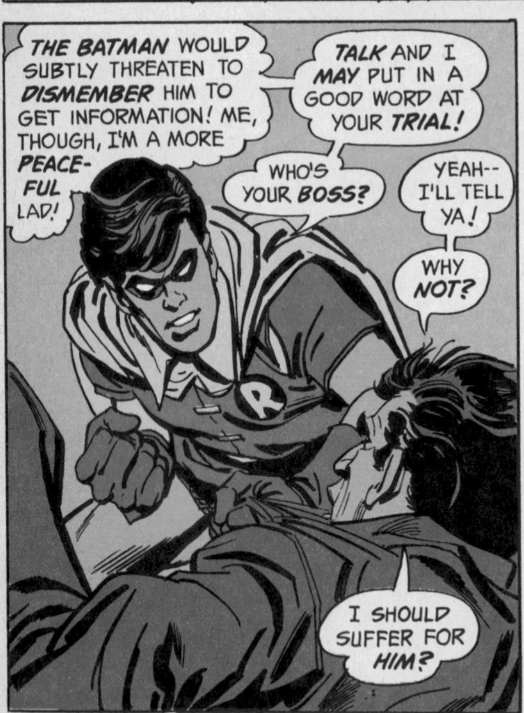
THE BATMAN WOULD SUBTLY THREATEN TO DISMEMBER HIM TO GET INFORMATION! ME, THOUGH, I'M A MORE PEACE-FUL LAD!
TALK AND I MAY PUT IN A GOOD WORD AT YOUR TRIAL!
WHO'S YOUR BOSS?
YEAH-- I'LL TELL YA!
WHY NOT?
I SHOULD SUFFER FOR HIM?

A LARD-LEGGED DUDE NAMED FORSTER APTENODYTES PAID US TO PUT THE SNATCH ON THE SNOT!
HE ARRANGED THE GIMMICK WITH THE BIRDS--

--AND OTHER THAN THAT, I KNOW NOTHIN'!
UNHH!
SOMEHOW, I FIND IT VER EASY TO BELIEVE YOU!
TAKE HIM--HE'S YOURS!

POLICE
HE'S GOING TO JAIL... AND I'M GOING TO GOTHAM CITY AS FAST AS MY CAMPER WILL CARRY ME!
...THE CITY--AND A CERTAIN CAVE--

SOON, ROBIN IS RELATING THE BIZARRE EVENTS TO HIS GUARDIAN AND MENTOR IN A HUGE CAVERN BENEATH A SUBURBAN MANSION...
THAT'S THE STORY! MAKE ANY SENSE TO YOU?
QUITE A BIT!
CONSIDER THE METHOD OF THE CRIME!
BIRDS, HIGHLY TRAINED NOT TO ATTACK THE KING--
--AND THE NAME THE HOOD GAVE YOU-- FORSTER APTENODYTES!
THE LABEL SCIENTISTS GIVE TO A CERTAIN BIRD IS--
--APTENODYTES FORSTERI...
...AND THAT BIRD IS THE EMPEROR PENGUIN!
IT ALL ADDS UP TO... HIM!
THE PENGUIN--!
YES, THE PENGUIN--
--NEXT TO THE JOKER, THE GREATEST CRIMINAL GENIUS WE'VE EVER TACKLED!
AUK! HOW DARE YOU TOUCH MY PRIVATE PET--?
HE'S A NOBLE CREATURE... DELICATE, SENSITIVE!
I MEANT HIM NO HARM!
5

LISTEN, BUMPTIOUS BRAT, YOU GET NEAR MY PET AGAIN AND I'LL WRECK YOU--
--CLEAR?
LET HIM BE!

HE'S ONLY A CHILD!
SURE... SURE! I'LL TAKE ORDERS FROM A SNIVELING SERVANT! THAT'LL BE THE DAY!
ONE MORE INTERFERENCE FROM YOU, WOMAN, AND I'LL SEND YOU TO THE EAGLE'S NEST!
YOU'LL DIE... YOU'LL DIE UGLY!

YOU MAY DIE ANYWAY-- THE INSTANT THE BRAT'S PRIME MINISTER RETURNS FROM EUROPE AND SIGNS THE PAPER GIVING RULING POWERS TO ME!
I'VE ALWAYS HAD A YEN TO BE AN EMPEROR ...LIKE MY ROYAL CHUM HERE...AND NOW I WILL!

A WHOLE COUNTRY-- MINE TO BOSS! A COUNTRY'S TREASURY --MINE TO LOOT!
HAPPY DAYS ARE JUST AROUND THE CORNER!

WILL THE OUTSIDER REALLY DO WHAT HE SAYS?
I'M AFRAID HE WILL... IF HE ISN'T STOPPED! BUT DO NOT WORRY! I'VE HAD EXPERIENCE DEALING WITH EVIL!
I SHALL PROTECT YOU!

TWO MORNINGS LATER... GOSSAMER FINGERS OF MIST CARESS THE STEEL-GRAY SEA AND THE WIND BITES PLAYFULLY AS A PAIR OF CAPED FIGURES SURVEYS AN AWESOME SCENE--
READY FOR A ROUGH CLIMB, ROBIN?
WITH THE YOUNG KING A CAPTIVE, WE DON'T DARE STORM THE FRONT OF HIS CASTLE!
SO WE ENTER VIA THE BACK-- UP THE SIDE OF THAT CLIFF!

I'M BEGINNING TO WISH I'D SPENT THIS SPRING VACATION WORKING ON MY STAMP COLLECTION!
YOU'RE SURE THE KING IS BEING HELD IN HIS OWN PALACE?
I'M NOT POSITIVE--

--BUT I'LL GIVE YOU BIG ODDS HE IS! REMEMBER...THE PENGUIN LOVES CRIME-FICTION-- HE ROOTS FOR THE BAD GUYS!
HE'S PARTICULARLY FOND OF EDGAR ALLAN POE'S "PURLOINED LETTER", THE STORY ABOUT A MISSING PAPER THAT'S WHERE THE HERO LEAST EXPECTS IT--

--RIGHT IN PLAIN SIGHT! NOBODY EXPECTS THE PENGUIN TO HIDE THE KING AT HIS PALACE!
ALSO... THE CASTLE IS CALLED "LU DLOM" IN THE NATIVE LANGUAGE --MEANING, APPROXIMATELY, "ROOST OF WINGS"!

"ROOST OF WINGS"... CHECK! THE PENGUIN WOULDN'T BE ABLE TO RESIST THAT!
ROBIN... LOOK! EAGLE'S NEST AND THREE ROPES DANGLING NEARBY!
I DON'T KNOW WHAT IT MEANS, BUT IT GIVES ME A CHILL!
7

SHEW! I THOUGHT WE'D NEVER REACH THE TOP--
QUIET! A COUPLE OF PLAYMATES ARE HEADING OUR WAY!
THE PENGUIN'S A NUT CASE, BUT HE PAYS GOOD--

--AND ME, I GO WHERE THE BREAD IS!
WE DO THE GOOD OLD STOMP-THE-GUARD ROUTINE?
WHAT ELSE?

ONLY PLEASE... NO BAD PUNS!
AWW... I HAVEN'T PUNNED FOR YEARS!--NOT SINCE I WAS A BOY WONDER!

US TEEN WONDERS ARE DIGNIFIED... MATURE!
I CAN'T TELL YOU HOW GLAD I AM!

HUNGRY, CHUM?
HAVE A KNUCKLE SANDWICH!

ROBIN... OWTCH!
SORRY! COULDN'T RESIST!

COME ON! THE PENGUIN MUST BE INSIDE!
LET'S NAIL HIM BEFORE YOU MAKE ANOTHER LOUSY JOKE!

MINUTES LATER, IN A LAVISH DINING HALL...
MMMM... FISH! SHELLFISH! SQUID! OCTOPUS! WE LOVE SEAFOOD--

DON'T WE, CHUM?
I'M COLD! CAN YOU NOT PROVIDE SOME WARMTH?

SILENCE, MOTOR MOUTH! WE LIKE THE COLD!
WHINE AGAIN, AND I'LL FEED YOU TO THE EELS!
AT LEAST PERMIT ME TO GIVE HIM A BLANKET--

--UNLIKE YOURSELF, HE IS WARM-BLOODED!
YOU'LL GIVE THE CHATTERING CHUMP EXACTLY ZERO UNLESS YOU HAVE MY PERMISSION--

--WHICH YOU HAVEN'T!
THE SERVING GIRL...! HER MOVEMENTS-- FLUID AS QUICKSILVER... UNMISTAKABLY GRACEFUL--
9

--AND THE VOICE... LIKE SUN-WARMED HONEY!
IT'S HER!

I'M TIRED OF YOUR INFERNAL INTERFERENCE! I BELIEVE I'LL TEACH YOU A LACHRYMOSE LESSON!

GET YOUR CLAMMY HANDS OFF HER--

--OR I'LL BEND YOU TILL YOU BREAK!
STAND BACK, BATMAN!
MY UMBRELLA'S FERRULE IS RAZOR SHARP! I'LL SKEWER THE FRANGIBLE FEMALE!

MY, MY! LISTEN TO THE DICTIONARY-RUN-AMOK THREATEN!
AUK!--HELPERS! HENCHMEN!

HELP! BRING GUNS ...KNIVES... AXES--
THE OLD BUMP-THE-BADDIES ROUTINE, BATMAN?
CORRECT! AND AFTERWARD, MAYBE WE'LL PLAY PULVERIZE-THE-PENGUIN!

YOU HOLLERED, BOSS?

SOK!
SOK!

AS WE USED TO SAY... THE JIG IS UP!
NOT JUST YET, YOU MORDANT MEDDLER! I HAVE AN ALLY-- MY PRECIOUS PET!

CHUM... ATTACK! SIC 'IM!
PENGUIN, YOU'VE GOT TO BE KIDDING! OR TOTALLY FLIPPED!
YOU THINK A CUDDLY REFUGEE FROM A TUXEDO TAILOR CAN BOTHER ME?
11

HOWEVER, WITH UNEXPECTED SPEED, THE PENGUIN'S "ALLY" SINKS HIS BEAK INTO THE BATMAN'S FOOT--

UNFRIENDLY BEASTIE, ISN'T HE?
COME HERE...
OWTCH!

B-BATMAN... SUDDENLY FEEL DIZZY!
ME... TOO...

YOU SURELY SHOULD! MY BUDDY'S BILL IS TIPPED WITH POISON... A CURARE EXTRACT!
YOU'LL SLEEP-- BUT NOT REST-FULLY, I SHOULD ADD!

BATMAN!

PERHAPS, IN THIS LAST TORTURED MOMENT OF CONSCIOUSNESS, THE BATMAN HEARS THE TEAR-FUL MURMUR, FEELS THE STRONG, VELVETY ARMS...
DARLING, DARLING--

YOU'RE FOND OF HIM, EH? EXCELLENT! YOU'LL JOIN HIM AT THE EAGLE'S NEST!
YOU'LL ALL THREE SWING, SUFFER... AND SCREAM!

STUNG BY SALT-LADEN WIND, THE TRIO AWAKENS AND...
WE CAUGHT OURSELVES A BAD CASE OF DANGER! WHAT'S THE PENGUIN'S PROGRAM, I WONDER--

--LEAVE US TO STARVE?
NO! OBSERVE THE NEST BELOW-- THE INFANT EAGLES! THEIR MOTHER WILL RETURN...
...AND SHE'LL THINK WE'RE THREATENING HER LITTLE ONES! SHE'LL CLAW US TO RIBBONS!

I REALIZE I SHOULDN'T BE MAKING SMALL TALK, TALIA, BUT--
YES... IT IS THE TRADITIONAL METHOD OF EXECUTION IN SWAWAK!
YOU RECOGNIZED ME?

ANYWHERE, ANYTIME! I OWE YOU MY LIFE!
I'M CURIOUS AS TO WHY YOU'RE ON KING PEEBLE'S ISLAND!
I POSED AS A SERVANT TO LEARN THE STATE OF SWAWAK'S TREASURY!
13

LIKE THE PENGUIN, I HOPED TO ROB-- USE THE MONEY TO FREE MY FATHER, RĀ'S AL GHŪL, FROM PRISON...TO REBUILD HIS ORGANIZATION-- HIS DREAM!
I DID NOT COUNT ON MEETING YOU!

HATE TO BREAK UP YOUR REUNION, GUYS--BUT MOMMA EAGLE IS ON THE SET... AND GIVING US THE BLOODY EYEBALL!
QUICK, ROBIN... SWING YOUR FEET UP TO MY SHOULDERS!

MADE IT! NOW WHAT--?
JUMP TO THE LEDGE ABOVE...
...USE THAT JAGGED EDGE ON YOUR ROPES!
MEANWHILE, I'LL KEEP MOMMA BUSY!

WHEW! THE HIGHER I GO, THE ROUGHER IT GETS!

TALIA...BEHIND ME! I'LL SHIELD YOU--
NO! I AM NOT HELPLESS!
BESIDES, I CAN BE USEFUL--!

THE TWO OF US WILL DIVIDE THE BIRD'S ATTENTION... AND DOUBLE OUR CHANCES!

AS THE BATTLE RAGES, THE PENGUIN OBSERVES FROM A RAMPART OF THE CASTLE--AND SQUAWKS IN THE FURY...
AUK! THE CRETINOUS CRUSADER AND HIS TROUBLESOME TEEN ARE CHEATING! QUICK--GIVE ME A RIFLE!

I'LL PUNCTURE THEIR PERFIDIOUS PERSONS--

YEOWWWCH!

AUK! I'LL TAN YOUR ROYAL HIDE--!
YOU WILL NOT STEP NEAR ME--NOR WILL YOU ATTEMPT TO HARM MY FRIEND THE SERVANT!
--OR I WILL LEAP FROM THE WALL TO THE ROCKS ON THE BEACH BELOW!
15

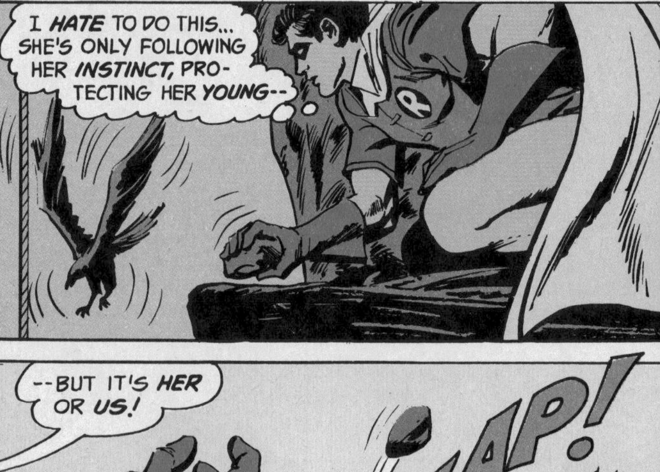

--BUT IT'S HER OR US!
ZAP!

OWLY, THE SUN SINKS, AND A CHILL TOUCHES THE ISLAND, AS...
COME ON, KIDDY KING-- I'M A FRIENDLY FELLA WHEN YOU UNDERSTAND ME! I'LL GIVE YOU CANDY--
THE AMERICANS HAVE AN EXPRESSION: "SCRAM, BUSTER!"

AUUK! I'LL COOK YOUR CONTEMPTIBLE CARCASS--!
NO!
YOU'RE THE ONE WHO'S COOKED, PENGUIN!

AUUK! THE BLASTED BATMAN!
I'M IN NO MOOD TO TRADE REPARTEE WITH YOU!
I'LL ASK YOU-- JUST ONCE-- SURRENDER!

MY FRIEND! THANK THE HEAVENS YOU'RE SAFE...
YOUR MAJESTY... BE CAREFUL-- YOU'LL FALL!

EXCITED, FULL OF DELIGHT AT SEEING TALIA, KING PEEBLE IV TOPPLES OFF AND DOWNWARD...
OH-- OH!!
17

NOR HAS THE BATMAN BEEN IDLE--

LAST OPPORTUNITY TO OBLITERATE OUR OPPROBRIOUS OPPONENT, MEN!

OBLITERATE?! I THOUGHT YOU WERE PLANNING TO "ALLITERATE" ME TO DEATH--

--NO MATTER! A REGIMENT OF THESE TIN THUGS COULDN'T STOP ME!

BACK OFF...OR I'LL BRUTALIZE YOU WITH MY BLADED BUMBERSHOOT!
CAN YOUR JAW-BREAKING WORDS!
I WARNED YOU... I'LL NOT BANDY WISECRACKS!
I DIDN'T FULLY REALIZE IT BEFORE...YOU'RE A SAD CASE! YOU'RE CRAZY--!
AUKK! THAT'S A LICENTIOUS LIE!
I'M ALMOST SORRY FOR YOU...
...CLINGING TO BIRDS BECAUSE YOU CAN'T STAND HUMAN COMPANY!

BUT I CAN'T FEEL MUCH PITY! MY ANGER WON'T LET ME!
19

BATMAN, IS EVERYTHING--

TALIA, YOU CAME TO *SWAWAK* TO COMMIT A CRIME!

YOU *DIDN'T*... AND YOU HELPED US PREVENT *GREATER* CRIMES!

MAYBE... JUST MAYBE YOU'VE EARNED YOUR *FREEDOM*--

LEAVE, TALIA! BECAUSE IF I TURN AROUND AND YOU'RE *STILL* HERE, I'LL HAVE TO MAKE A DECISION THAT COULD *RUIN* ME!

FOR *BOTH* OUR SAKES, *GO!*... PLEASE!

BATMAN... ROBIN... YOU ARE INDEED *SPLENDID!* I SHALL *REWARD* YOU... *RUBIES, DIAMONDS... ANYTHING!*

NO, YOUR YOUNG MAJESTY... ANY REWARD WOULD BE EITHER TOO *MUCH* ...OR NOT *ENOUGH!*

THE SKY DIMS, AND THE LONG SHADOWS OF NIGHT CREEP ACROSS A PATH THAT IS HARD AND, PERHAPS, WITHOUT END. SOMEWHERE IN THE DISTANCE, GULLS MOAN A SONG OF WELCOME TO THE DARKNESS...

20

AN ALMOST LEGENDARY FIGURE, THE COWLED SHADOW OF THE BATMAN PROWLS THROUGH THE NIGHT, PREYING UPON THE CRIMINAL PARASITE LIKE THE WINGED CREATURE WHOSE NAME HE HAS ADOPTED!
CREATED BY BOB KANE
SO MUCH FOR PROF. STRANGE!
YEAH! FUNNY HOW HE WOULDN'T GIVE UP THE BATMAN'S SECRET I.D.!
GUESS HE WAS ONE OF THOSE TURKEYS WHO'S SCARED OF BATS! I DON'T UNDER-STAND GUYS LIKE THAT!
S-2681
TURKEYS? NO, NO TURKEYS N THIS ISSUE--BUT THERE'S 'NOTHER SORT OF JAILBIRD WAITING IN THE WINGS. IN FACT, EVEN THOUGH WE'RE JUST DEALING WITH THUGS SO FAR, WE'VE NAMED OUR TALE--
"THE MALAY PENGUIN!"
TEVE ENGLEHART * STORY
MARSHALL ROGERS * ART
TERRY AUSTIN * EMBELLISHER
M. SNAPINN * LETTERER
JULIUS SCHWARTZ * EDITOR

SLAM
SPLASH

WHERE'D HE COME FROM? WHAT IS THIS?

DON'T FREEZE, BRUNO! HE'S GOT ROBIN WITH HIM!
I NEED HELP!

BUT HE-- I JUST MENTIONED HIS NAME--
SOK
SORRY, BRUNO! TIME'S UP!

KPOW KPOW
WHAT WAS THAT YOU PUSHED OFF THE PIER, MURDOCK?

ANSWER ME!
NO! GET AWAY! AAAGH! MY HAND!

I COULDN'T EAR YOU BEFORE IN HE FOG, SO OU'RE GOING O REPEAT IT OR ME NOW!

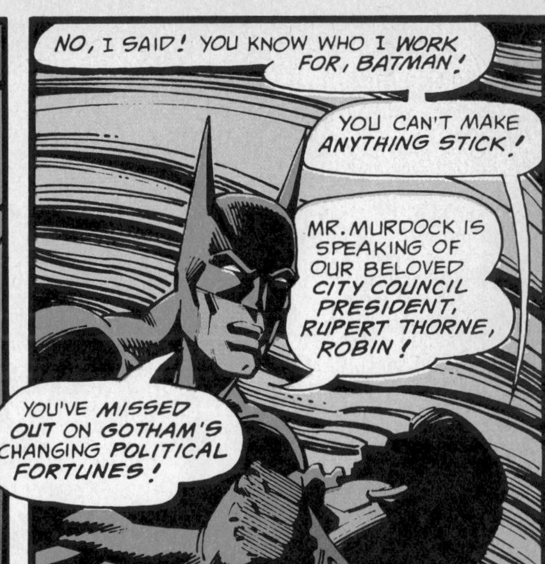
NO, I SAID! YOU KNOW WHO I WORK FOR, BATMAN!
YOU CAN'T MAKE ANYTHING STICK!
MR. MURDOCK IS SPEAKING OF OUR BELOVED CITY COUNCIL PRESIDENT, RUPERT THORNE, ROBIN!
YOU'VE MISSED OUT ON GOTHAM'S CHANGING POLITICAL FORTUNES!

BUT I'VE READ THE APERS--BETWEEN THE LINES! DOES THORNE REALLY CONTROL THE POLICE?
NO--NOT WITH COMMISSIONER GORDON IN CHARGE! HE CONTROLS THE COURTS!
AND THE POLICE IN MATTERS OF CITY POLICY--

EEEEEEEEEEEEE
-LIKE WHETHER THE BATMAN'S TILL WELCOME IN GOTHAM CITY!

HERE COME THE POLICE--AND I'M READY TO MEET THEM WITH OPEN ARMS! HOW ABOUT YOU, BATMAN?

PL

EEEEE
EEEEEEE
EEEEE
PIER 31 WAREHOUSE
LET'S GET OUT OF HERE!
3

HOWEVER, LAST ISSUE, WE SAW BOSS THORNE MURDER HUGO STRANGE IN HIS PERSONAL CAMPAIGN TO DESTROY THE BATMAN--A FACT THE DYNAMIC DUO HAS YET TO DISCOVER! AND NOW HUGO STRANGE LIES ON THE BOTTOM OF THE RIVER!

THAT'S NOT THE ONLY SECRET WE KNOW, EITHER...

--TO THE
ENGUIN!

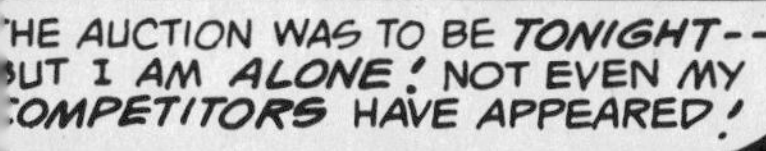
HE AUCTION WAS TO BE TONIGHT--
UT I AM ALONE! NOT EVEN MY
OMPETITORS HAVE APPEARED!

IS THIS A GAME? AND IF SO--WHAT ARE THE RULES?

WELL, I HAVE LITTLE TIME TO DEVOTE TO THE MATTER NOW, WITH MY PRIMARY PLANS PROCEEDING APACE!
LEARNING THE BATMAN'S SECRET WOULD HAVE BEEN GLORIOUS, BUT IT SEEMS NOT TO BE!
IF ONLY I KNEW WHO MY RIVALS WERE--!

A HAHAHAHA HAHA
T RAINS DOWN LIKE ICE CUBES, THAT LAUGH--
-THE MAD LAUGH OF--
THE JOKER!

SHOW YOURSELF--
--YOU GRINNING GARGOYLE!

5

THE PENGUIN FEARS NO SANE MAN--BUT THE JOKER IS HARDLY THAT!
IT'S HIGH TIME I TOOK MY LEAVE!

AT LEAST, I KNOW HE DIDN'T DIVERT STRANGE! HE WOULDN'T RETURN HERE IF HE HAD!
WE HAVE NO NEED TO CROSS SWORDS--
--AND THAT SUITS ME PERFECTLY!
SHAKE A LEG, BOYS! WE HAVE PLACES TO GO!

Gotham News

READ THE NEWS WEEKLY
THUMP

SUPERMAN
REED GALLERIES TO EXHIBIT LEGENDAR
MALAY PENGUIN
BY MAUREEN LIBE

AND, IN THE REED GALLERIES.
HOW COULD YOU DO SOMETHING LIKE THIS, REED?

MY DEAR BATMA WHAT ARE YOU TALKING ABOUT

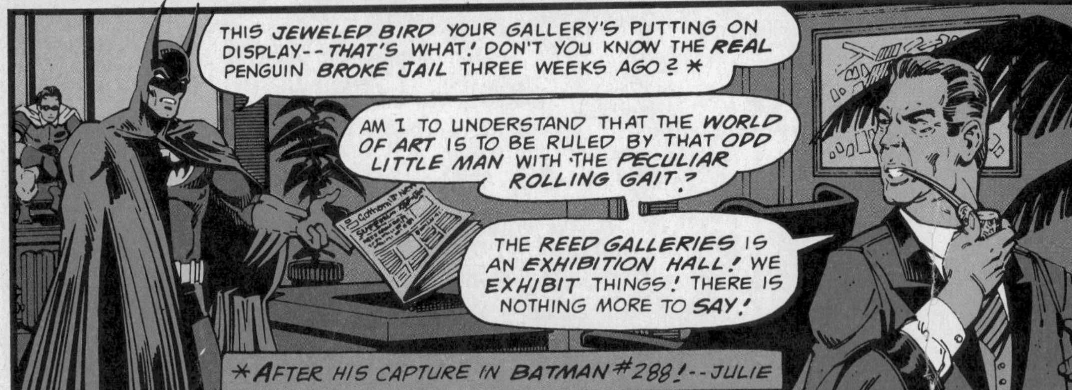
THIS JEWELED BIRD YOUR GALLERY'S PUTTING ON DISPLAY--THAT'S WHAT! DON'T YOU KNOW THE REAL PENGUIN BROKE JAIL THREE WEEKS AGO? *
AM I TO UNDERSTAND THAT THE WORLD OF ART IS TO BE RULED BY THAT ODD LITTLE MAN WITH THE PECULIAR ROLLING GAIT?
THE REED GALLERIES IS AN EXHIBITION HALL! WE EXHIBIT THINGS! THERE IS NOTHING MORE TO SAY!
* AFTER HIS CAPTURE IN BATMAN #288! --JULIE

WHAT CONCERN IS IT OF YOURS, ANYWAY? YOU NO LONGER HAVE ANY OFFICIAL STATUS IN THIS CITY!
LISTEN, MR. REED--!
NO, YOU LISTEN! I CAN'T SAY I APPROVE OF THE CITY'S RESOLUTION, BUT I WILL NOT BE DICTATED TO IN MY OWN GALLERY! I ASSURE YOU, OUR SECURITY IS QUITE SUFFICIENT!

SEE HERE--
--THE MALAY PENGUIN REPOSES IN ITS OWN ROOM--
--TO BE VIEWED ONLY AT A DISTANCE THROUGH MAGNIFYING WINDOWS!

SURROUNDING THE BIRD ITSELF--
CLICK
--IS A RING OF LASERS AND ELECTRONIC EYES!

THAT CAN BE BEATEN! THE SHADOW-THIEF DID SO*--!
CLICK!
*IN JLA #139 --JULIE

AH! BUT FIRST, THE PENGUIN WOULD HAVE TO WALK ACROSS THE FLOOR-- WHICH IS MONITORED BY SEISMO-GRAPHS TO DETECT VIBRATION!
HE COULDN'T FLY BECAUSE THERE ARE MICROPHONES TO PICK OUT ANY UNTOWARD NOISE-- EVEN THE WHIRR OF WINGS!
WHAT ABOUT TELEVISION CAMERAS?

CAM-RAS?
BATMAN, LET'S BE REALISTIC HERE! THERE IS SUCH A THING AS OVERKILL-- AND THERE IS SUCH A THING AS A BUDGET!
WHO DO YOU THINK THE PENGUIN IS ANYWAY-- A GHOST?

I THINK THE PENGUIN IS A MAN WHO LOVES TO PLAY GAMES--CHALLENGING GAMES! HE LOVES TO MATCH WITS FOR HIGH STAKES--PARTICULARLY PRICELESS BIRDS!
I THINK, MR. REED, THAT THE PENGUIN IS NOT A MAN TO BE UNDER-ESTIMATED--BUDGET OR NO BUDGET!
7

SUMMARIZE IT, PLEASE, ALFRED!
WELL, SIR, SINCE HUGO STRANGE LEFT ALL THE MONEY HE DRAINED FROM YOUR HOLDINGS HERE AT THE OFFICE WHEN HE DISAPPEARED, THEY FEEL MOST OF HIS DEALINGS CAN BE NULLIFIED!
WALL STREET WILL BREATHE MORE EASILY WITH WAYNE ENTERPRISES BACK IN ITS ACCUSTOMED POSITION!

THAT'S GOOD! WHAT ABOUT THE MAIL?
NOTHING IMPORTANT.
THANK-YOU'S, REQUESTS-- ANNOUNCEMENT OF A BOARD MEETING IN PARIS BY YOUR SECURITY EXCHANGE--

PARIS, HUH? THAT WOULD SOUND GOOD ANY TIME BUT NOW!
I'LL SEND BROOME! HE'S A GOOD MAN!
GOOD NIGHT, ALFRED!

GOOD MORNING SIR!
I'LL AWAKEN YOU AT NOON!

GOTHAM
ENERAL--?
YES, SILVER'S IN HERE!* THEY'VE STARTED TO ALLOW HER VISITORS!
M GENERAL HOSPITA

*SILVER ST. CLOUD, BRUCE'S CURRENT FLAME, WAS ALSO CAPTURED BY HUGO STRANGE LAST TIME! --JULIE

HELLO, SILVER--
HI, BRUCE! WOW! YOU'RE LOOKING GOOD!
THEY'VE KEPT ME HERE FOR TWO DAYS SO FAR-- AFRAID I GOT SOME OF THAT MONSTER SERUM ALL THOSE OTHER POOR PEOPLE GOT! I THOUGHT YOU'D BE IN BED, TOO!

NO SUCH LUCK!
I'M A WORKING MAN!

HI! YOU MUST BE
RUCE'S WARD, DICK!
UM...YEAH! I WANT TO APOLOGIZE FOR BRUSHING YOU OFF THE OTHER NIGHT--!*
*DICK ONLY PRETENDED TO DO THAT LAST ISSUE, SO HE COULD CHANGE TO ROBIN! --JULIE
NEVER MIND!
SUPPOSE I DID SOUND PRETTY LOONY!

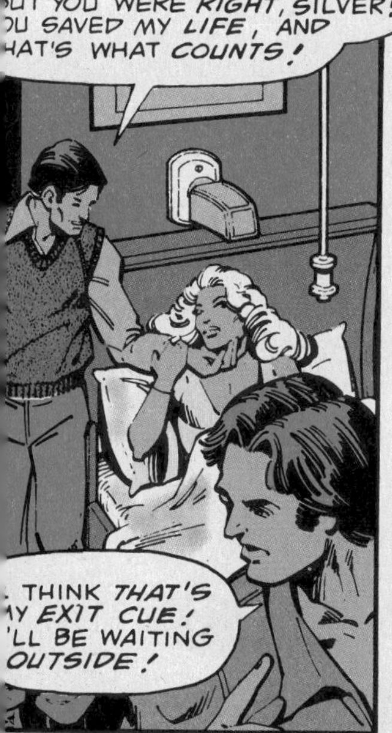
UT YOU WERE RIGHT, SILVER!
OU SAVED MY LIFE, AND
HAT'S WHAT COUNTS!
THINK THAT'S
MY EXIT CUE!
'LL BE WAITING
OUTSIDE!

OOO-WHEE!
9

THAT TAKES CARE OF BRUCE'S DAYLIGHT HOURS!

LATER, WHEN NIGHT MANTLES THE CITY, HE GREETS HIS OTHER LOVE...

...ADVENTURE!

THE GALLERIES LOOK PRETTY QUIET, BATMAN!

WE'LL JUST WATCH FOR A WHILE!

ROBIN! COMING OUT OF THE THEATER...!

GOT YOU, BATMAN! I'D RECOGNIZE THAT WADDLING WALK ANYWHERE--

--THE PENGUIN!

EGAD! B and R!

DON'T YOU EVER GET TIRED OF BREAKING JAIL, PENGUIN?

NOT AS TIRED AS I GET BEING PUT THERE, BATMAN!

ZZZ

ZZZZZZZZ

LET ME EXHIBIT HOW I DID IT--WITH MY BUZZ-UMBRELLA!

WITHOUT WORD OR LOOK, THE DYNAMIC DUO RESPONDS AS ONE!

ZZZZZZZZZZZZZZZZZ

PFAH! MISSED!

NOW, LET US TURN FOR A MOMENT TO MATTERS AT THE FAMED TOBACCONISTS' CLUB... MATTERS WHICH WILL ALSO AFFECT THIS SAGA MOST PROFOUNDLY...

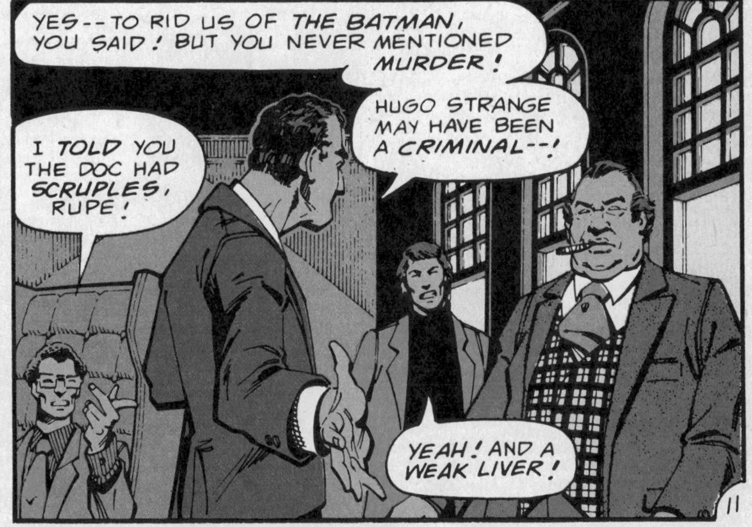

WH-WHAT--?
YOU HAVEN'T BEEN ON THE COUNCIL FOR VERY LONG, DOCTOR! I SUPPOSE I SHOULD HAVE STARTED WORRYING...
...WHEN PHOSPHORUS SPOOKED YOU SO EASY! *
*DETECTIVE #469!--JULIE

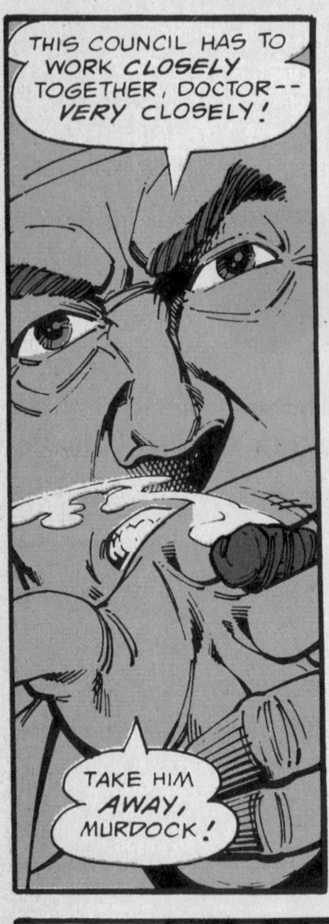

THIS COUNCIL HAS TO WORK CLOSELY TOGETHER, DOCTOR--VERY CLOSELY!
TAKE HIM AWAY, MURDOCK!

BUT THEN, SUDDENLY...
GO ON--TAKE HIM, THORNE! TAKE HIM AS YOU TOOK ME!
BUT SOON--I SHALL TAKE YOU!
WHA--? WHAT--?!?

SOMETHING THE MATTER, RUPE?

YOU--YOU DIDN'T SEE--
--ANYTHING?
SEE ANYTHING? WHATTA YOU MEAN?

I THOUGHT--I MEAN--
--FORGET IT! WHAT ARE YOU ALL GAWKING AT?

EANWHILE, BACK AT THE BATMAN--

A BATTLE OF WITS--

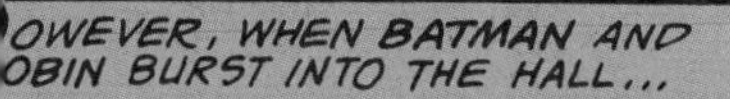

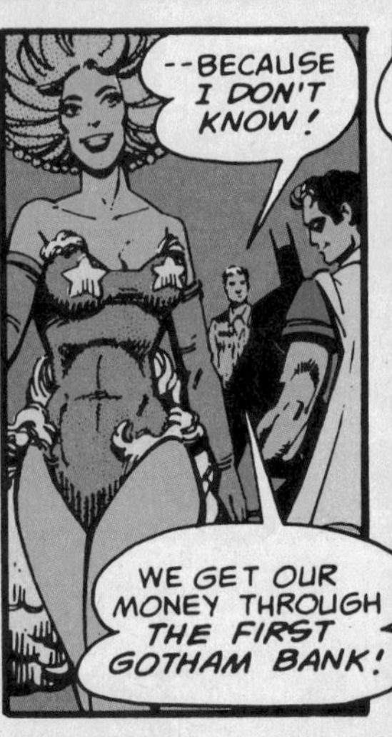

THINK YOU'VE GOT THE ANSWER, FRIENDS? THEN PLAY ALONG WITH US A FEW MOMENTS LONGER, AS WE SHIFT TO THE FOLLOWING EVENING...

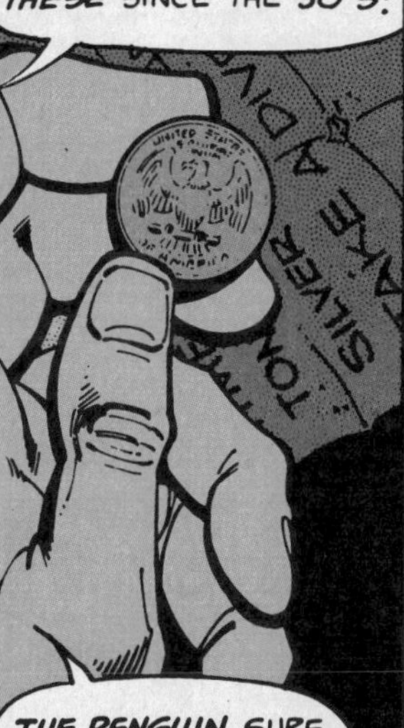

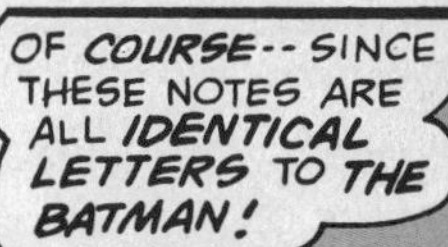

BATMAN,
WE NEED STALL NO LONGER!
TIME IS ON THE WING!
TONIGHT I SHALL LIFT THE
SILVER BIRD--AND YOU WILL
TAKE A DIVE!
DISRESPECTFULLY
YOURS,
The Penguin

GOTHAM INTERNATIONAL AIRPORT--
SKREEE

THE BATMAN!
SKREEEEEEE
GET AWAY FROM THE PLANE! WE'RE ABOUT TO TAKE OFF!
BUT THE DARK KNIGHT MAKES NO REPLY!

HE SPRINTS UP THE STAIRWAY--
--DUCKS PAST THE STEWS--

--AND POUNDS PURPOSEFULLY THROUGH THE CLUSTERED CABIN--

--UNTIL HE REACHES THE COCKPIT!
GOOD LORD! THE WORD'S OUT ON THE BATMAN!
HE'S HIJACKING THE PLANE!
WRONG!

HE IS!
AWRRK!
THE PENGUIN!
YOU WERE RIGHT--
--BUT--
--I DON'T GET IT!
I WAS SO SURE HE WAS AFTER THE MALAY STATUE!

THAT'S WHAT WE WERE SUPPOSED TO THINK, ROBIN! IE SPARED NO EXPENSE TO FOCUS OUR ATTENTION ON THAT BIRD--
-- BACKING THE MUSICAL, AS YOU SURMISED--
--LURKING AROUND IE THEATER UNTIL E SPOTTED HIM -- ALL OF THAT!
E HAD ME FOOLED, O -- FOR A WHILE!

BUT THOUGH THE PENGUIN PLAYS GAMES, HE ALWAYS PLAYS FAIR! THINK OF THE WORDS HE USED WHENEVER HE SENT US A MESSAGE-- OUT OF THEIR CONTEXT!
"PITCH," "ROLL," "BANK"--AND THEN "STALL," "WING," "LIFT," AND "DIVE"!
OF COURSE...!
THEY'RE ALL FLIGHT WORDS!
AND THERE WAS NOTHING ABOUT THE MALAY STATUE INVOLVING FLIGHT--NOT EVEN THE BIRD ITSELF, BECAUSE PENGUINS CAN'T FLY--
--UNLESS THEY STEAL A "SILVER BIRD" CALLED AN AIRPLANE!

N AS THE SECOND E CAME, I REALIZED EN DECOYED--AND AIRPLANE I KNEW WORTH HIJACKING S ONE--FILLED WITH MEMBERS OF THE SECURITIES EXCHANGE, ON THEIR WAY TO PARIS!
INCREDIBLE! WHAT A PLAN!
AND YET-- IT SEEMS HARD TO IMAGINE THE PENGUIN PASSING UP THE MALAY BIRD!

WHO SAID ANYTHING ABOUT PASSING IT UP, TWERP?
I STOLE IT TWO WEEKS AGO, BEFORE IT EVEN GOT TO THIS COUNTRY!
THE ONE IN THE GALLERY IS A FAKE!

COME ON, PENGUIN! YOU'RE GOING BACK TO YOUR CAGE!
INCREDIBLE! I'M OUT ON MY OWN...
...MAKING MY OWN WAY IN THE WORLD, AND NOT DOING A BAD JOB OF IT, EITHER...
...BUT WHEN IT COMES TO THE BATMAN, I'VE GOT A LONG WAY TO GO!
Fin

MEOW-DO-YOU-DO? ALTHOUGH THE BATMAN CAUSED CAT-ASTROPHE TO MY LATEST PLANS, HE CAN NEVER KEEP THE PRINCESS OF PLUNDER LOCKED UP PURR-MANENTLY! JUST THINK OF ALL THE TIMES HE'S FACED THE CLAWS OF...
The CATWOMAN!
MY REAL NAME IS SELINA KYLE, BUT IN MY FIRST ENCOUNTER WITH THE BATMAN (BATMAN #1; SPRING, 1940) I WAS KNOWN ONLY AS THE CAT!
I FIRST WORE A COSTUME IN BATMAN #3; FALL, 1940. IT DID HIDE MY LOVELY FACE, THOUGH!
I THINK I IMPROVED ON IT A BIT WITH THIS "BLACK CAT" OUTFIT FROM BATMAN #10; APRIL-MAY, 1942.
BY THE MID-1940'S, I'D SWITCHED TO SOMETHING MORE ATTRACTIVE... WHICH I WORE FOR SEVERAL YEARS! THIS SHOT IS FROM BATMAN #84; JUNE, 1954!
BUT TIMES CHANGE... AND SO DID MY COSTUME! THIS ONE FROM BATMAN #197, DEC., 1967... SOMEWHAT RESEMBLED THE ONE JULIE NEWMAR WORE WHEN SHE PORTRAYED ME ON TELEVISION!
FINALLY IN BATMAN #210; MARCH, 1969, I FIRST DONNED THE FETCHING FELINE OUTFIT I NOW WEAR! TELL ME... WHICH DO YOU THINK MAKES ME LOOK MY BEST?

GOTHAM CITY FIRST METHODIST CHURCH, JULY 6, 8:45 P.M....
...AND DO YOU, SELINA KYLE, TAKE THIS MAN, BRUCE WAYNE, TO BE YOUR LAWFULLY WEDDED HUSBAND?
I DO... OH, *YES*, I DO!

I NOW PRONOUNCE YOU MAN AND WIFE... YOU MAY KISS THE BRIDE.
DARLING...
BRUCE DEAREST... *choke* I-I'VE NEVER BEEN AS HAPPY AS I AM AT THIS MOMENT!

BRAVO! AT LAST!
CONGRATULATIONS, YOU TWO!
THOUGHT IT WOULD NEVER HAPPEN!
HOORAY!

YOU'RE A LUCKY MAN, BRUCE!
DON'T I KNOW IT!
AND I'M GOING TO EXERCISE AN ANCIENT PRIVILEGE...
...AND *KISS* THE NEW BRIDE!

TERROR TRAIN!

NNOOOOOOOO EEEEEEEEEEEE!

POW POW! BLAM!

..NO!! =Gasp!=

GOTHAM CITY AMTRAK, FIFTY MILES DUE WEST, JULY 6, 8:45 P.M. ...

BRUCE JONES, STORY
TREVOR VON EEDEN & PABLO MARCOS, ART
TODD KLEIN, LETTERS
HELEN VESIK COLORS
DICK GIORDANO, EDITOR

YES? I--
YOU'LL PLEASE COME WITH ME, MISS KYLE... QUIETLY...
SAY, WHAT IS THIS? WHO ARE YOU?
YOU PICKED A BAD TIME FOR THIS, BUSTER... I JUST LEFT THE MAN I LOVE AT A TRAIN STATION IN GOTHAM CITY--PERHAPS FOREVER--
--AND I'M NOT IN THE MOOD FOR THIS...
...NOT IN THE MOOD AT ALL!
WAUGH!
NOW SUPPOSE WE FIND OUT JUST WHO YOU ARE...
...WHERE YOU UGH! COME FROM!
...AND WHAT YOU WANT.
YOU CAN START WITH ANY OF THE ABOVE!
BUT WITHOUT WARNING, THE COMPARTMENT DOOR OPENS BEHIND SELINA...
WHA--
3.

AH, CATWOMAN, AT LAST! GLAD YOU COULD MAKE IT!
PLEASE...ER... HAVE A SEAT...
THE NAME'S =UMPHH= SELINA KYLE...
YES, OF COURSE, FORGIVE ME, AND FORGIVE THE WAY I HAD YOU BROUGHT HERE. WE WEREN'T CERTAIN YOU'D...AH...COOPERATE.
THUD

I'M DETECTIVE SERGEANT RICHARD STUART, MISS KYLE, I--
I'M CLEAN, SERGEANT.
EH? YES, OF COURSE. WE KNOW THAT. THIS ISN'T AN ARREST, MISS KYLE... IT'S MORE LIKE A... PROPOSAL.

HENRY?
HAVE A LOOK AT THIS, MISS KYLE...

THE VANISHING TRAINS CASE... YES, I'VE HEARD OF IT.
THERE'S BEEN A THIRD DISAPPEARANCE?
NOT YET. BUT AMTRAK 419 IS SCHEDULED TO RUN TOMORROW AT TWELVE NOON: DESTINATION, CHICAGO. WE WANT TO BE SURE IT DOESN'T SHARE THE SAME FATE AS 417 AND 418.
AND YOU WANT MY HELP?
2ND PASSENGER TRAIN VANISHES! POLICE AND FBI BAFFLED!
WE WANT THE BEST, CATWO--UH, MISS KYLE. YOU'RE THE BEST.

I'M FLATTERED.
SO WHAT WOULD YOU HAVE ME DO?
HERE'S A MAP OF THE AREA THE TRAINS COVER--OR ARE SUPPOSED TO COVER. AS YOU KNOW, THE LAST TWO VANISHED COMPLETELY SOMEWHERE BETWEEN GOTHAM AND CHICAGO, ILLINOIS...ONLY TO TURN UP FIVE DAYS LATER, INTACT, ALL PASSENGERS ACCOUNTED FOR...

WHAT DID THE PASSENGERS SAY?
VARYING REPORTS: SOME CLAIMED TO HAVE SEEN 'GHOSTS' OR 'DEMONS', MOST COMPLAINED OF MEMORY LOSS...
...BUT ALL AGREED THAT AT SOME POINT ALL THE LIGHTS WENT OUT, FOLLOWED BY A LENGTHY PERIOD OF BLACKNESS.

HMM. ANY TUNNELS ALONG THE WAY WHERE A TRAIN MIGHT BE SIDETRACKED?
ONLY ONE, BUT IT'S NOT LONG ENOUGH TO HIDE A THIRTY-SIX CAR TRAIN IN.
WE'VE CHECKED OVER EVERY INCH OF THAT TRACK, HAD GUARDS POSTED EVERY OTHER MILE. FRANKLY, WE'RE STUMPED!
PETE, THAT FILM READY?

"THERE'S THAT TUNNEL I MENTIONED. AS YOU CAN SEE, THE ENGINE IS WELL OUT OF THE OTHER SIDE BEFORE THE CABOOSE IS EVEN NEAR THE ENTRANCE..."

"NOW WATCH THIS AND GET READY FOR A JOLT!"

"I-IT'S FADING...FADING INTO THIN AIR!"

"UM-M-M...AND IT'S *NOT* TRICK PHOTOGRAPHY!"

5.

OKAY, SERGEANT, I'LL TAKE YOUR CASE! I'LL GET MY COSTUME OUT OF MOTHBALLS!
GREAT! HOW CAN WE HELP YOU?
GET ME RECORDS OF ALL THREE TRAINS DATING BACK TO THE DAY THEY WERE BUILT. AND AFTER THAT--

--GET ME A TICKET ON BOARD THE 419!

TIME: 2:25 P.M.
PLACE: AMTRAK RAILROAD CAR FIFTY MILES OUTSIDE OF GOTHAM.
TRAIN: THE 419.
SO FAR, SO QUIET...

ACCORDING TO THESE BLUEPRINTS AND DATA THAT DETECTIVE STUART GAVE ME, SOME OF THESE CARS WERE BUILT DURING THE SECOND WORLD WAR AND WERE REFURBISHED FOR PRESENT DAY USE BY AMTRAK.
9
HERE COMES THAT TUNNEL STUART SHOWED ME IN THE MOVIE...
THE LAST TRAIN DISAPPEARED SHORTLY AFTER EMERGING FROM THE OTHER SIDE.

WOW! BLACK AS PITCH IN HERE! CAN'T SEE M HAND BEFORE MY--
HEY! SHOULDN'T I BE SEEING THE TUNNEL EXIT BY NOW?
SOMETHING SCREWY GOING ON HERE...

WHAT IN BLAZES! A GRAVEYARD! WE'RE MOVING THROUGH A GRAVEYARD!
HAHAHAHAAAAA
AHAHAH
HA
HAHA
EEEEEE
EE
HAHAHAHAHA HA HA HA HA HA
GHOSTS! MOMMY, I'M SCARED!
AH AH AH AH AH
HA HA HA
WHAT TH--
IDN'T NYONE ER TELL YOU SN'T POLITE FRIGHTEN HILDREN-- OOF!
MY HAND WENT RIGHT THROUGH HIM!
HA HA HA HA HA HA
WELCOME ABOARD THE PHANTOM EXPRESS, CATWOMAN! IT'S A SHAME...
THAT VOICE ...FAMILIAR SOME-HOW...
...SO SOON!
...YOU HAVE TO LEAVE US...
AGH!
WEAKNESS SEEPING INTO MY VEINS... O STRENGTH... C-CAN'T FIGHT IT...
HA HA HA HA HA HA HA HA HA HA HA HA HA HA HA HA HA HA HA HA HA HA
NEXT: IN THE LAND OF THE DEAD!
7

THE TRAINS WERE DISAPPEARING ONE BY ONE, FIRST THE AMTRAK 417, THEN THE 418; ENGI
CARS, CABOOSE, THE ENTIRE TRAIN, JUST VANISHED INTO THIN AIR SOMEWHERE BETWEEN G
AND CHICAGO. THE POLICE WERE STYMIED. THE FBI WAS IN A TAILSPIN. THE PUBLIC WAS
PANICKED, EVEN THOUGH BOTH TRAINS AND PASSENGERS HAD EVENTUALLY SHOWN UP AT
CHICAGO DESTINATION INTACT, UNHARMED. NOTHING HAD BEEN STOLEN, NOTHING HAD BEEN
SMUGGLED INTO THE WINDY CITY.

BUT PASSENGERS HAD CLAIMED TO HAVE SEEN "GHOSTS" ABOARD BOTH TRAINS, AND M
HAD COMPLAINED OF LOSS OF MEMORY. WHAT **WAS** HAPPENING? WAS THE RAILWAY RE
"HAUNTED"? CATWOMAN DIDN'T THINK SO. SHE HAD VOLUNTEERED TO RIDE THE 419 AND
GET TO THE BOTTOM OF THIS. BUT SHE GOT TO THE BOTTOM OF SOMETHING FAR DEEPE

In the Land of the DEAD

DERGROUND YARD! THAT'S 20! SO THE R TRAINS E HIJACKED!
BUT WHY? AND BY WHOM?

ONE WAY TO FIND OUT!
WHOK
UH!

ER, LYLE! F--AGGH!
NICE CATCH, LYLE!
UUULMPH!
LET'S SURROUND HER, PETE...
S'MATTER, LYLE? LOSE YOUR GUN?
CHUFF!
REALLY, BOYS, YOU'RE MAKING THIS *FAR* TOO EASY!
PERHAPS *I* CAN EVEN THE ODDS A BIT!
WH...?

AGHH!
NICE WEAPON, THIS CAT-O'-NINE-TAILS OF YOURS--
--I'LL SEE IF I CAN'T MAKE IT STANDARD ISSUE ON THE FORCE!
SERGEANT STUART! SO YOU'RE THE BRAINS BEHIND ALL THIS! IT FIGURES!
PERHAPS YOU'D CARE TO PROVIDE ME WITH SOME DETAILS
MY PLEASURE. YOUR TRAIN, THE 419, ALREADY WENT AHEAD TO CHICAGO WITHOUT YOU! AND TWENTY EYEWITNESSES SWEAR THEY SAW YOU HANGED!
YOU SEE, YOU REALLY ARE DEAD!
CUTE, STUART, CUTE. BUT GET TO THE BOTTOM LINE. WHY?
"IN 1945, DURING WORLD WAR II, THERE EXISTED A CLEVER, CUNNING, BRILLIANT MAN WHO WAS ALSO A SPY FOR THE GERMAN GOVERNMENT.
HE WAS KNOWN AS THE "JEWELER" BECAUSE HE STOLE SECRET FORMULAS FROM THE AMERICANS AND TRANSCRIBED THEM, IN CODE, ONTO THE FACES OF DIAMONDS SO THAT THEY COULD NEVER BE DESTROYED.. THAT MAN WAS MY FATHER.
"TOWARD THE END OF THE WAR, H CAME BY A FORMULA THAT WOULD ASSURE GERMANY'S VICTORY, THE FORMULA FOR MAKING A HYDROGEN BOMB HE INSCRIBED IT ONTO THE FACE OF A CAT'S-EYE DIAMOND...BUT BEFORE HE COULD LEAVE THE COUNTRY, HE REALIZE THAT HE WAS BEING FOLLOWED...
"HE DUCKED INTO A SMALL PET SHOP AND SURREPTITIOUSLY TAPED THE DIAMOND TO THE INSIDE OF THE COLLAR OF A BEAUTIFUL PERSIAN CAT...
"JUST OUTSIDE THE PET SHOP, HE WAS PICKED UP BY THE FBI...
...BUT SINCE HE WAS CLEAN, TWENTY-FOUR HOURS LATER HE WAS RELEASED..."
3

E RETURNED IMMEDIATELY
O THE PET STORE. THERE HE
OUND A SIGN POSTED ON
HE DOOR--
GONE TO CHICAGO FOR CAT SHOW
"AS HE LEFT THE SHOP, HE SAW THE PROPRIETOR HEADING TOWARD THE TRAIN STATION, AN ANIMAL CAGE BENEATH HIS ARM!...
..THE PERSIAN CAT WAS GONE!
"MY FATHER FOLLOWED HIM TO THE STATION, BOARDED, WAITED UNTIL THE MAN WAS NAPPING, THEN STOLE THE CAT. THE MAN AWOKE AND GAVE CHASE. MY FATHER ATTEMPTED TO ESCAPE BETWEEN THE MOVING CARS..."
SIL
SHORT FIGHT ENSUED ATOP ONE
F THE CARS, DURING WHICH MY
ATHER WAS KNOCKED OVER THE
DGE TO HIS DEATH!
"THE MAN WHO KILLED HIM, SELINA KYLE, WAS YOUR FATHER!"
NOTHING WAS FOUND ON MY FATHER'S BODY, NO ID, NO MONEY, NO DIAMOND! THE NEXT WEEK GERMANY FELL TO THE ALLIES. MY FATHER HAD DIED IN DISGRACE IN THE EYES OF HIS COUNTRYMEN! I EMIGRATED TO AMERICA AS A BOY. MY WHOLE LIFE HAS BEEN DEDICATED TO AVENGING MY FATHER!
BEGAN AN ATTEMPT TO RECOVER THE
AMOND, KNOWING MY FATHER'S PROPENSITY FOR
HIDING THE INSCRIBED JEWEL DURING DANGER AND
COMING BACK LATER TO RECOVER IT.
FIRST I TOOK A JOB ON THE RAILROAD, THINKING I COULD SEARCH THE TRAIN HE'D TRAVELED ON...
BUT THEN I DISCOVERED THAT THAT TRAIN HAD BEEN DISASSEMBLED AND THE CARS FROM IT USED ON THE FOUR SEPARATE AMTRAK TRAINS THAT RUN THE CHICAGO ROUTE TODAY. SO I JOINED THE GOTHAM POLICE FORCE. MY PLANS WERE SIMPLY TO "KIDNAP" EACH TRAIN, ONE AT A TIME...
NATURALLY, AS DETECTIVE SERGEANT STUART, I MADE SURE I WAS ASSIGNED TO THE CASE OF THE "VANISHING TRAINS"...
I WOULD THEN CHECK EACH CAR THOROUGHLY AND SEND IT ON ITS WAY, PASSENGERS UNHARMED, NOTHING SEEMINGLY STOLEN!
I'M STILL WAITING...
HM...?
4

AH YES! HOW DID I MAKE THE TRAINS "VANISH" INTO THIN AIR?
IT ISN'T HARD, REALLY, WHEN YOU KNOW HOW!
SO QUIT GLOATING AND TELL ME!
1 "THE SECRET IS IN THAT SMALL TUNNEL I SHOWED YOU IN THE FILM.
REAL TRAIN
TUNNEL
HOLOGRAPH TRAIN
Amtrak
2 "FOR AS THE REAL TRAIN ENTERS THE TUNNEL MOUTH, IT'S IMMEDIATELY SIDE-TRACKED INTO AN UNDERGROUND PASSAGE..."
REAL TRAIN
Amtrak
3 "THE TRAIN SEEN EXITING THE TUNNEL IS A HOLOGRAPHIC PROJECTION TURNED TO THE SAME SPEED AS THE REAL TRAIN. A REAL TRAIN ENTERS, A "GHOST" TRAIN EXITS!
WHEN THE HOLOGRAPH IS TURNED OFF, THE TRAIN APPEARS TO VANISH!
I SEE. CLEVER. AND THE "GHOSTS" ON BOARD ARE HOLOGRAPHS TOO?
EXACTLY, AS ARE THE TOMBSTONES OUTSIDE THE TRAIN WINDOW. OH, AND ALSO THE "NOOSE" THAT "HANGED" YOU!
UH-HUH... AND HOW EXACTLY WAS I STRANGLED?
NERVE GAS, THE SAME AS THE PASSENGERS. SO ABOUT THE HEAD AND SLIGHT MEMORY LOSS, BUT DO HAVE TO OUR LITTLE TRACKS.
AND NOW I'LL BID YOU ADIEU SELINA KYLE...
WAIT A MINUTE! WHERE DO I FIT IN?
YOUR DEATH WILL AVENGE MY FATHER'S HONOR. AS DETECTIVE STUART I WAS ABLE TO CONVINCE THE COMMISSIONER THAT I SHOULD RIDE THIS LAST TRAIN, THE 420, ALONE. I WILL NOW SEARCH THE REMAINING CARS, FIND THE DIAMOND, AND RETURN THE TRAIN TO CHICAGO, PRETENDING THAT, LIKE THE OTHER PASSENGERS, I SAW ONLY GHOSTS...
AFTER THAT, I'LL TAKE THE DIAMOND ITS FORMULA TO GERMANY, WHERE MY FATHER'S NAME WILL BE VINDICATED. GERMANY WILL RISE ONCE AGAIN THE FOURTH REICH!'

LL, SELINA, OLD GIRL, YOU DO GET MIXED UP
TH SOME GOOFBALLS! AND IF YOU DON'T GET
TIED FROM HERE BY THE TIME STUART FINDS
AT DIAMOND, HE'S NOT GOING TO BE THE
LY ONE WITH A SPLIT PERSONALITY!

TWO HOURS LATER...

I FOUND IT! I FOUND IT! START THE TRAIN! WE LEAVE IMMEDIATELY!

AND AS THE 420 ROARS DOWN THE TRACK...

FAREWELL, MISS KYLE! SORRY YOU WERE TOO TIED UP TO JOIN US IN CHICAGO!

(HEH-HEH!) THE WHEELS PASSED RIGHT OVER HER! GOODBYE, CATWOMAN! HELLO, GERMANY...

--A BRILLIANT, NEW, POWERFUL GERMANY!

B-BUT THE TRAIN! I-I SAW IT CRUSH YOU!

COME NOW, YOU DON'T THINK YOU'RE THE ONLY ONE CAPABLE OF MAKING A HOLOGRAPHIC IMAGE, DO YOU? I HAD PLENTY OF TIME TO RIG YOUR VIDEO CAMERAS WHILE YOU SEARCHED FOR YOUR PRECIOUS DIAMOND...

THE 420 ROARS OUT OF STUART'S SECRET UNDERGROUND PASSAGE INTO THE DAY-LIGHT...
Amtrak
GIVE IT UP, STUART. YOU CAN'T ESCAPE, THERE'S NOWHERE TO GO...
SUDDENLY...
MY GOD! ANOTHER TRAIN COMING FROM THE OPPOSITE DIRECTION! WE'LL BE KILLED!
YOU IDIOT! YOU'VE SHUNTED US ONTO THE WRONG TRACK!
NO! NO! I CAN'T DIE! NOT NOW!
STUART, DON'T! WAIT!
AS THE 420 FLIES BY THE SWITCH, CATWOMAN'S CAT-O'-NINE-TAILS LASHES OUT AND--
IF I CAN PUT THAT OTHER TRAIN ON THE TRACK NEXT TO US...
THE SWITCH IS MADE... BUT THE APPROACHING TRAIN FINDS A NEW TARGET...
MY LEG! BROKEN IN THE FALL!
C-CAN'T MOVE!
NOOOOOOOOO!
FAREWELL, STUART...
...AND THANKS, DAD, FOR SAVING THE WORLD THE FIRST TIME... I'M GLAD I COULD REPAY THE FAVOR!
7

THERE ARE OTHER CREATURES WHO STALK THE GOTHAM NIGHT THAN THE DREADED..
BATMAN
ONE SUCH CREATURE IS THE WOMAN WHO WAS BORN SELINA KYLE.
NEVER SCRATCH A CAT
DAMN HER.
GERRY CONWAY WRITER * DON NEWTON + AFREDO ALCALA ARTISTS
BEN ODA LETTERER ADRIENNE COLORIST * LEN WEIN EDITOR
J-8433

GRROWWWMM?
MY SENTIMEN EXACTL DIABLO

DOES SHE TAKE ME FOR A FOOL?
I GAVE HER FAIR WARNING TO LEAVE MY MAN ALONE, BUT DID SHE LISTEN?

RRIPPPPP
SHE DID NOT!
HISSSSSSSSS

THAT, MS. VALE, WAS A VER SERIOUS MISTAKE.
ONE YOU SOON WILL COME TO REGRET.

I'VE FINALLY FIGURED OUT JUST WHAT IT IS I LIKE ABOUT YOU, BRUCE.
YOU MAKE ME LAUGH.
THIS MORNING AT BREAKFAST, I FELT AS IF MY WHOLE WORLD WERE COLLAPSING*--
*SEE LAST MONTH'S DETECTIVE FOR DETAILS. --Len.

UT AFTER A DAY WITH YOU RKING AROUND NEW ENGLAND, FEEL SIXTEEN AGAIN.
HAT'S YOUR CRET, MR. AYNE?
I'M RICH.
RICH PEOPLE DON'T TAKE ANYTHING SERIOUSLY.
HA.

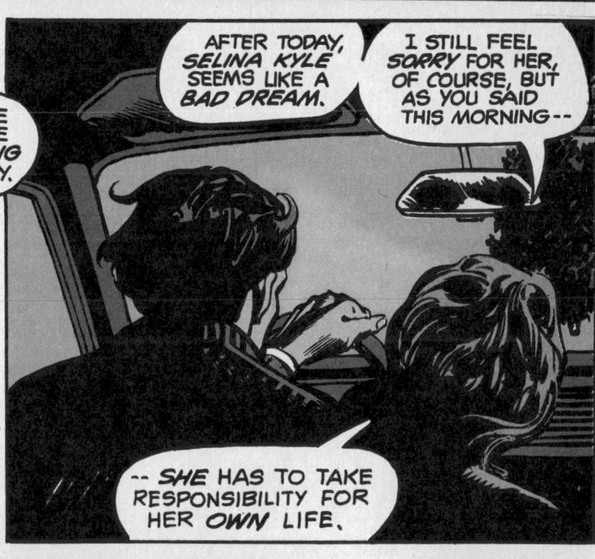
AFTER TODAY, SELINA KYLE SEEMS LIKE A BAD DREAM.
I STILL FEEL SORRY FOR HER, OF COURSE, BUT AS YOU SAID THIS MORNING--
-- SHE HAS TO TAKE RESPONSIBILITY FOR HER OWN LIFE.

AT'S WHAT I D... BUT IS T REALLY T I FEEL?
OVED SELINA... D HER LEAVING T ME DEEPLY.
BUT SHE DID LEAVE--BY HER OWN CHOICE-- AND NOW VICKI AND I HAVE--

EH?
VVVRRROOOOMM
"SELINA!"
3

IT LUNGES FROM THE NIGHT LIKE SOME GREAT BRIGHT-EYED PANTHER, ITS ODDLY OLD-FASHIONED DESIGN HIDING A HIGH-POWERED ENGINE THAT SNARLS WITH ALMOST ANIMALISTIC HUNGER...
BRUCE, THAT CAR--
RRRROAARR
IT'S HER, VICKI!
HANG ON WHILE I TRY TO--
A WET ROAD, A PATCH OF OIL ON THE TARRED SURFACE:
SCREEEEEECH
THE CAR SKIDS, WHEEL LOOSE AND OUT OF CONTROL--
KRASH!

SPWHOOM!
SINKING FAST-- SHORE MUST DROP OFF HERE -- LIKE A CLIFF!
CRASH KNOCKED VICKI OUT! HAVE TO GET HER TO THE SURFACE!
DAMN HER--
DAMN CATWOMAN!
RROWWRRR
BRUCE...
OH, PLEASE, NO!
FORGIVE ME...
MMMROWWRRR
5

DOOR *JAMMED*--!

HAVE TO PULL VICKI THROUGH THE *WINDOW!*

CAN'T HOLD MY *BREATH* MUCH *LONGER*--HARD TO *FOCUS*--!

WHAT--?

CATWOMAN!

NOT TAKING ANY *CHANCES*, ARE YOU?

YOU WANT TO MAKE *SURE* SHE'S FINISHED!

HOW COULD I EVER HAVE THOUGHT I *LOVED* YOU?

CAN'T BE SURE IN THIS LIGHT--
-- BUT IT LOOKS LIKE SOMEBODY'S OUT THERE!
KEEP DREAMING.
THERE'LL BE NOTHING DOWN THERE BUT SCRAP-- HUH?
WE SAW YOU CRASH-- ED THOUGHT NOBODY COULD MAKE IT THROUGH A WRECK LIKE THAT, BUT ME--
HEY, DON'T SAY THERE'S SOMEBODY ELSE STILL DOWN THERE--?
SHUT UP AND GET THIS KID TO THE TRUCK.
SHE LOOKS LOUSY--!
JEEPERS!
OVER HERE, MISTER!
RRRRRRRRRRRR
7

GOTHAM GENERAL HOSPITAL:
NOON.
HI, STRANGER.
HAVE A GOOD REST?
BRUCE...
I FEEL LIKE I'VE SLEPT FOR HOURS.
MAKE THAT TWO DAYS.
TWO--? BRUCE, THIS IS A HOSPITAL...
WHAT HAPPENED TO ME?
A MILD CONCUSSION... BUT YOU'RE GOING TO BE FINE.
REMEMBER ANYTHING ABOUT THE CRASH--?
ALL I REMEMBER IS DREAMING I WAS ASLEEP... AND THAT YOU WERE WITH ME, BESIDE ME...
YOU WERE, WEREN'T YOU?
BRUCE NODS, BUT VICKI IS ALREADY ASLEEP ONCE MORE...
TISSUE
OUTSIDE IN THE HALL, THREE FRIENDS STAND WAITING ANXIOUSLY, AND EACH RELAXES VISIBLY AT THE SIGHT OF WAYNE'S EXPRESSION...
SHE'S ALL RIGHT-- THANK GOD.
ANY WORD ABOUT CATWOMAN?
WE DID AS YOU ASKED, BRUCE. BARD AND GORDON, INVESTIGATIONS HAS HANDLED THIS ALONE, NOT REPORTING IT TO THE POLICE.
WE'VE HAD HER APARTMENT STAKED OUT FOR FORTY-EIGHT HOURS... BARBARA IS THERE NOW...
...BUT SO FAR SELINA HASN'T APPEARED.
ALL THAT MEANS IS SHE HASN'T GONE IN OR OUT.
SHE COULD BE HOLED UP INSIDE.
BRUCE, I HAVE TO KNOW--
JUST WHAT ARE YOU PLANNING?
YOU'RE WASTING YOUR TIME, JASON.
TAKE IT FROM AN OLD EX-COMMISSIONER OF POLICE--BRUCE CA STONEWALL WITH TH BEST OF THEM.

ADVICE--
THIS
I'VE BEEN A DETECTIVE FOR YEARS, SINCE 'NAM, AND I KNOW--
ANY OTHER NEWS, JASON?
BOSS THORNE-- INDICTED FOR POLICE COMMISSIONER PAULING'S MURDER.*
GENTLEMEN, I FEEL BETTER ALREADY.
Gazette
OSS THORNE ARRAIGNED PD CHIEF'S
*LAST ISSUE --Len.
THAT'S NOT ALL, BRUCE.
I GOT A CALL THIS MORNING--
HIS HONOR, THE MAYOR, WANTS TO SEE ME THIS AFTERNOON.
WELL, WELL-- I CAN'T IMAGINE WHY!
AYNE NSION:
USK.
IN THE BATCAVE...
I WISH YOU'D RECONSIDER, SIR. YOU'RE STILL RECOVERING FROM YOUR GUNSHOT WOUNDS*--
AND YOU HAVEN'T HAD A REAL NIGHT'S SLEEP IN TWO DAYS.
AT LEAST LET ME COME WITH YOU, BRUCE!
*RECEIVED LAST ISSUE. --Len.
9

SORRY, DICK, BUT THIS IS PERSONAL.
BESIDES, YOU'VE BEEN HELPING ME TOO MUCH LATELY-- YOU EVEN TOOK MY PLACE TWICE IN THE PAST FEW WEEKS*--
--AND THAT CAN'T BE DOING YOUR RELATIONSHIP WITH THE TITANS ANY GOOD.
BRUCE, MY FIRST DUTY AS ROBIN IS TO YOU--
WRONG.
*SEE OUR PAST TWO ISSUES. --Len.

YOUR FIRST DUTY IS TO YOURSELF.
BE RESPONSIBLE FOR YOURSELF, DICK--

--AND ALL THE REST WILL FOLLOW.

THAT'S SOMETHING CATWOMAN MUST COME TO UNDERSTAND.
SHE'S TRIED TO MAKE VICKI AND ME RESPONSIBLE FOR HER HAPPINESS.

LIFE DOESN'T WORK THAT WAY.

C'MON, BRUCE, YOU KNOW BETTER.
WE ARE RESPONSIBLE FOR EACH OTHER.

YOU RAISED ME... TAUGHT ME HOW TO BE A MAN... TOOK RESPONSIBILITY FOR MY LIFE.
AND IT WAS GOOD FOR YOU, TOO, BRUCE.
I THINK--HAVING ME UNDERFOOT ALL THOSE YEARS--KEPT YOU SANE.
TIMES CHANGE, DICK... PEOPLE CHANGE.
ANYWAY AS I SAID--
THIS ONE IS PERSONAL.

'VE NEVER SEEN HE MASTER QUITE O COLD, YOUNG SIR.
EXCEPT WHEN HE SPEAKS OF JOE CHILL--
--THE MAN WHO MURDERED HIS PARENTS. WHEW!
SELINA AND I HAVE NEVER GOTTEN ALONG, BUT SHE'S NOT THAT BAD--NOT ANYMORE.

SOMETHING'S HAPPENING TO BRUCE, ALFRED.
IT'S BEEN SETTLING IN FOR A LONG TIME.
AND IT'S NOT GOOD.

ELINA KYLE'S APARTMENT BUILDING:
NIGHT.

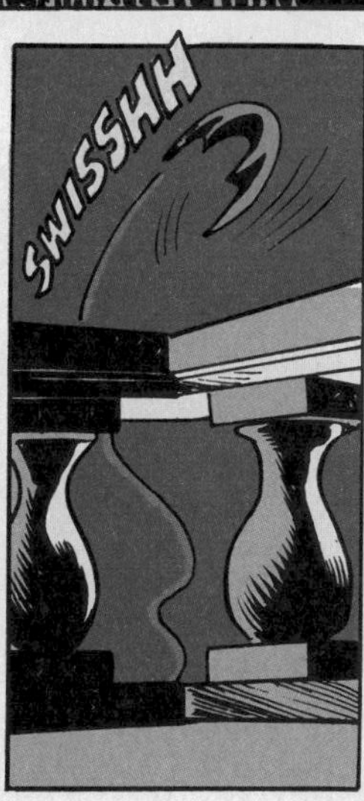
SWISSHH

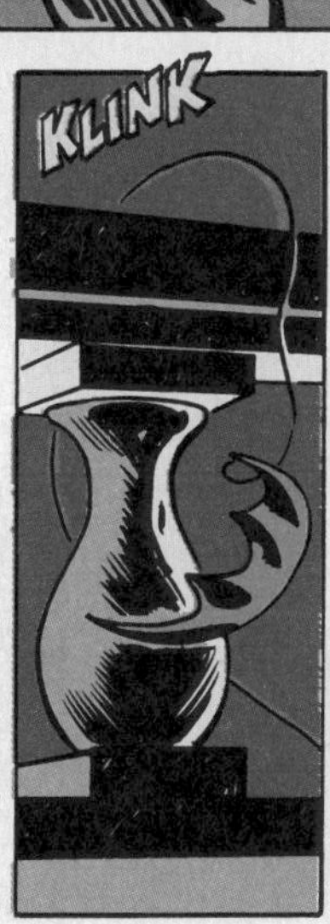
KLINK

11

GROWWR

HISSSSS

SELINA'S PANTHER!

ITS EYES-- WILD, VICIOUS!

GOING TO LEAP--

OUR HUNDRED POUNDS
F MUSCLE AND FURY
T HIM, SNARLING.

HE HAS NO CHANCE TO DODGE.

GRROWWRR

IT TAKES ALL HIS SKILL JUST TO KEEP THE PANTHER'S FANGS FROM HIS THROAT.

CRASH!

AWWWWRRR
WHAM
--THIS HURTS ME MORE THAN IT DOES YOU!

S OUT--
CONSCIOUS.
AND I FEEL LIKE A WELL-USED *SCRATCHING POST!*
CLICK
FIRST, TRYING TO KILL *VICKI,* AND NOW, *THIS*--
--LEAVING A WILD *PANTHER* LOOSE IN *YOUR APARTMENT!*
HMMM?
SELINA, WHAT'S *HAPPENED* TO YOU?
WELL, WELL...
THIS PUTS A DIFFERENT *LIGHT* ON THINGS.

BILLS ARE LIKE A DIARY.
THEY CAN REVEAL A PERSON'S SECRETS-- HIS AMBITIONS, HIS FRUSTRATIONS--

CATAMONT WAREHOUSE INC.
NOTICE:
Selina Kyle TENANT
ACCORDING TO AGREED UPON TERMS, RENT PAID IN FULL ON SIX MONTHS LEASE.
--HIS PAST, AND HIS FUTURE.
JACKPOT.

GOTHAM CITY HALL...
I'M GOING TO ENJOY THIS.

I HAVEN'T HAD A GOOD PIPE IN SIX MONTHS, SINCE HILL UP THERE FIRED ME...
THEY ALL TASTED BITTER, SOMEHOW.
BUT I'LL TELL YOU SOMETHING, BARBARA... JASON...
...THIS ONE TASTES SWEET.

DAD'S FINALLY HIMSELF AGAIN, JASON.
THANK YOU.
ALL HE NEEDED WAS A NUDGE--
--AND A CAUSE.

BARBARA, THORNE KILLED A MAN BEFORE WITNESSES--
AND NOT JUST ANYONE... HE SHOT HIS OWN HAND-PICKED POLICE COMMISSIONER!
NOT ONLY THAT--

--YOUR FATHER AND I HAVE FOUND STRONG EVIDENCE LINKING THORNE TO HAMILTON HILL'S MAYORAL CAMPAIGN.
WE HAD THE BATMAN'S HELP, BUT IT WAS JIM GORDON WHO KEPT PUSHING TILL WE LEARNED THE TRUTH.
NOW HILL WANTS TO SEE HIM...
WHAT I WOULDN'T GIVE TO SEE THAT--!
Shoes

CITY HALL, THIRD FLOOR...

I'M STILL THE MAYOR, GORDON.
IF YOU DON'T RESPECT ME, RESPECT THE OFFICE.
YES, I'VE HAD BAD NEWS...
LOOK AT THIS.

WHEN WORD GOT OUT THAT THORNE HAD HAD A PART IN YOUR CAMPAIGN, THIS WAS BOUND TO HAPPEN.

DAMN IT, MAN, A RECALL ELECTION WILL TEAR THIS CITY APART. I NEED TO DEFUSE IT--HERE AND NOW!
I'M HEADING INTO A ROUND OF SENSITIVE UNION NEGOTIATIONS --THERE'S A NEW BOND ISSUE THE CITY'S OFFERING TO THE MAJOR BANKS--
--AND I'M PERSONALLY SPEARHEADING THE DRIVE AGAINST THIS NEW FEDERALISM INSANITY!
SO?
17

SO? WE'RE TALKING ABOUT THIS CITY'S FUTURE, GORDON.
IF I'M IMPEACHED, THAT FOOL ARTHUR REEVES MIGHT BE ELECTED IN MY PLACE--AND WE BOTH KNOW THAT WOULD BE A DISASTER.
WHY DO YOU THINK I ACCEPTED THORNE'S HELP?
FOR THE GOOD OF GOTHAM CITY!
YOU'RE MAKING ME CRY.
MEN LIKE YOU ALWAYS THINK THEY'RE INDISPENSABL
"FOR THE GOOD OF GOTHAM CITY--"
YOU MEAN FOR THE GOOD OF HAMILTON HILL!
BUT YOU KNOW I'M RIGHT ABOUT REEVES... AND ABOUT THROWING OFF THIS RECALL DRIVE.
YES, DAMN YOU...
WELCOME BACK... COMMISSIONER GORDON!
TWILIGHT, ON GOTHAM'S WEST SIDE...
CATAMONT
WAREHOUSE
1801
SELINA NEVER COULD RESIST A PUN ON "CAT."
THIS WAREHOUSE IS WHERE SHE MUST HAVE KEPT HER CATILLAC WHILE SHE WAS OUT OF GOTHAM...
...ALL THOSE MONTHS, AFTER SHE LEFT ME.

SAFE BET I'LL FIND ER *HERE*...

SKRITCH

... SHE HAS *NOWHERE ELSE* TO GO.

AND WHOSE FAULT IS *THAT*?

HERS-- OR MINE?

HISSSS

WHAM!

SELINA!

19

SHE'S THE ONLY ONE YOU CARE ABOUT!
YOU WANT TO SEND ME TO JAIL-- GET RID OF ME--
--SO YOU CAN BE WITH HER!
CRATES TO THE SIDE--!
HAVE TO TWIST-- LAND ON THEM TO BREAK MY FALL--
--AND PRAY THEY'RE NOT FILLED WITH MACHINERY!
SKARUNCH!
UNNHHH!

IS THIS WHAT YOU WANT, CATWOMAN?
TO KILL ME, THE WAY YOU TRIED TO KILL VICKI VALE?
IF I WANTED HER DEAD, SHE'D BE IN A COFFIN!
I LOVED YOU--
BUT WHEN I NEEDED YOU, YOU'D FOUND SOMEONE ELSE!
ME.
ARE YOU?
CAN YOU HATE THE WAY I CAN HATE?
SWAK
TWO DAYS I'VE HID HERE--
--WANTING YOU AND HATING YOU.
AFRAID TO MOVE-- BECAUSE OF YOU!
MY LIFE IN RUINS-- BECAUSE OF YOU!
KRAK!
EVERYTHING LOST-- BECAUSE OF YOU!
AAAHHH!
21

I WANT TO KILL YOU!

KWHAM

WHAT... WAITING FOR...?

LOOKS LIKE... GOT YOUR CHANCE...

MY CLAWS ARE STEEL-TIPPED... RAZOR-SHARP.

I COULD CUT YOUR THROAT.

IT WOULD BE SO EASY.

SNIK
SNIK
SO
EASY.
MY
GOD.
NO.
BRUCE... I ALMOST KILLED YOU.
I WAS THAT CLOSE.
NOT SO CLOSE.
YOU'VE GOT A STRONG KNEE-- BUT I'VE GOT A STRONGER JAW.
YOU NEED A CATHARSIS.
LET'S JUST SAY I GAVE YOU ONE!
SO MUCH HATE.
WAS IT REAL?
AS REAL AS THE LOVE WE KNOW.
I FINALLY UNDERSTOOD THE ANGUISH YOU'VE BEEN FEELING--
--WHEN I SAW THAT YOU'D FORGOTTEN YOUR PANTHER, LOCKED AWAY ALONE FOR TWO DAYS.
IT MADE ME REALIZE THE TRUTH OF SOMETHING ROBIN SAID:
WE ARE RESPONSIBLE FOR EACH OTHER. YOU HURT ME BY LEAVING GOTHAM... I HURT YOU BY STARTING UP WITH VICKI.
LIFE CAN TAKE PEOPLE IN OPPOSITE DIRECTIONS. IT'S NOT FAIR, IT'S THE WAY THINGS ARE.
NEITHER OF US INTENDED THE HURT WE GAVE.
BUT FOR THE HURT I GAVE YOU, SELINA, I'M SORRY...
SHE NODS, HOLDING HER TEARS, KNOWING AT LAST THAT THEY'VE REACHED THE END.

From THE BATMAN'S CRIME-FILE

COBBLEPOT, OSWALD CHESTERFIELD
Alias THE PENGUIN.

SUBJECT OF THIS FILE: The PENGUIN'S

THE PENGUIN MUST ALWAYS BE CONSIDERED ARMED AND WITH MEANS OF ESCAPE AT HAND SO LONG AS HE HAS ONE OF HIS TRICK UMBRELLAS HANDY.

BANG!

IN HIS VERY FIRS
APPEARANCE
(*DETECTIVE COMIC*
#58; DEC., 1941), T
PENGUIN, MAS-
QUERADING UNDE
THE NAME OF
MR. BONIFACE,
USED UMBRELLAS
WHICH SHOT *BULLE*
KNOCKOUT GAS
AND *ACID!*

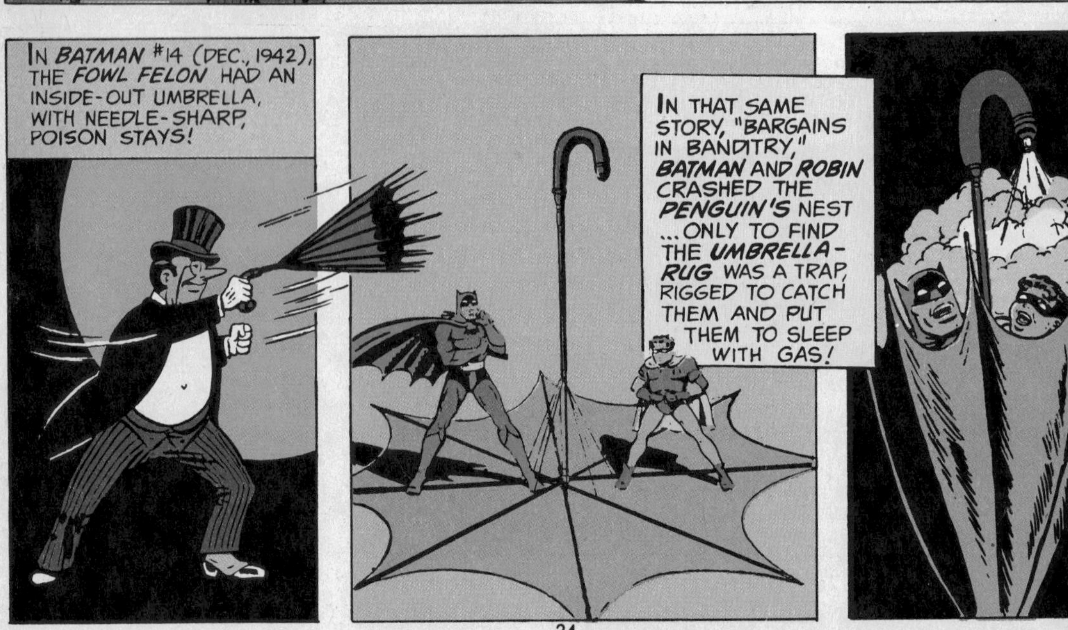

UNIQUE UMBRELLAS!

"THE THREE ECCENTRICS" (*BATMAN* #21; FEB.-MAR., 1944) GAVE THE *BEAKED BADMAN* A CHANCE TO USE HIS *REAR-VIEW UMBRELLA* TO SPOT THE PURSUING MANHUNTER!

TWO UMBRELLAS WERE INTRODUCED IN "CRIME ON THE WING" (*BATMAN* #33; FEB.-MAR., 1946). ONE TURNED UMBRELLA SILK AND RIBS INTO A WEB TO CATCH *BATMAN*...

...WHILE THE OTHER, DROPPED "ACCIDENTALLY," WAS A BOOBY-TRAP WHICH SHOT GAS AT *BATMAN* WHEN HE TRIED TO USE IT ON THE *PENGUIN*!

TRANSPORTATION? "THE PENGUIN'S NEST" (*BATMAN* #36; AUG.-SEPT., 1946) INCLUDED A *PARACHUTE-UMBRELLA* CONCEALED IN A *HAT*, AND A *POGO-STICK-UMBRELLA*!

AND THIS ONE FROM "THE PENGUIN ON PAROLE" (*BATMAN* #38; DEC.-JAN., 1946) WAS A COMBINATION *HELICOPTER* AND *TEAR-GAS GUN*!

A MORE MODERN ESCAPE-GIMMICK WAS THE *ROCKET-UMBRELLA* USED IN "PARTNERS IN PLUNDER" (*BATMAN* #169; FEB., 1965)!

HERE WE HAVE THE ULTIMATE UMBRELLA... A ROBOT-CONTROLLED MODEL THAT DID THE ROBBING FOR ITS CREATOR, WHILE HE STAYED IN HIS LAIR!

"THE PENGUIN TAKES A FLYER--INTO THE FUTURE" (*BATMAN* #190; MARCH, 1967).

LADIES AND GENTLEMEN--I *BESEECH* YOU... GIVE A REPENTANT JAILBIRD THE OPPORTUNITY TO MAKE *AMENDS!*

NO LONGER WILL I BE A BIRD OF *PREY*-- BUT A CONSTRUCTIVE OCCUPANT OF THE SOCIAL *NEST*--

SET FREE THIS CAGELING SO THAT HE MIGHT MAKE *RESTITUTION*--

57601

I AM A CHANGED MAN, FELLOW CITIZENS... FOR I HAVE FOUND THE *LOVE* OF A GOOD WOMAN!

MAX ALLAN COLLINS
STORY

NORM BREYFOGLE
ARTIST

ALBERT DEGUZMAN
LETTERER

ADRIENNE ROY
COLORIST

DENNY O'NEIL
EDITOR

THE PAROLE BOARD THANKS YOU FOR YOUR IMPASSIONED PRESENTATION, MR. COBBLEPOT-- YOU'LL BE INFORMED OF OUR DECISION SHORTLY.
THANK YOU. I SINCERELY THANK YOU.

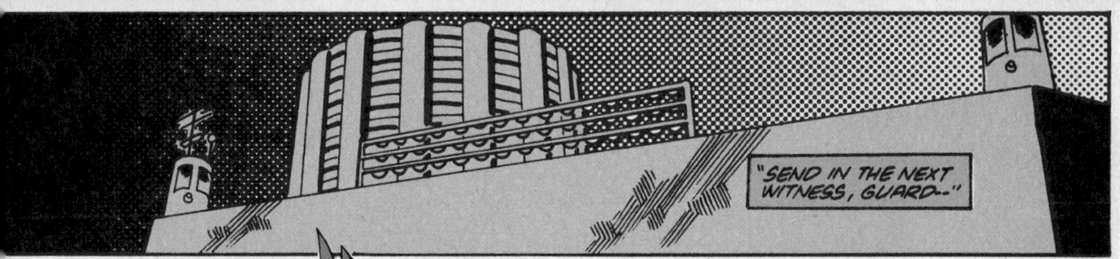
"SEND IN THE NEXT WITNESS, GUARD--"

AWK! WHAT ARE OU DOING HERE?
E COME TO ER MY INSIGHTS YOUR CHARACTER THE BOARD MBERS.
Whisper

BUT MY DEAR FELLOW, I'VE CHANGED-- WHERE ONCE A FOUL HEART ROOSTED, NOW BEATS A VIRTUAL VALENTINE OF VIRTUE!

SPARE THE BIRDSEED FOR THE PIGEONS, PENGUIN--
B-BUT...
COME ALONG, PENGUIN--YOU'RE NOT A FREE MAN YET!

AT THE REQUEST OF COMMISSIONER GORDON, WE'VE GRANTED YOUR REQUEST TO BE HEARD IN THE CASE OF OSWALD C. COBBLEPOT--

ALIAS THE PENGUIN--YES. AND THANK YOU FOR HEARING ME. NOW--

YOU SHOULD KNOW AT THE OUTSET THAT SEVERAL BOARD MEMBERS HAVE FILED PROTESTS AGAINST YOUR APPEARANCE HERE--

"PROTESTS? WHY, WITH ALL DUE RESPECT, NO ONE KNOWS THAT SCHEMING LITTLE VULTURE BETTER THAN..."

NO ONE DOUBTS YOUR FAMILIARITY WITH MR. COBBLEPOT--OR YOUR BIAS--
AREN'T YOU PEOPLE FORGETTING THE FACTS? THE PENGUIN IS NOT ONLY A MASTER THIEF, HE'S A CON MAN--DON'T LET HIM FOOL YOU!

"WHY, HE'S BEEN IN AND OUT OF GOTHAM PRISON FOR TWENTY YEARS--THAT CUSTOM PRISONER'S UNIFORM HE'S ALLOWED TO WEAR IS PRACTICALLY AN ANTIQUE!"

IF IT WERE UP TO ME...
BUT IT ISN'T. YOU HAVE NO OFFICIAL AUTHORITY. THERE ARE, IN FACT, THOSE OF US WHO VIEW YOU AS A VIGILANTE--

PERSONALLY FIND LUDICROUS THAT HAVE EVEN ALLOWED E PRESENCE OF A ASKED OUTLAW TO ULLY THE DIGNITY OF ESE PROCEEDINGS...

SLAM
THAT BAD, HUH?

WANT TO TALK ABOUT IT?
ACTION IS WHAT'S CALLED FOR. TALKING'S FOR THE BIRDS.

BUT, GEE-- WHAT IF THE PENGUIN'S REALLY REFORMED? SHOULDN'T WE GIVE HIM THE BENEFIT OF...

"ROBIN, LESSON FOR THE DAY: LEOPARDS DON'T CHANGE THEIR SPOTS; AND PENGUINS DON'T CHANGE THEIR PLUMAGE--"
OKAY, PENGIE-- YOU'RE OUTA HERE! FLY THE COOP, ALREADY!
4

AND SOON A DAPPER PAROLEE IS MAKING A SOCIAL CALL--
Candy
MY HEART FLUTTERS LIKE A FLEDGLING! COURAGE, PENGUIN, COURAGE...

OSWALD! YOUR PAROLE CAME THROUGH! WHY DIDN'T YOU SEND WORD ?!?
Candy
NO CARRIER PIGEONS ALLOWED IN STIR, MY DEAR.

DOVINA, MY DEAR--YOUR PICTURE DIDN'T DO YOU JUSTICE!
OH--OSWALD--HOW WELL I FEEL I KNOW YOU, FROM YOUR LOVELY LETTERS--

IMAGINE--WHAT BEGAN AS A SIMPLE EXCHANGE MISSIVES, HATCHED IN THE PERSONAL COLUMN OF THE ORNITHOLOGICAL NEWS...

HAS SPREAD ITS WINGS INTO... DARE I SAY IT? A ROMANCE IN FULL FLIGHT!
SAY IT, MY LOVE! SAY IT!

AFTER A PROPER COURTSHIP, DEAR DOVINA, YOU MAY EXPECT A PROPOSAL OF MATRIMONY...
AND YOU MAY EXPECT AN AFFIRMATIVE RESPONSE.... ONE CONDITION--
Candy

NYTHING,
Y LOVE!
NYTHING!
YOU MUST, AS WE AGREED IN OUR MANY LETTERS, WADDLE THE STRAIGHT AND NARROW PATH!
I WILL NOT MARRY A CRIMINAL-- I WISH TO BE A MATE, NOT AN ACCOMPLICE.
'LL PROVE MYSELF
ORTHY, DOVINA! I'LL
AKE YOU PROUD!
I KNEW YOU WOULDN'T SQUAWK AT MY REQUEST!
ND AS NIGHT DESCENDS UPON
E CITY OF GOTHAM, DARK AS
RAVEN'S WING, A FAMILIAR
EACON SUMMONS A DARK
KNIGHT--
YOU THINK THE PENGUIN'S AT IT AGAIN?
I HARDLY THINK GORDON WOULD CALL US IN ON A ROUTINE MATTER!
6

BATMAN! YOU'RE NOTHING IF NOT PROMPT--
WE WERE ON PATROL NEARBY. WHAT'S THE PENGUIN DONE?

WHY, NOTHING--THIS IS JUST A ROUTINE MATTER..., RASH OF LIQUOR STORE ROBBERIES...

CRIME IS CRIME. BATMAN AND ROBIN GO TO WORK...
LIQUOR

SMALL-TIMERS.
EIGHT LIQUOR STORES IN ONE NIGHT ISN'T SO SMALL-TIME. ESPECIALLY NOT TO THE EIGHT LIQUOR STORE OWNERS.

BATMAN, CUT ME A DEAL AND I'LL CLUE YA IN ON SOMETHING BIG--
I'LL CUT YOU A DEAL. SPILL AND YOU KEEP YOUR TEETH.

HEY, ISN'T IT A LITTLE EARLY FOR YOU TO BE UP? IT'S NINE O'CLOCK IN THE MORNING!
I HAVEN'T BEEN HOME YET.

I HEARD YOU NABBED THOSE LIQUOR STORE HEISTERS. THANKS FOR THE PROMPT SERVICE.

FINE. NOW GIVE ME SOME. WHAT'S THE PENGUIN UP TO? I HEAR HE'S PUT THE WORD OUT FOR HIS OLD CRONIES TO HOOK UP WITH HIM...

WE HAVEN'T HEARD THAT. FAR AS WE KNOW, PENGUIN'S GONE STRAIGHT--HE'S OPENED AN UMBRELLA FACTORY.
OH, PLEASE!

"LOOK," GORDON SAYS, "WE'VE BEEN WATCHING MR. COBBLEPOT LIKE A HAWK--HE SHUTTLES FROM HIS LOVE NEST WITH MISS DOVINA PARTRIDGE, TO THIS FACTORY HE'S OPENING, AND BACK AGAIN... THAT'S THE WHOLE STORY!"
GOTHAM UMBRELLA WORKS

PECK
"WHAT'S THE STORY ON HIS GIRL-FRIEND?" BATMAN ASKS. "GOOD FAMILY BACKGROUND--VERY UPRIGHT LADY," SAYS GORDON. "SHE AND PENGUIN FELL IN LOVE BY MAIL--"
WELL, I MUST FLY, MY LOVE! AN HONEST DOLLAR CALLS!
8

KNOK KNOK
OH, DEAR-- OSWALD MUST'VE FORGOTTEN SOMETHING!

OSWAL... OH. IT'S YOU.

MAY I COME IN?
CERTAINLY. I'VE WANTED A WORD WITH YOU FOR SOME TIME.

SEE HERE, YOUNG MAN--MY OSWALD IS REFORMED. HE NEVER STOLE FOR THE MONEY-- AFTER ALL, HE INHERITED A FAMILY FORTUNE! HE ONLY WANTED ATTENTION-- APPROVAL--

"THE PRISON PSYCHIATRIST SAID OSWALD'S PENCHANT FOR COLLECTING WAS A SIMPLE ANAL RETENTIVE TENDENCY WHICH CAN BE OVERCOME BY THERAPY AND LOVE!"

MISS PARTRIDGE--I PROMISE YOU I WILL NOT
PERSECUTE "OSWALD." IF HE AND I TANGLE,
REST ASSURED HE WILL HAVE DESERVED
MY ATTENTION--

"WHAT YOU REFER TO AS 'COLLECTING,' I REFER TO AS 'STEALING.' AND IF HE BEGINS 'COLLECTING' AGAIN, I'LL CAGE HIM AGAIN."
RELLA WORKS
GOOD DAY, GENTLEMEN.
HIYA, BOSS.

U STRIKE
E AS AN
NORABLE
VIDUAL. I
L TRUST
OUR
GMENT.

OH, OSWALD... OSWALD... DO BE A GOOD BOY...

GHT FOLLOWS
AY. BATMAN
FOLLOWS
PENGUIN.
WHAT'S GOING ON DOWN THERE ?
I DON'T KNOW.

"BUT IF THAT UMBRELLA FACTORY IS FOR REAL, I'LL EAT MY CAPE--"
GOTHAM UMBRELLA WORKS
10

I THINK YOU'RE RIGHT--THOSE SECURITY GUARDS LOOK LIKE THUGS--AND WHY WOULD AN UMBRELLA FACTORY NEED ARTILLERY LIKE THAT?
LET'S HAVE A LOOK--

"THOSE SECURITY GUARDS ARE THUGS, ROBIN--DON'T YOU REMEMBER? THEY WERE STOOGES OF PENGUIN'S WHO WALKED ON A TECHNICALITY--"

AND IN THE PENGUIN'S WAREHOUSE--
HOW'S THINGS GOIN', BOSS?

YOU'RE NOT DOUBLING ANYTHING, PENGUIN, EXCEPT YOUR PRISON SENTENCE!

BATMAN! YOU JUST COULDN'T RESIST FOULING MY NEST, COULD YOU? GET HIM, BOYS--

DON'T FLY AWAY, PENGUIN--
I'M NOT, DEAR FELLOW-- I'M MERELY SEEKING A PLACE TO PERCH--

I'LL ENJOY WATCHING MY EMPLOYEES DISPATCH YOU AND YOUR RED-BREASTED BRAT--BREAKING AND ENTERING IS ILLEGAL, YOU KNOW--

BREAKING AND ENTERING? IS THAT WHAT WE'RE DOING?
IGNORE HIM-- HE'S JUST TRYING TO RUFFLE OUR FEATHERS--

HEY, HE'S GONE--

12

CHIRP! CHIRP! CHIRP! CHIRP! CHIRP!
IT'S SOME KIND OF ALARM!
STAY DOWN HERE AND KEEP AN EYE OUT--I'M GOING UP AFTER HIM--

CHIRP!
COPS!
WE GOTTA SPLIT--

CHIRP! CHIRP! CHIRP!
PENGUIN! I KNOW YOU'RE UP HERE--

INDEED I AM--AND WITH MY TRUSTY BUMBERSHOOTER, .357 MAG!

I HOPE YOU'RE SATISFIED. YOU'VE RUINED ME. MY ONE TRUE LOVE WILL BE FOREVER LOST TO ME--
THEN YOU SHOULDN'T HAVE GOTTEN BACK INTO CRIME--

AH, BUT I DIDN'T, DEAR FELLOW. THIS BUSINESS IS QUITE LEGITIMATE--

I HAVE BROUGHT MY MASTERY OF THE UMBRELLA-MAKER'S ART TO ASSEMBLY-LINE PRODUCTION--"
GOTHAM UMBRELLA WORKS

THEN WHY THE HEAVILY ARMED GUARDS?
TO KEEP PRYING EYES OUT--

OF COMPETITORS?
NO! WAK! WAK! OF YOURS... AND THE POLICE!

YOU SEE, MOST OF MY EMPLOYEES ARE LIKE ME-- EX-CONS WHO CAN'T GET A BREAK! AND FLOCKING TOGETHER WITH SUCH BIRDS OF A FEATHER PUTS ME...

AH, I SEE THAT MY BOYS HAVE FOR THE MOST PART FLOWN. YOU MAY TAKE ME IN NOW... AND THIS IS NOT A GUN. MERELY AN UMBRELLA-- ALBEIT OF AN EXTREMELY HIGH QUALITY.
IN VIOLATION OF PAROLE.
14

AND THAT, LADIES AND GENTLEMEN, IS MY STORY--

SYMPATHETIC AS WE MIGHT BE TO MR. COBBLEPOT'S GOOD INTENTIONS, HE IS STILL IN VIOLATION OF HIS PAROLE.
NEXT CASE.

BOARD ROOM
SLAM
THAT BAD, HUH?

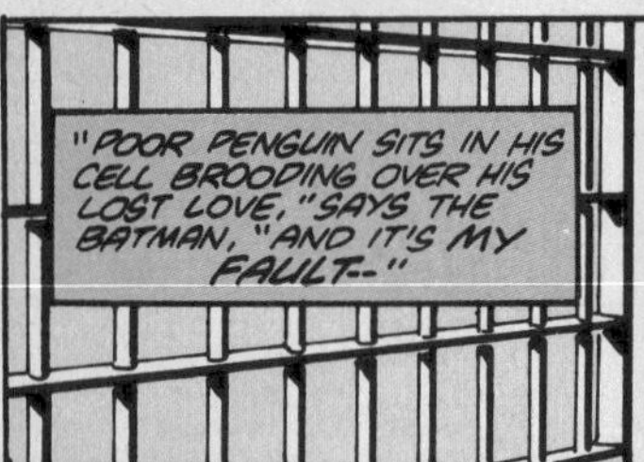
"POOR PENGUIN SITS IN HIS CELL BROODING OVER HIS LOST LOVE," SAYS THE BATMAN, "AND IT'S MY FAULT--"

BUT MAYBE I CAN DO SOMETHING TO MAKE UP FOR LAYING THIS PARTICULAR EGG--
15

SOON--
YOU GOT A VISITOR, PENGUIN--

SO THEN YOU WILL MARRY ME? YOU RECOGNIZE THAT MY HEART WAS IN THE RIGHT PLACE? HOW...?
A LITTLE BAT TOLD ME.
THE E

"EYRIE"
QUICK FOOTSTEPS STRIKE THE CAMPUS ROAD LIKE DRUMBEATS.
HESE DRUMBEATS ARE SOON DROWNED OUT BY A FASTER, MORE FRENZIED CADENCE--
--THE SOUND OF BEATING WINGS!
THE DRUMMING IS ACCOMPANIED BY SHRILL CRIES--
--CRIES THAT SEEM TO SAY, "KILL... KILL...
--KILL!"
JOEY CAVALIERI
WRITER
KLAUS JANSON
ARTIST/colorist
JOHN COSTANZA
letterer
DENNIS O'NEIL
EDITOR

YOU ELECTED A PRESIDENT WHO PROMISED TO GET THE GOVERNMENT OFF OUR BACKS... NOW... TAKE THE NEXT STEP!
HOW MUCH LONGER WILL YOU DEPEND ON THESE SO-CALLED "HEROES" TO MAKE YOUR WORLD A BETTER ONE? HOW MUCH LONGER CAN YOU DEFER YOUR RESPONSIBILITY TO SOCIETY TO THESE SELF-STYLED SAVIORS?
THE "SUPER-HERO" IS AN AFFRONT TO THE COMMON MAN... AN INSULT TO THE TALENTS AND CAPABILITIES OF THE COMMON MAN TO COPE WITH THE WORLD AS HE FINDS IT!
TOO LONG HAS THE COMMON MAN BEEN HELD BACK BY THE PRESENCE OF THESE "SUPERMEN." TOO LONG HAVE THEIR EFFORTS BEEN STIFLED BY THOSE WHO WOULD BETTER THEMSELVES AT OUR EXPENSE!
ELIMINATE THE SUPER-HERO... AND WITNESS THE TRIUMPH OF THE COMMON MAN!

OU MUST DECIDE WHO WILL ONTROL YOUR LIVES... YOUR DESTINIES!
WILL IT BE MEN WHO WEAR MASKS AND HIDE THEIR IDENTITIES FROM THE WORLD...
...OR WILL IT BE YOU? WHO WILL TAKE COMMAND?
WE WILL! WE WILL! WE WILL!

WHAT A PACK OF INGRATES, HUH?
IT'S ENOUGH TO MAKE A GUY WANNA HANG UP HIS CAPE AND STAY HOME!

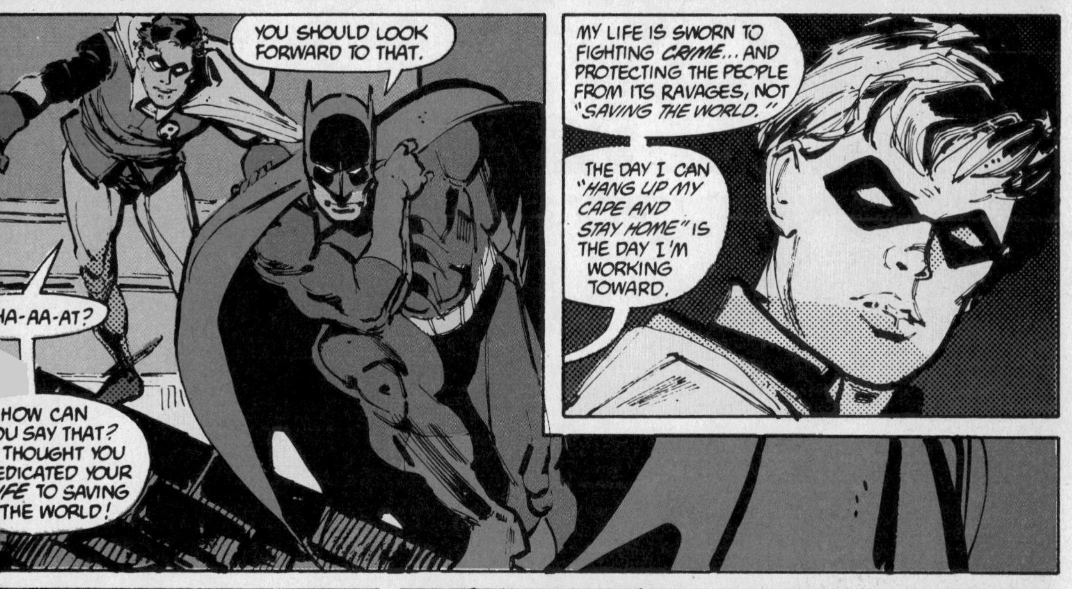
YOU SHOULD LOOK FORWARD TO THAT.
HA-AA-AT?
HOW CAN OU SAY THAT? THOUGHT YOU EDICATED YOUR IFE TO SAVING THE WORLD!
MY LIFE IS SWORN TO FIGHTING CRIME... AND PROTECTING THE PEOPLE FROM ITS RAVAGES, NOT "SAVING THE WORLD."
THE DAY I CAN "HANG UP MY CAPE AND STAY HOME" IS THE DAY I'M WORKING TOWARD.

THE TIME HAS COME TO STOP LOOKING OUTSIDE OURSELVES FOR HELP!
PEOPLE MUST LEARN TO HELP THEMSELVES!

HELP! HELP!!
3

A REMARKABLE BIRD OF PREY, THE FALCON.
THE TYPICAL PEREGRINE CAN DIVE AT A SPEED OF EIGHTY MILES AN HOUR--

IMAGINE THE SPEED, THEN, OF A FALCON TWICE NORMAL SIZE--

--A BIRD IN SHORT--
--THAT IS A MONSTER!

THE BIRD'S GETTING AWAY!
MEET ME BELOW!

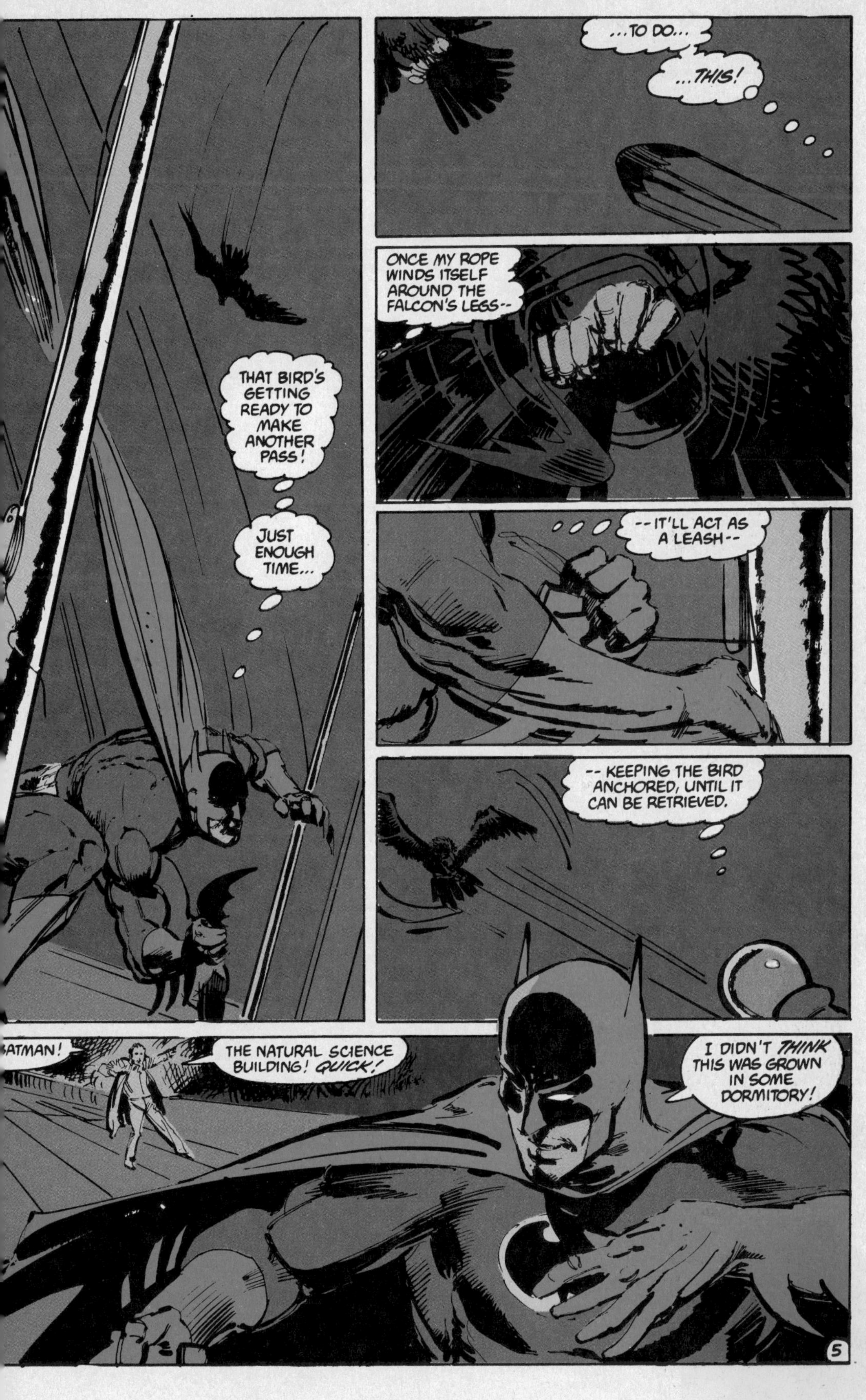
THAT BIRD'S GETTING READY TO MAKE ANOTHER PASS!
JUST ENOUGH TIME...
...TO DO...
...THIS!
ONCE MY ROPE WINDS ITSELF AROUND THE FALCON'S LEGS--
--IT'LL ACT AS A LEASH--
--KEEPING THE BIRD ANCHORED, UNTIL IT CAN BE RETRIEVED.
ATMAN!
THE NATURAL SCIENCE BUILDING! QUICK!
I DIDN'T THINK THIS WAS GROWN IN SOME DORMITORY!
5

WE'VE BEEN BROKEN INTO! THEY'RE STILL THERE--GETTING AWAY WITH *EVERYTHING!*
I'M RIGHT BEHIND YOU, BATMAN!

NOT *THIS* TIME. YOU'D BETTER MAKE SURE THE WOUNDED STUDENT GETS MEDICAL ATTENTION.
BUT THE CAMPUS POLICE CAN TAKE CARE OF THAT! WHY DO YOU ALWAYS LEAVE ME BEHIND FOR ALL THE *UNIMPORTANT* STUFF?

REMEMBER WHEN I SAID OUR PURPOSE WAS TO PROTECT PEOPLE FROM CRIME? WHAT MAKES YOU THINK IT'S ANY LESS VITAL THAN PURSUING CRIMINALS?
ENSURING THAT THE VICTIMS OF CRIME ARE TAKEN CARE OF ALWAYS COMES FIRST.
KEEP IN MIND--

"-- WHAT'S *REALLY* IMPORTANT."
WHAT'S IMPORTANT ABOUT THIS?

IMPORTANT? I'LL TELL YOU WHAT'S IMPORTANT.

IF I HAD TO CHOOSE BETWEEN THAT BOX AND YOU--

--YOU'D HAVE TO GO!

THESE COMPUTER DISKS HOLD THE NOTES TO THE GRAND AND GLORIOUS BREEDING EXPERIMENT THAT PRODUCED THESE PRIZE PEREGRINES!

NEVER BEFORE HAVE FALCONS OF SUCH SIZE BE--

IDIOTS! CRETINS!

GET THIS MAMMOTH MONSTROSITY AWAY FROM ME!

ORRY, BOSS. HE BIRD MUST'VE VANTED THAT OX AS MUCH S *YOU* DO.

WE PRETTY MUCH GOT A HANDLE ON 'EM NOW.

SEE HAT OU DO.

E LOST *ONE* ALCON THROUGH OUR INCOMPETENCE. E CAN'T AFFORD *NOTHER* SUCH LOSS.

DR. BAIRD HERE WOULDN'T LIKE IT...

BUT I'M SURE THERE'S A LOT HE WOULDN'T LIKE... SINCE HE'S BECOME A PRECIOUS *PART* OF OUR PLUNDER... *HMMMM?*

WH-WHAT... WHAT DO YOU MEAN?

7

WHAT I MEAN IS, THEY'RE VERY VALUABLE BIRDS... BECAUSE THEY'RE EXPERIMENTAL... UNIQUE...
BUT THEY WON'T REMAIN SO, IF YOU CAN BREED MORE LIKE THEM! THAT'S WHY WE'RE ABSCONDING WITH YOUR LAB NOTES...
AND YOU AS WELL!

KIKK
NO! NO!

ALL MY WORK!
I CAN'T LET THIS HAPPEN!

I DON'T RECALL THROWING IT OPEN TO A VOTE.

EGG ON YOUR FACE? WEAR IT AND LIKE IT.
YOU'RE NOT GOING TO BE MUCH TROUBLE. WE KNOW YOU BETTER THAN YOU KNOW YOURSELF. EVEN IF YOU COULD OFFER RESISTANCE, YOU WON'T... FOR FEAR WE'LL HARM YOUR FALCONS.

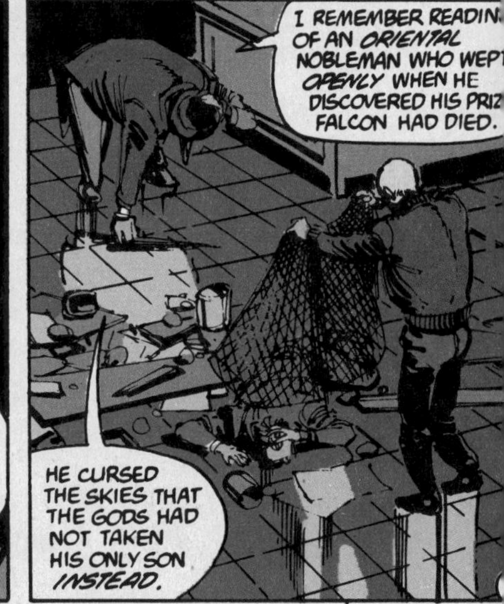
I REMEMBER READIN OF AN ORIENTAL NOBLEMAN WHO WEP OPENLY WHEN HE DISCOVERED HIS PRIZ FALCON HAD DIED.
HE CURSED THE SKIES THAT THE GODS HAD NOT TAKEN HIS ONLY SON INSTEAD.

NO, MY FRIEND.
I'M WAGERING YOU'LL REMAIN VERY COOPERATIVE!

COOPERATIVE INDEED... WITH HIS TESTIMONY AT YOUR TRIAL.
DRAT! THIS WILL BE A WASTE OF PRECIOUS TIME!
NOW WE'LL HIT TRAFFIC FROM THE RALLY ON THE WAY BACK!

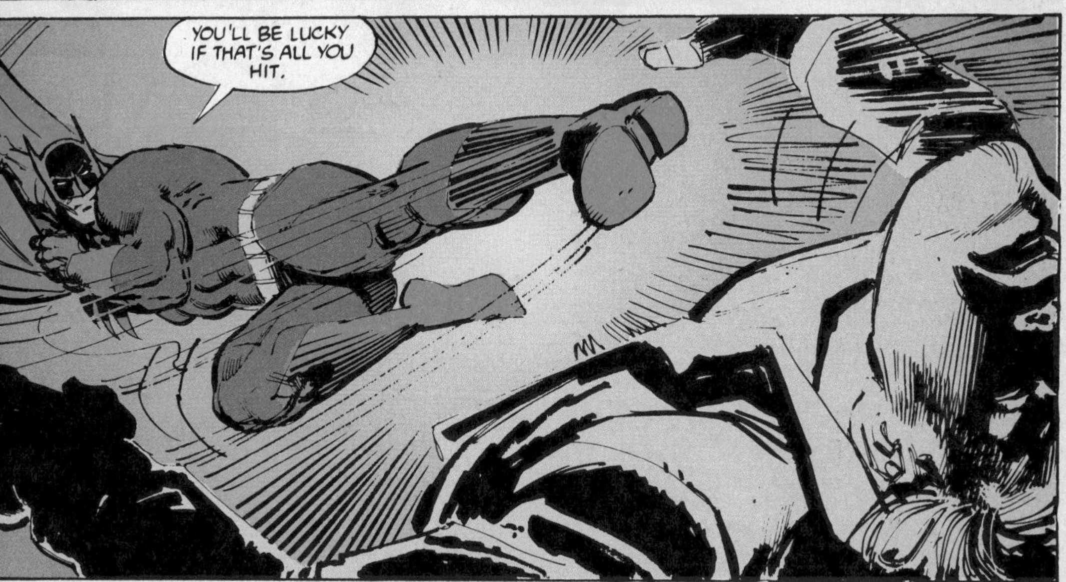
YOU'LL BE LUCKY IF THAT'S ALL YOU HIT.

THE BOSS IS ALLERGIC TO BATMAN. BREAKS OUT IN A RASH WHENEVER HE'S AROUND.
SO DON'T LET 'IM GET TOO CLOSE, HEAR?

NORMALLY, THESE HOOKSTICKS ARE USED TO BRING FALCONS DOWN FROM TREES BY LOOPING THE LEATHER THONGS ON THEIR LEGS...
9

...BUT I CAN FIND ANOTHER USE FOR IT!
...FOR THE TIME BEING...
...IT WILL MAKE AN IMPROMPTU VERSION...
...OF A BO STICK!

WELL DONE, BATMAN. TRULY ENTERTAINING. MORE EXCITING THAN FOURTH OF JULY FIREWORKS!
BUT IF YOU TRULY WANT TO SEE A PYRO-TECHNICAL DISPLAY--

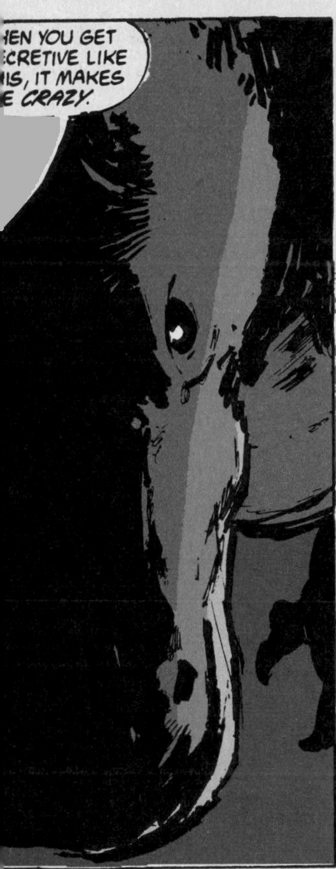

HEN YOU GET ECRETIVE LIKE IS, IT MAKES E CRAZY.

I MEAN, IF YOU HAVE EVEN THE SLIGHTEST IDEA WHERE THE PENGUIN COULD HAVE TAKEN THOSE BIRDS, I WISH YOU'D LET ME IN ON IT!
TO ME, IT'S LIKE A VARIATION OF AN OLD JOKE. "WHERE DOES A TWENTY-FIVE POUND FALCON GO TO EAT?"

"ANYWHERE HE WANTS TO!" GET IT?
DO YOU GET IT? THAT'S THE POINT. WHERE WOULD THOSE FALCONS WANT TO GO?
I THINK I'VE LEARNED ENOUGH ABOUT THEIR NESTING HABITS, AND THEIR NEEDS AS BIRDS OF PREY, TO BE NEARLY CERTAIN.

EVEN IF YOU DO, I DON'T KNOW WHAT YOU WANT WITH THESE BIRD CALLS.
I'M NOT SURE I'D WANT THOSE THINGS TO BE TOO TERRIBLY ATTRACTED TO ME. IF I HAD TO SHARE A NEST WITH A BIRD LIKE THAT--
SKREEK
SKREEK
11

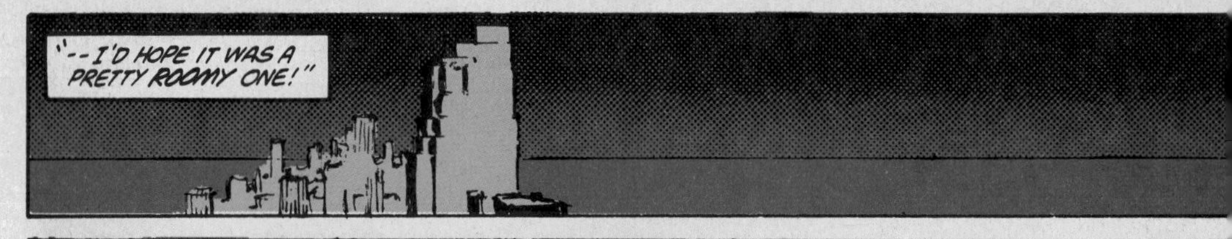
"--I'D HOPE IT WAS A PRETTY ROOMY ONE!"

A VERY CLEVER BIT OF WORK!
TELL ME, HAVE WE HEARD ANYTHING SINCE OUR RANSOM DEMAND?

NOTHING YET. IT STILL TAKES TIME TO HEAR FROM HALFWAY 'ROUND THE WORLD!

WHAT MAKES YOU THINK YOU'LL COLLECT?
YOU MUST BE JOKING-THAT ARAB SHEIK FRIEND OF YOURS IS MADE OF MONEY!
AFTER ALL, HE HAD NOTHING BETTER TO DO WITH HIS DOUGH THAN TO ENDOW GOTHAM UNIVERSITY --AND YOU--WITH ENOUGH FOR YOU TO GENETICALLY PRODUCE THAT PACK OF PRODIGIOUS PEREGRINES!

SO HE'S GOT EIGHT HOURS TO COME ACROSS--OR HIS EXPERIMENTAL GIFT TO THE SPORT OF FALCONRY WILL BE WIPED OFF THE DISKS... AND THE LANDSCAPE...
...AND YOU ALONG WITH IT!

NOT TO MENTION A WONDERFULLY UNEXPECTED DIVIDEND ON MY INVESTMENT--

"-- THE END OF BATMAN!"
MY DEDUCTION WAS SOUND.
FALCONS IN URBAN AREAS CAN AND DO MAKE THEIR NESTS IN SKYSCRAPERS, SOMETIMES AS HIGH AS THIRTY STORIES UP.
TRUST THE PENGUIN TO CONTRIVE A DRAMATIC HOME FOR HIS HOSTAGES!
AND TRUST HIM TO TAKE A PARTICULAR PRIDE IN HIS CHARGES AS WELL!
SEEMS LIKE SOMEONE I KNOW'S WADDLED OUT FOR A MOONLIGHT STROLL.
13

ANOTHER MINUTE AND--
--THE PENGUIN--
--WILL FIND HIMSELF--
--AN ENDANGERED SPECIES!

OH, NO! I SHOULD HAVE EXPECTED AS MUCH FROM HIM!
IT'S--

SPRANNG!

--A DECOY!

CUCKOO! CUCKOO!
THE ALARM!
THE BAT'S TAKEN THE BAIT!

ELCOME, BATMAN... MY MAKESHIFT MPLE TO THE GOD PERSONIFIED THE SACRED FALCON.
HERE, AS IS WRITTEN IN THE EGYPTIAN CURSE--

"--DEATH WILL COME ON SWIFT WINGS!"

ANAGED HIDE HIS BLE KNIFE... NOTHER FEW CONDS, NOW...

...JUST AS LONG AS THEY KEEP WATCHING OUT THE WINDOW... AND NOT AT ME!

YOU HAVEN'T A CHANCE, BATMAN!
CHANCE FAVORS THE PREPARED... AND I CAME PREPARED!

I BROUGHT THIS FROM THE BAT CAVE... FIGURING I'D EVENTUALLY HAVE TO FEND OFF THE FALCONS!

IT'S WORKING JUST AS I HOPED IT WOULD!
SKREEEEEEEE
I PRE-RECORDED THE CRY OF A FALCON THAT SIGNALS "DANGER." IT'S THEIR OWN CODE TO FLEE FROM AN ATTACKER... THE BIRDS ARE NOW ACTUALLY AFRAID OF ME!

THE PENGUIN THOUGHT HE WAS FUNNY TRIPPING ME UP. WE'LL SEE WHO LAUGHS THIS TIME.
HE DOESN'T SEEM SO INTERESTED IN ME AT PRESENT... WHICH GIVES ME THE OPPORTUNITY TO BORROW...

...THIS FALCON LURE. FALCONERS USE THEM TO ATTRACT THE BIRDS... IT'S MADE TO LOOK LIKE THE FALCONS' QUARRY!
NOW TO GET MY FILE DISKS!

THOSE FALCONS HAVE TURNED CHICKEN!
IT'S THE NOISEMAKER HE BROUGHT ALONG!
GET IT AWAY FROM HIM! GET IT!

FOR PITY'S SAKE, MOVE FASTER! THAT'S BATMAN IN THAT BIRDCAGE, NOT SOME BUDGIE!
EEEEE

THE GOOD DOCTOR HAS A PLAN IN MIND, I SEE--
SKRE

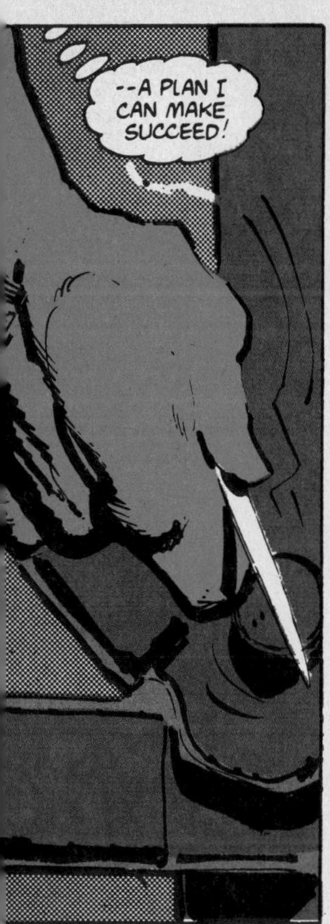
--A PLAN I CAN MAKE SUCCEED!

NO! NO!!
THOSE BIRDS ARE OUR FORTUNE! DON'T LET THEM GET AWAY!
YOU NEEDN'T WORRY, PENGUIN! THEY WON'T BE GOING VERY FAR!
FIRST THEY'RE ATTRACTED TO THE BRIGHT BOX--
17

...AND NOW THEY'RE ATTRACTED TO YOU!
GAHH!
I'VE PRIDED MYSELF ON MY RAPPORT WITH BIRDS--

--BUT NOW... I'M NOT SURE I LIKE IT!

DON'T JUST STAND OUT THERE, YOU MENTAL DEFECTIVES--
--GET THEM OFF MY TAIL!
BU' WHADDABOUT TH' BATMAN?

GOOD QUESTION.
THUNK

"WHAT ABOUT THE BATMAN?"
OFTEN ASK MYSELF THAT QUESTION.

VE COME
D THE
NCLUSION...
HELP! HELP!!
...THAT IT SHOULD REMAIN ONE OF LIFE'S GREAT MYSTERIES.
19

CALL THEM OFF!
CALL THEM OFF!!

I SHOULD THINK YOU WOULD BE MORE *APPRECIATIVE,* PENGUIN...

...SEEING AS HOW YOU'VE FOUND YOURSELF ON THE RECEIVING END OF THE GOLDEN RULE...

...BUT IF IT WILL MAKE YOU *HAPPIER...*
MUCH.

AND I CERTAINLY
HOPE TO *RETURN*
THE FAVOR AT THE
EARLIEST
OPPORTUNITY!

SO WHEN AND UNTIL
THAT DAY PRESENTS
ITSELF, I BELIEVE I'LL
SIMPLY BID YOU A
CIVIL--

--*Adieu.*

NOT A VERY
TRUSTING
INDIVIDUAL,
ARE YOU?
21

THE FOLLOWING MORNING...
THE "SUPER HERO" IS AN AFFRONT TO THE COMMON MAN...
...AN INSULT TO THE TALENTS AND CAPABILITIES OF THE COMMON MAN TO COPE WITH THE WORLD AS HE FINDS IT!

TOO LONG HAS THE COMMON MAN BEEN HELD BACK BY THE PRESENCE OF THESE "SUPERMEN"... TOO LONG HAVE THEIR EFFORTS BEEN STIFLED BY THOSE WHO WOULD BETTER THEMSELVES AT OUR EXPENSE!
ELIMINATE THE SUPER HERO... AND WITNESS THE TRIUMPH OF THE COMMON MAN!

GODFREY'S RALLY AT GOTHAM UNIVERSITY WAS WELL-ATTENDED. CAMPUS SECURITY CLAIMED ALMOST A THOUSAND STUDENTS HEARD GODFREY SPEAK...
AND SOME WITNESSES CLAIM EVEN BATMAN AND ROBIN WERE ON HAND AS WELL.

YOU THINK HE'S RIGHT, BRUCE?
I THINK HE'S RIGHT ON AT LEAST ONE IMPORTANT POINT...
LAST NIGHT, THAT BAIRD FELLOW DID A FINE JOB OF HOLDING HIS OWN AGAINST THE PENGUIN...

I THINK THE "TRIUMPH OF THE COMMON MAN" IS ASSURED...
...WHETHER OR NOT THERE'S A BATMAN TO HELP HIM.
THE END

END NOTES

By Robert Greenberger

ıtman probably has the most eresting, colorful and deadly ues gallery in comic books (that ıor in comic *strips* reserved for ·k *Tracy*). In our first volume st of Batman's best-known foes ›eared, however briefly. The er, Catwoman, Penguin, Two- :e, et al., all made an appear- e; yet it was felt that since the er was indeed Batman's greatest and inspiration for an armload classic confrontations, the wn Prince of Crime deserved own volume.

n reviewing material for this ume, it was apparent that ough Batman has many memo- le enemies, after fifty years, the ılity of their stories did not ays stand up well to the test of ıe. As a result, with a nod ·ard the summer, 1992 release *Batman Returns*, this volume ıld concentrate on meetings ween the Caped Crusader and Penguin and Catwoman.

'o the casual reader, the various ɛrpretations of the characters y seem quite inconsistent from inning to end; this section of volume will attempt to sort out ıe of that continuity. While the ıguin went from deadly to com- -but-deadly to just-plain-dead- the Catwoman has been many ıgs.

n the beginning, the Cat- nan was a beautiful cat burglar, led after screen star Hedy ıarr. In short order, though, as tumed characters became the m in comics, she donned a cat's ıd mask and plagued the ıamic Duo. By the mid-1940s, familiar purple-and-green out- had been designed, and was d right through the 1950s. ile that in itself is not necessar- confusing, it should be noted t Selina Kyle's personality has n under constant revision. ıile she seemed your basic ale criminal through the 1940s, ırns out that she was a normal young woman, who had been injured in an airplane accident and survived sans her memory. Lost and aimless, she turned to crime and, for a decade, plagued Gotham City as the Cat, later Catwoman. Ultimately, another blow to the head restored her memory and she foreswore crime. That story, pre- sented in BATMAN #62 (1950), was a very early attempt at charac- terization and continuity, some- thing virtually unheard of in comics at that time. She appeared infrequently from 1950 to 1952, helping Batman when circum- stances demanded it (such as her brother's sudden arrival as a cos- tumed criminal), but returning to crime in the story presented here, "The Crimes of the Catwoman."

During her formative appear- ances in BATMAN and DETEC- TIVE COMICS, Catwoman dis- played an attraction for Batman that fans recall most about her. As a result, she was often willing to spare Batman or Robin's life—a perfect example of which is con- tained in our first volume, "The Jungle Cat-Queen." Creator Bob Kane admits today that Catwoman was invented for the originality of having a female antagonist and to play off that attraction between opposites. Very rarely did either

admit their feelings for the other, but the underlying sexual tension was there.

None of the stories used on the *Batman* television series were based on comics, and therefore do not appear here, but during the first two seasons, it was quite obvious that sexy Julie Newmar and Adam West were enjoying the sexual tensions (within the limits of network standards of that time). Such tensions were heightened as a subplot in the *Batman* feature film where Adam West was paired with Lee Meriwether, a more sultry Catwoman. Such male/female byplay was abandoned altogether when Eartha Kitt assumed the skintight cat-suit in the third and final season.

Still, the television series helped spark the return of Catwoman, who was absent for far too long in the comics. During the late 1950s and early 1960s, editor Jack Schiff abandoned the costumed criminals and had the Cowled Crusader and his youthful sidekick deal with aliens and bizarre foes such as Clayface. Some of the rationale behind this was a result of the arrival of the Comics Code Authority and the feeling that such grotesque villains as the Joker and Two-Face would be unacceptable. If they went, the entire rogues gallery would go, too. In 1967, in another then-rare incidence of continuity, an issue of DETECTIVE COMICS concluded with a jailed Selina Kyle reading a headline about Batman and Batgirl, giving her reason to break free and claim the Darknight Detective for herself. That story, of course, is in this volume.

The 1960s also gave birth to a concept that has either enchanted or baffled readers and in some ways has forced writers to abandon some of the more interesting characters of the past. Parallel worlds, Earth-1 and Earth-2, were introduced to explain whatever happened to the original super-heroes of comics' Golden Age. The two parallel worlds continued to grow until even editors and writers had their heads spinning. All was washed away during DC Comics' 50th anniversary in 1985, but before that cataclysmic event, the Golden Age Batman and Catwoman were allowed to fin proclaim their love and marr the memorable "The Autol graphy of Bruce Wayne," repri in volume one. A side note to f this union produced a daugh Helena Wayne, who became costumed crimefighter called Huntress when her mother killed. That origin story was final appearance of that orig Catwoman.

Confusing enough was w became of the modern-day C woman. In the 1970s she was ju costumed foe relying on crimes, and few of her stories v of any particular note. O though, did have Batman stop wonder for a few panels about two women in his life, Catwo and Talia, daughter of Rā' Ghūl. Both were on the "wr side of the law and he coul fathom his attraction to them- what to do about it.

In the early 1980s, Selina returned, swearing she reformed and, with Bruce Way help, became a legitimate busir woman. She even began rom ing Wayne while occasion fighting side by side with Batman. This led to some v memorable subplots from wri Len Wein and Marv Wolfman, they did not lead to very str Catwoman-oriented stories for collection. This interpretatio the character did lead to a sh lived series of backup features s ring the adventurous Catwon The first two installments are sented here, representing the of that run.

Frank Miller turned everyo head when his classic THE DA KNIGHT RETURNS burst on comics scene in 1986. There, story projects what happens w Bruce Wayne is 50 and is fo out of retirement one last ti Catwoman appears in the st characterized as a harde embittered prostitute. This Miller to write a brand-new o and characterization for Catwoman in the acclaimed B MAN: YEAR ONE, from M and artist David Mazzucch Kyle was now a thrill-seeking titute with a young lesbian l who decided to don a cat-suit tman one better. The media, ›ugh, painted her as an assistant Batman, so she swore she would ıke people remember her as an lividual. That first confronta- n set the stage for a new round sexual politics and violent bat- s. Since that story was a flash- :k to Batman's roots, it was felt : modern-day Catwoman need- to be a villain as well, and Mike Barr and Alan Davis obliged in hrowaway two-parter involving : Joker.

The new version of Catwoman nanded further exploration and, er a brief run in ACTION)MICS WEEKLY, Mindy well, J.J. Birch and Michael Bair vided the four-part miniseries itled CATWOMAN: HER SIS- R'S KEEPER. Like THE DARK IGHT RETURNS and BAT- AN: YEAR ONE, this story nains available in trade paper- k.

)nly recently has this revamped twoman been given additional y in the comics, and so it was med that these stories were too h for inclusion in this volume. doubt, though, with the movie twoman played by Michelle iffer, comics writers and artists l once again want to explore dark relationship between the and the Cat.

'he Penguin's comics history is different, with little attention l to his roots, the character sidered a comical fellow driven :rime in order to exact revenge n those who taunted him. Tim ton, director of both *Batman* s, has stated that he found the chological underpinnings for Penguin to be very weak, and is true. Only in recent years e comics writers made an mpt to deal with the Penguin way that makes him a credible at to Batman.

riginally, the Penguin was por- ed as a deadly villain with a k trigger finger, but by 1943, was devolved into a gimmicky with a penchant for umbrellas bird crimes. He has been rded by some as Batman's sec- best-known foe, and that can raced directly back to both his norable visual appearance and superb portrayal on the television series by Burgess Meredith. Danny DeVito's performance is expected to make everyone reconsider the Penguin, which can only help the character in the comics.

As seen in our first volume, the Penguin was played largely for comic relief. That collection reprinted his appearance from the 1940s comic strip and an early rivalry with the Joker.

The writers of the 1940s seemed to enjoy the Penguin's gimmicks, given his relatively frequent appearances in BATMAN, DETECTIVE COMICS, and even occasionally in WORLD'S FINEST COMICS. Unfortunately, except for those gimmicks, few of the stories hold up today.

Throughout his appearances, the Penguin relied on his vanity and his criminal and mechanical genius to challenge or thwart the Dynamic Duo. He was invariably defeated and ended up in prison. As the 1950s rolled on, his appearances became less frequent; he was seen in one story in 1953, not again until 1956, and then, until 1965, he was totally missing. With the development of the TV series, starting in 1965, editor Julius Schwartz cautiously reintroduced members of the rogues gallery. The Joker, of course, was first, and the Penguin soon followed.

Interestingly, Schwartz kept the costumed foes in BATMAN while DETECTIVE was reserved for non-costumed opponents, keeping to the series name. This rule was occasionally ignored when the TV series' success had the Joker making appearances very often. During the 1960s, the Penguin was limited to two appearances, both included here, and then there were none until the 1970s.

Those 1970s appearances were inconsistent, with the two best in this volume. After that, he was again a gimmicky foe with no serious attempt at characterization or justification.

In the 1980s, the Penguin appeared very seldom but writer Doug Moench, trying to make the best of the situation, included a revelation that the Penguin was actually able to withstand arctic temperatures, just like his namesake. Moench and artist Don Newton tried hard with the Penguin but still couldn't come up with anything substantial.

It wasn't until the late 1980s that editor Denny O'Neil felt the time had come to remedy that. Under his guidance, Joey Cavalieri reinterpreted the character in the story seen here. Then O'Neil undertook the task to further redefine the Penguin when he wrote the very first DETECTIVE COMICS ANNUAL. The Penguin was used in a deadly manner, reminiscent of those very first appearances, but since that annual was connected with two others, it could not be collected here. Since then, O'Neil has asked his writers to keep the Penguin a fearsome foe and not just a comical caricature.

The 1990s seem destined to retain the sharped-edged interpretations of both the Penguin and Catwoman. Both have been remade for today's audiences, assuring that some of these modern-day appearances will also lay claim to the title of *greatest* Batman stories.

Robert Greenberger, currently Manager-Editorial Scheduling, has been a contributing editor to DC's Greatest Stories series since its inception.

CREATING THE GREATEST

by Paul Kupperberg

ALFREDO ALCALA

Alfredo Alcala was one of the wave of Philippine artists whose work b appearing in DC Comics in the late 1960s and early 1970s. Alfredo lent his illustrative style to a variety of DC stories, from short stories in the comp then-popular mystery line to the universe-spanning activities of the super- to the realm of the supernatural, including work on BATMAN, ARAK, H BLAZER and numerous other titles. Alfredo's work has also appeared at M in such titles as *Conan*.

TERRY AUSTIN

Terry Austin began his career assisting inker Dick Giordano and quickly m on to establish himself as one of the comics field's preeminent and most p inkers in his own right. Terry's inks have graced the work of a number of th pencillers in comics, including Marshall Rogers on Batman in DETEC COMICS and John Byrne on Marvel Comics' *X-Men*. In addition to his work inker, Terry has also applied his talents as a writer on Marvel's *Cloak and Dagg*

NORM BREYFOGLE

Norm Breyfogle was quickly recognized as *the* Batman artist for the 1990s he took over the pencilling of DETECTIVE COMICS just a few short year Since then, Norm has added the inking of his own work and painting repertory and, in 1992, won the plum assignment of artist on DC's fourth m ly Dark Knight title, BATMAN: SHADOW OF THE BAT.

E. NELSON BRIDWELL

E. Nelson Bridwell went from being one of comics' earliest fans in the 19 a position as assistant to editor Mort Weisinger in 1965. Renowned for his clopedic knowledge of comics history, Nelson was soon serving as DC's unc "continuity cop" during an era when editors and writers were only just begi to tie together DC's more than quarter century of history. In addition to hi torial duties, Nelson was also a prolific writer. His credits include a run o Batman syndicated newspaper strip, SHAZAM!, THE INFERIOR FIVE, SECRET SIX, SUPER FRIENDS, and many stories for the Superman fam titles. Nelson continued writing and editing for DC until his death in 1987.

JACK BURNLEY

Jack Burnley began cartooning for the King Features Syndicate at the t age of 14 and, throughout the 1930s, illustrated sports and other features, i ing short stories by Damon Runyon. Burnley began his comic book car Hillman Publications in 1939 and soon moved over to DC, where he work Superman before moving on to create Starman. Jack's distinctive style wa seen on numerous covers and features throughout the 1940s, including Ba in both the comic books and the syndicated newspaper strip. Jack left DC a comic book industry in 1947 to return to newspaper work, working for *Th Francisco Examiner* until his retirement in 1976. Since 1981, Jack Burnle lived in Virginia.

JOEY CAVALIERI

Joey Cavalieri began in comics as an editor in DC's Special Projects Grou was soon scripting such features as Green Arrow, The Huntress, and Batma also edited LOONEY TUNES and TINY TOONS magazines, and is curren editor at Marvel Comics.

MAX ALLAN COLLINS

Max Allan Collins is the author of over two dozen mystery novels, incl the Shamus Award-winning *True Detectives* and the film novelization o *Tracy*. Max has written the syndicated newspaper comic strip *Dick Tracy* si creator, the late Chester Gould, retired in 1977. He is the co-creator of Ms and Wild Dog for DC and has also scripted Batman.

:RRY CONWAY

;erry Conway was still a teenager when he published his first science- fiction el and broke into comic-book writing soon after, in the early 1970s, for vel Comics. For Marvel, Gerry wrote virtually every character on their roster, uding a long run on *Spider-Man*, as well as serving in various editorial capaci- . For DC, Gerry has written almost as many features, including Batman, cules Unbound, Steel, Firestorm, Superman, and many others. Gerry current- rites for Marvel Comics while he pursues a successful career in Hollywood.

'EVE ENGLEHART

teve Englehart has been writing comics for over twenty years, his work earing in the top titles for both Marvel and DC Comics, including Batman, erman, Green Lantern, *Fantastic Four*, *The Avengers*, *Master of Kung Fu*, and *er-Man*. Steve was also one of the pioneer creators to work in the indepen- t comics field.

LL FINGER

ill Finger was one of the true innovative talents and legendary figures of the ics industry. He collaborated with Bob Kane on the creation of Batman and ted the first two episodes of the Dark Knight's appearances in DETECTIVE MICS. Bill went on to script features for many publishers, including Plastic ı (for Quality Comics), Green Lantern, Wildcat, Vigilante, Johnny Quick, erman, Superboy, Blackhawk, Tomahawk, Robin, Challengers of the :nown, Batman (in comic books and in the syndicated newspaper strip), as as Captain America and ALL WINNERS COMICS (for Timely). Bill also te for radio and television, contributing scripts to *Mark Trail*, *77 Sunset Strip*, *Roaring Twenties*, *Hawaiian Eye*, and, naturally enough, two episodes of the *nan* TV program in 1966. He also wrote television commercials and co-wrote feature film, the 1969 cult film *The Green Slime*. Bill Finger was still writing)C Comics at the time of his death in 1974.

.RDNER FOX

.s much as any writer, Gardner Fox helped create the tone and feel of the nan stories of the 1960s. Gardner was an attorney who began his prolific and ›vative second career as a writer in the late 1930s on Batman and went on to ıte such Golden Age classics as the original Flash, Hawkman, Starman, tor Fate, and the Justice Society of America. His influence extended through- the 1950s and 1960s when, until his retirement from DC Comics in 1968, he ted and/or wrote such memorable features as the Justice League of America, m Strange, The Atom, Hawkman, and, of course, Batman, all under the aus- s of legendary comics editor Julius Schwartz. Until his death in 1986, Gardner continued writing comics and novels. He published over 100 books in ıerous genres, some under the pseudonyms of Jefferson Cooper and Bart ımers, as well as many fantasy novels under his own name.

E GIELLA

ıker Joe Giella began his career in the 1940s as an inker for Hillman lications and Timely Comics, the company that was to become Marvel in : years. Joe first worked for DC Comics in 1951 where, in the 1960s, his ue style of embellishment became associated with some of the company's test heroes, including Batman (over the work of penciller Sheldon Moldoff), Flash (with artist Carmine Infantino), and The Atom (with penciller Gil e). Giella, who also pencilled and inked a run of the Batman syndicated spaper strip during the 1960s, retired from comics in the early 1980s.

:K GIORDANO

ick Giordano was part of the creative team that, more than any other, helped ge the face of comic books in the late 1960s and early 1970s. Along with er Dennis O'Neil and penciller Neal Adams, Dick helped bring Batman back is roots as a dark, brooding "creature of the night," and brought relevance to ics in the pages of GREEN LANTERN/GREEN ARROW. Dick began his er as an artist for Charlton Comics in 1952 and became the company's editor- ief in 1965. In that capacity, he revamped their line by adding an emphasis ıch "action heroes" as The Question, Captain Atom, Thunderbolt, and The Beetle (characters now published by DC Comics). In 1967, Dick came over C for a three-year stint as editor, bringing with him many of the talents who would help shape the industry of the day, including Dennis O'Neil, Jim A and Steve Skeates. The winner of numerous industry awards, Dick continu be a major influence in comics, both as one of the most respected artists i business, as well as in the position of DC's Vice President-Editorial Director.

SID GREENE

Artist Sid Greene got his start in comics in 1941 and was soon drawing fea for such publishing houses as Timely and Novelty. Sid came to DC in 1 where he did the bulk of his work throughout the 1960s and 1970s, penci and/or inking a wide variety of genre stories and such features as Star Ro Johnny Peril, The Atom, Elongated Man, Hawkman, The Justice Leagu America, The Flash, Hourman, and, of course, The Batman. His credit Marvel Comics from the late 1970s include *Ka-Zar* and *S.H.I.E.L.D.*

EDMOND HAMILTON

The late Ed Hamilton had a long and active career in both comics and fiction, beginning in the 1930s and continuing through the ensuing dec until his death in the 1980s. During the 1940s, Ed wrote for numerous c book companies, including scripts for such features as Batman, Superman, Green Lantern. Among his most well known and best regarded work for DC his efforts on the cult favorite Legion of Super-Heroes. Ed Hamilton was als author of numerous pulp stories and science-fiction novels.

FRANCE EDDIE HERRON

Eddie Herron was one of the mainstay DC writers of the 1940s, 1950s, 1960s, with a list of credits that includes a wide variety of characters and ge Eddie's work appeared extensively in the science fiction, mystery, and super- titles, including MYSTERY IN SPACE, STRANGE ADVENTURES, SU MAN, and, of course, BATMAN.

BRUCE JONES

Bruce Jones is both a writer and accomplished artist whose work has app in the pages of numerous DC, Marvel, and independently published comic b In addition to his writing credits on the Catwoman tales in BATMAN, B work has also appeared in Marvel's *Ka-Zar*.

BOB KANE

Bob Kane created Batman in 1939 after three years spent pencilling and i comic book features for a variety of publishers, including the legendary Eisne Studios, as well as a stint working on the Betty Boop animated cartoons f Fleischer Studios. Bob contributed most of the pencilling and cover art, as w significant amounts of inking, to the early years of the Batman feature in DE TIVE COMICS and BATMAN. In 1943, Bob discontinued most of his book work to concentrate his talents on the daily syndicated newspaper stri remained connected with the Batman comic book until 1968. During the 1 Bob also created the animated cartoon series, *Courageous Cat & Minute* and *Cool McCool*. Since the late 1960s, Bob Kane has been involved in num one-man art shows in galleries and museums nationwide, as well as the creati limited-edition lithographs. Now living in California, Bob served as a cons on the 1989 movie *Batman* and the current *Batman Returns*.

PABLO MARCOS

The work of artist Pablo Marcos has appeared in the comics of numerous lishers in America and abroad for many years. As either penciller or inker, h worked for DC, Marvel, Atlas, and other publishers on such features as Ba Conan, Star Trek, Green Arrow, and Warlord. Pablo's work currently appe many titles for DC.

SHELDON MOLDOFF

Sheldon Moldoff, who began his career at DC Comics in 1938, came to p nence in comics in the early 1940s with his work on the Hawkman feat FLASH COMICS under the signature "Shelly." Shelly's early style, remin of the work of Alex Raymond and Hal Foster, was distinctive in its own earning him work on a variety of adventure and humor features for DC and publishers throughout the 1940s and 1950s. In 1943, Shelly began what was a 25-year association with the Batman feature in both BATMAN and DE

/E COMICS, and his style as both penciller and inker was so dominant, he ·ed to define the look and style of the Batman feature for the duration of his . Shelly left comics in the late 1960s to work on animation storyboards for h cartoon series as *Courageous Cat & Minute Mouse* and *Cool McCool*.

ON NEWTON

)on Newton was one of the best known and most popular artists in comic ·k fandom in the late 1960s and early 1970s before turning professional for arlton Comics, where his work appeared in their horror titles and in *The ntom*. Don began working at DC Comics soon after as the penciller of SHAZ-1!, The Original Captain Marvel. He also had a long run as the penciller of man in BATMAN and DETECTIVE COMICS, as well as on Aquaman, DC MICS PRESENTS, and Green Lantern Corps. Don was still working for DC he time of his death in the mid-1980s.

V NOVICK

rv Novick began his comic book career at the dawn of the Golden Age. ong his earliest work was the first appearance of The Shield in 1940 for MLJ gazines, later Archie Comics. Irv was also the artist on Steel Sterling and er features for MLJ and numerous other publishers. He later came to work for ' Comics, working on stories for the war anthologies and features, including PTAIN STORM, and, later, on super-hero titles. During the 1960s, Irv's work featured in such titles as BATMAN and DETECTIVE COMICS. He was r to have a long run as penciller on THE FLASH.

ENNIS O'NEIL

)ennis O'Neil was a journalist who broke into comic books in 1965 at Marvel nics, where he worked on such features as Millie the Model and The Two-n Kid before moving over to Charlton Comics under editorial director Dick rdano. At Charlton he wrote a variety of features under the pseudonym rgius O'Shaunessey," a name he later took with him when he moved over to Comics in 1967, accompanying Dick Giordano on his move to the company. ny scripted several features at his new creative home, including Justice gue of America, Wonder Woman, Bat Lash, Superman, The Creeper, and ptain Marvel. Denny is best remembered for his groundbreaking work in rning the Batman to his dark and gritty roots as a "creature of the night" with sts Neal Adams and Giordano and, with that same team, bringing the touch ealism and relevance to the pages of GREEN LANTERN/GREEN ARROW. er a stint as a writer and editor at Marvel Comics, Denny returned to DC, re he wrote The Question, THE BATMAN movie adaptation, and is the edi-of the Batman line of comics.

IARLES PARIS

nker Charles Paris began his career inking Mort Meskin on the Johnny Quick Vigilante features for DC in the 1940s, but he is best known for his work on man, a feature he inked from 1947 through 1964 over such pencillers as Jack nley, Fred Ray, Sheldon Moldoff, and Dick Sprang. After Batman (including ny of the Batman Sunday newspaper strips of the 1940s), Charlie went on to other DC features, including Metamorpho, many issues of THE BRAVE D THE BOLD, including the first appearance of the Teen Titans. Charlie red from comics in 1968 to travel and paint.

RRY ROBINSON

rry Robinson was a 17-year-old about to start college when he met Batman tor and artist Bob Kane at a summer resort, a chance meeting that resulted in reer that persists to this day. Jerry began as Kane's assistant, and soon graduat-o both pencilling and inking the feature. Among his many contributions to Batman mythos of the 1940s was a definition of the strip's look and style, the tion of the visual look of the Joker, and the naming of Robin, the Boy nder. After leaving Batman, Robinson went on to work on Vigilante and ny Quick for DC, the Green Hornet and other features for Harvey Comics, a variety of features for other publishers, including Atlas and Western lishing. In 1961, he began writing and drawing political and social commen- strips for the Chicago Tribune-New York News Syndicate and *Classroom fs and Flubs* for *The New York Daily News*. Since 1977, Jerry has headed the toonists and Writers Syndicate, which syndicates cartoons and features to 40 countries around the world.

MARSHALL ROGERS

A former architecture student, Marshall Rogers began working at DC in mid-1970s, pencilling a variety of mystery and super-hero short stories. He qu ly rose to artistic prominence with his assignment to the Batman featur DETECTIVE COMICS with writer Steve Englehart and inker Terry Austi run many fans consider the definitive portrayal of the Dark Knight.

GEORGE ROUSSOS

George Roussos began working as an art assistant to Batman creator Bob K in 1940, inking backgrounds and doing lettering on the strip. George event began inking Batman over such pencillers as Dick Sprang, and was soon cilling on his own for other DC features, including Air Wave. George was als innovative color artist, contributing his sense of color to hundreds of stories the years. George left DC for Marvel Comics in 1972 where he still work cover colorist.

ALVIN SCHWARTZ

Writer Alvin Schwartz had his first story published when he was 12 and hooked for life, his poetry appearing in literary magazines while he was still a school student. Schwartz began writing for comics in 1941 for Street and S Publications and came over to DC a short time later after meeting DC e Sheldon Mayer. Alvin wrote for such features as Green Arrow, The New Legion, Wonder Woman, and the Flash, as well as Captain Marvel storie Fawcett Comics. In addition to these stories, he also wrote numerous continu for the 1940s Batman syndicated strip as well as the comic books, and such tures as Aquaman, Slam Bradley, A Date with Judy, Star-Spangled Superman, Superboy, the Superman newspaper strip, and many others. He wrote extensively outside of comic books, including novels under his own r and the name Robert W. Tracy. Alvin Schwartz left comic books in the 1950s to set up the consulting firm Human Factors Analysis.

LEW SAYRE SCHWARTZ

During the 1950s, Lew Sayre Schwartz was one of numerous Batman a who served to fill the large demand for material starring the Caped Crusade his Boy Wonder sidekick in DETECTIVE COMICS, BATMAN, and WOR FINEST COMICS.

DICK SPRANG

Dick Sprang was one of the earliest artists hired by DC to draw Batman i early 1940s when the demand for stories outstripped Dark Knight creator Kane's studio's ability to produce material. Dick's dynamic, energetic style unique among all the Batman "ghost" artists, and his 25-year run on the Ba titles (with regular forays into the pages of WORLD'S FINEST COMICS) h define the look of the character throughout the 1950s. Dick retired from co freelancing in 1961 and currently lives in Arizona where, in between cre giant-sized full-color painting reproductions of his famous Batman covers the 1940s and 1950s, he contributes the occasional illustration or cover to D

CHIC STONE

Inker Chic Stone's credits date back to the 1950s and the American C Group. His work gained recognition in the pages of the Marvel Comics o early 1960s when it appeared over such pencillers as Jack Kirby and Don Chic was also an accomplished penciller, his work appearing in issues of Marvel Comics, as well as at DC on Batman.

TREVOR VON EEDEN

Trevor Von Eeden began his pencilling career at DC Comics while still a school student in the mid-1970s when he was picked to draw Black Light Trevor has continued drawing since, with work appearing in a number of tit DC, including the Catwoman feature in BATMAN and his recent work on Canary and Green Arrow.

(Paul Kupperberg is an Editor at DC Comics and a member of its Development Gr

DAVE STEVENS